D1859711

THE BHAGAVADGITA

AS A

PHILOSOPHY OF GOD-REALISATION

Owing to the antiquity and rarity of this book, certain pages are regrettably absent, and readability is compromised due to the blurring of the original text. If you possess any insights regarding the availability of these missing sections, kindly inform us. Your assistance is crucial in ensuring the completion of this significant work for the benefit of future generations.

THE BHAGAVADGITA

AS A

PHILOSOPHY OF GOD-REALISATION

(Being a Clue through the Labyrinth of Modern Interpretations)

R. D. RANADE

GYAN

Published by

GYAN

Gyan Publishing House
5, Ansari Road
Daryaganj, New Delhi-110002
Phone: 011-47034999, 9811692060
E-mail: books@gyanbooks.com

Distribution Network
gyanbooks.com
India, USA, Canada, UK, Australia

© Publisher

All rights reserved. No part of this work may be reproduced, stored, adapted, or transmitted in any form or by any means, electronic, mechanical, photocopying, micro-filming, recording or otherwise, or translated in any language, without the prior written permission of the copyright owner and the publisher.

ISBN: 978-93-6280-000-8 (HB)
First Published, 1959

2nd Impression 2024

Printed at: Gyan Press, Delhi.

The book is sold subject to the condition that it shall not, by way of trade or otherwise, be lent, resold, hired out, or otherwise circulated without the prior publisher's written consent.

THE BHAGAVADGITA AS A PHILOSOPHY OF GOD-REALISATION
Author: R. D. RANADE

The late Dr. Ramchandra Dattatreya Ranade

Birth
3-7-1886

Death
6-6-1957

THE BHAGAVADGĪTĀ

AS A

PHILOSOPHY OF GOD-REALISATION

(Being a clue through the labyrinth of modern interpretations)

Dr. R. D. RANADE,

M. A., D. Litt.

1959

TABLE OF CONTENTS

PART II

VEDĀNTIC AND MYSTICAL INTERPRETATIONS OF THE BHAGAVADGĪTĀ

PART III

THE LABYRINTH OF MODERN INTERPRETATIONS

CONTENTS

CONTENTS

PART IV

THE CLUE THROUGH THE LABYRINTH

Scheme of Transliteration

अ a   आ ā   इ i   ई ī   उ u   ऊ ū

ऋ ṛ   ऌ ḷ   ए e   ऐ ai   ओ o   औ au

अनुस्वार ṁ   विसर्ग ḥ

क k   ख kh   ग g   घ gh   ङ ṅ

च c   छ ch   ज j   झ jh   ञ ñ

ट ṭ   ठ ṭh   ड ḍ   ढ ḍh   ण ṇ

त t   थ th   द d   ध dh   न n

प p   फ ph   ब b   भ bh   म m

य y   र r   ल l   व v   श ś

ष ṣ   स s   ह h

क्ष kṣ   ज्ञ jñ

THE BHAGAVADGĪTĀ
AS A
PHILOSOPHY OF GOD-REALISATION

BEING A CLUE THROUGH
THE LABYRINTH OF MODERN INTERPRETATIONS

GENERAL INTRODUCTION

The question of the supreme teaching of the Bhagavadgītā has engaged the attention of scholars throughout the centuries. As the title of the present work will show, God-realisation according to us is the supreme teaching of the Bhagavadgītā. This has not been properly insisted on by any of the great scholars that have gone by. We shall see presently how both in ancient and modern times they have produced a labyrinth out of which the only way to escape is by holding securely in our hands the thread or clue of God-realisation.

The present work is divided into five parts. The first part deals with the ancient systems with which the Bhagavadgītā comes into relation. The second part deals with the thought of the middle ages where we find the great Vedāntic scholars and spiritual teachers throwing light on the meaning of the Bhagavadgītā. The third part deals with a veritable labyrinth that has been produced in the interpretation of the Bhagavadgītā by modern scholars during the last century and a half. The fourth part deals with our solution of the problem in terms of contemporary thought and mode of procedure. The last part deals, in a general way, with the conception of the Sublime which has been outlined in the Bhagavadgītā and which has assumed great importance with eminent European philosophers, linking it up with the conception of the Divine.

It will be necessary for us here to cast a glance at the main points of discussion in these five parts in order that the reader may be able to appreciate better the entire argument of the work. The first part will deal with the Upaniṣads, the Sāṁkhya–Yoga and the Brahmasūtras. Particular attention is drawn in the Upaniṣad Section to the realisational value of the Īśa, to the reality of the Aśvattha in the Kaṭha as against its unreality in the Bhagavadgītā, and to the prototype of the Viśvarūpa of the Bhagavadgītā in the Muṇḍaka.

Under Sāṁkhya and Yoga we are pointing out how the word Avyakta, used by the Upaniṣads and the Sāṁkhya philosophy to designate Prakṛti, has been used by the Bhagavadgītā to designate Akṣara Puruṣa or Paramagati, how the Triguṇas play no less an important part in the Bhagavadgītā than in the later Sāṁkhya philosophy, having their physiological correspondence with the cerebral, cardiac and muscular functions, and lastly, how the word Kaivalya has been used to indicate Isolation in Sāṁkhya, Vision of the Self by the Self in Yoga and Unison in Vedānta.

In regard to the Brahmasūtras and their relation to the Bhagavadgītā, this much is certain that there is inter-quotation and inter-reference. It is evident that the Brahmasūtras do refer to the Bhagavadgītā in that famous Sūtra अतश्चायनेऽपि दक्षिणे and that the Bhagavadgītā refers to Brahmasūtras in the expression ब्रह्मसूत्रपदैश्चैव, but what Brahmasūtras it refers to cannot be determined. Hence the question of the priority or posteriority of the Bhagavadgītā and Brahmasūtras remains a very difficult problem to solve.

Part II of our work deals with the main points of discussion between the great Vedāntic commentators such as Śaṁkara, Rāmānuja, Madhva and Vallabha, as well as with that eminent mystical exponent of the Bhagavadgītā, Jñāneśvara, who might easily be regarded as the greatest commentator on the Bhagavadgītā that has ever lived. The three principal problems from the Vedāntic commentators with which we shall be dealing are the nature of the Absolute or God, the character of Asat or Not-Being, which they interpret variously, as well as the meaning of Naiṣkarmya or transcendence of actions which also they interpret differently to suit their own philosophical convenience.

Under Jñāneśvara we shall see particularly how he discusses poetico-philosophically the nature of the Absolute which he likens to the Cit-Sūrya, his analysis of the principal mystical emotions which is a contribution to the psychology of religion, as well as his greatest contribution to thought, namely, his doctrine of asymptotic approximation to Reality, which is a veritable landmark in the history of the philosophy of mysticism.

Part III and Part IV constitute the central portion of our work. Part III discusses the chief doctrines about the interpretation of the Bhagavadgītā that have been advanced by scholars during the last century and a half, while part IV deals with our examination of them expressed in terms of contemporary thought and modes of reasoning. We shall begin part III with the consideration of the interpolationist theories of Garbe, Holtzmann and Otto, each scholar coupling his interpolationalism with a philosophical theory of his own, namely, theism, pantheism and holy-ism. Dr. Bhandarkar's devotionalism is a very mature product, concerned with the investigation of Aikāntika Bhakti in the Nārāyaṇīya and its parallel in the Bhagavadgītā. In addition, he has the credit of disproving the theory of Christian influence on the Bhagavadgītā by his investigation into inscriptional, historical and philological evidences. The theory of

Christian influence on the Bhagavadgītā was put forth by three great Christian scholars, Weber, Lorinser and Lassen; but Farquhar was inclined to take a saner and a more sympathetic view of the philosophies and religions of other lands than his predecessors. Lokamanya Tilak was concerned primarily to show the superiority of Karma to Jñāna, Bhakti and Yoga. In regard to the first, by his theory of ज्ञानोत्तर कर्म and by his sympathy with the theory of ज्ञानकर्मसमुच्चय, he tries to prove the superiority of Karma. In regard to the second, he tells us that the essential nature of Bhakti consists in doing actions in a devotional spirit, while in regard to Yoga, he tells us that no real Karma is possible unless we possess the Yogic equanimity. With regard to Mahatma Gandhi's doctrine we know how he defines Anāsakti as the central Sun round which revolve the three planets of devotion, knowledge and works—Bhakti, Jñāna and Karma—while he regards Ahiṁsā itself as an aspect of Anāsakti. His analysis of Anāsakti is remarkable in resolving it into three component parts of desireless action, dedication and surrender. Under the theories advanced by some other modern eminent thinkers, we have the doctrines of socio-theism, triune unity and the world as a puppet-show as the essential teaching of the Bhagavadgītā. Dr. Otto's doctrine of Numenism is based on the conception of the Numen which means supernatural divine power, the Īśvara of the Bhagavadgītā in his scheme being wholly transcendent, and pre-determination and instrumentalism being the two foci round which Numenism moves. Finally, in Aurobindo, we find the doctrine of ascent of matter into spirit, of which his doctrine of Avatāra is a specification, as well as his interpretation of the Gnostic Ideal which claims our sympathy. In regard to the Bhagavadgītā, he puts forth certain doctrines which might to all appearances look heterodox, but which might be supported by the Absolutistic philosophy, namely, doctrines such as those of the Bhagavadgītā not being a book of ethics at all but of spiritual life, of the impossibility of all desireless and disinterested action, and of the abandonment of all standards of duty in favour of the supreme duty of self-surrender. When we consider all the above different interpretations of the Bhagavadgītā, we might easily find ourselves perplexed and may not know how to escape from this labyrinth. Is there a clue which might enable us to come out of it?

Part IV deals with our own constructive effort for the interpretation of the Bhagavadgītā in terms of the supreme clue of God-realisation. The clue has been missed by the great interpreters of the past, and hence we lay stress on it in terms of contemporary thought and ways of reasoning. We shall speak first of the antinomies in the Bhagavadgītā as in Kant. We shall find almost the same antinomies in the Bhagavadgītā, namely, those concerning God, the world and causality. Then we proceed to a discussion of the Categorical Imperative in the Bhagavadgītā as in Kant, namely, duty for duty's sake, its three specifications here being those of non-attachment, skill and sacrifice (असंग, कौशल and यज्ञ). In regard to Super-moralism, which is a favourite doctrine with certain eminent modern moralists, we shall find that the Bhagavadgītā advises us to rise above qualities and actions and to reach निस्त्रैगुण्य and नैष्कर्म्य, while in regard to Beatificism, it gives us an insight into the relation of beatification to equanimity, at the same time suggesting that beatification is itself Brahman. So far as the criteria of the reality of God-experience are concerned, three very important criteria emerge from the

Bhagavadgītā—supersensuousness, central initiation and continuity, which might easily be regarded as a great contribution to psycho-epistemology. As regards the method of meditation, the Bhagavadgītā makes original suggestions in respect of meditation on metaphysical conceptions, such as the Sūtra, Vaiśvānara and Tajjalān, as well as on moral and social virtues. Finally, in regard to the Sublime Vision of God, which is the supreme goal according to the Bhagavadgītā, we find in the description of the विश्वरूपदर्शन, experiences such as those of splendour, wonder, terror and joy, which link it up with a universal philosophy of the Sublime.

Part V deals with the relation of the Sublime to the Divine. We will show here how the Sublime leads to the Divine, taking illustrations from metaphysics, science and morality, thus supporting the upshot of the teachings of the Bhagavadgītā which we have noticed at the end of the last part. (1) Under metaphysics, we deal with Otto, whose 'Idea of the Holy' puts forth the doctrine of the *Mysterium Trimendum* and regards the Numinous as a complex of the feelings of mystery, wonder, power, terror, reverence and joy, which are closely allied to the feelings expressed in the eleventh chapter of the Bhagavadgītā referred to at the end of the last part. Then we pass on to Kant who has done more for the Sublime than any other philosopher and whose Critique of Judgment is almost the final word about the nature of the Sublime. We disagree with him a little, however, when he puts the Sublime in between taste and teleology, while we regard the Sublime as higher than teleology. His classical distinction between the mathematical Sublime and the dynamical Sublime is illustrated in the universe in the distinction between magnitude and force; but greater than any other force, as Kant tells us, is the force of inner consciousness. Anaximander, a great ancient Greek philosopher, has already linked up the questions of the Infinite and the Divine, the *Apeiron* and the *tò Thêion*. (2) After the treatment of the Sublime in metaphysics, we go on to its treatment in the realm of science, taking examples from geology, meteorology and astronomy where respectively the phenomena of the earthquakes, the Aurora Borealis and the heavenly alligator are supurb illustrations of the Sublime in nature. (3) Finally, we proceed to the Sublime in morality. No greater statement has been made by Kant than when he says that there is nothing more sublime in the world than the moral. This is, of course, in his early works, the three Critiques. But when we come to his *Opus Postumum*, a posthumously published work, we find statements which are incomparably higher than what we find in the Critiques referred to. Here he demolishes his old conceptions of the Summum Bonum and the Categorical Imperative. The Summum Bonum, he tells us here, cannot lead us to God ; it remains only a conception. The Categorical Imperative instead of remaining a nudity is here regarded as the Command of the Inner Being, the voice of the *Imperantis* who holds universal sway. And finally, 'what is strangest of all' he tells us in cryptic terms, 'I am myself this Being'. We thus see how the ideas of the Sublime, the Moral and the Divine may be connected together in any great system of philosophy. We shall show how these are connected together in the development of the doctrine of the Bhagavadgītā.

PART I

THE RELATION OF THE BHAGAVADGĪTĀ TO THE ANCIENT PHILOSOPHICAL SYSTEMS

CHAPTER I

THE RELATION OF THE BHAGAVADGITA TO THE UPANIṢADS

The Upaniṣads have been veritably the source of the teachings of the Bhagavadgītā. The Bhagavadgītā is indebted to almost all the Upaniṣads in this connection. It will not be possible for us to do justice to this multiple indebtedness. We shall confine our review to the five Upaniṣads, namely Īśa, Kaṭha, Muṇḍaka, Chāndogya and Śvetāśvatara. The relation of the Bhagavadgītā to the Nṛsiṁha-Uttara-Tāpanīya Upaniṣad will be dealt with later in the course of this work.

Īśopaniṣad

The first point to be noted in connection with the indebtedness of the Bhagavadgītā to the Īśopaniṣad consists in the teaching by the Īśopaniṣad as regards activism. It has, however, been further developed by the Bhagavadgītā. The Īśopaniṣad does make mention of non-contamination by action; but the further teaching of autonomy, which we find in its developed form in the Bhagavadgītā, is its original contribution to thought. The Īśopaniṣad tells us

कुर्वन्नेवेह कर्माणि जिजीविषेच्छतं समाः ।
एवं त्वयि नान्यथेतोऽस्ति न कर्म लिप्यते नरे ॥ Īśa. Up. 2.

It tells us that we are born here below in this mortal world in order to do action. But we should also see that we do not become entangled in it. The conception of autonomy in the Kantian sense was developed long ago in the Bhagavadgītā. We know from the Bhagavadgītā, for example, that we should do our duty for duty's sake:

कार्यमित्येव यत्कर्म नियतं क्रियतेऽर्जुन। XVIII, 9.

This is its contribution to the philosophy of activism. In fact, the Īśopaniṣad supplies the basis of activism to the Bhagavadgītā, upon which it erects the structure of autonomy.

The second point of connection between the Īśopaniṣad and the Bhagavadgītā is that even though there are some passages referring to self-realisation in the Bhagavadgītā, we find the doctrine of self-realisation almost in its full-fledged form in the Īśopaniṣad. It is indeed far higher in realisational value than the Bhagavadgītā. Look at this verse :—

तदेजति तन्नैजति तद्दूरे तद्वन्तिके।
तदन्तरस्य सर्वस्य तदु सर्वस्यास्य बाह्यतः॥ Īśa. Up. 5.

"It moves and it does not move; it is far and it is near; it is both inside and outside; it is both transcendent and immanent." According to Īśopaniṣad, all such contradictions are reconciled in self-realisation. There is another verse in that Upaniṣad which tells us how its author was first able to see the lustre of God, then the Form of God, and finally to identify himself with that Form.

तेजो यत्ते रूपं कल्याणतमं तत्ते पश्यामि योऽसावसौ पुरुषः सोऽहमस्मि।

Īśa. Up. 16.

In fact, this doctrine of lustre, form and the identity of the Form with one's own self has been excellently stated in the Īśopaniṣad.

Kaṭhopaniṣad

One of the most striking ideas that we find in the Bhagavadgītā, namely, the idea of Aśvattha in the fifteenth chapter of that work, owes its origin and inspiration to the Kaṭha, where we have that famous verse:

ऊर्ध्वमूलोऽवाक्शाख एषोऽश्वत्थः सनातनः ।

तदेव शुक्रं तद् ब्रह्म तदेवामृतमुच्यते ॥ Kaṭh. Up. II, 6. 1.

But there is one fundamental difference between the descriptions of the Aśvattha in the Kaṭha and in the Bhagavadgītā. In the Bhagavadgītā we read,

ऊर्ध्वमूलमधःशाखमश्वत्थं...अश्वत्थमेनं सुविरूढमूलमसंगशस्त्रेण दृढेन छित्त्वा ।

XV, 1...3.

It is the business of man here below to cut down this tree of unreality. In fact, the Aśvattha is the tree of unreality and equivalent to Saṁsāra in the Bhagavadgītā. On the other hand, to the Kaṭhopaniṣad the Aśvattha is real and is equivalent to Brahman. We have a conception of Igdrassil, or the ash tree, in the Scandinavian mythology where we are also told that it is our business to cut down that tree. The ash tree is not far different from the Aśvattha. So there is a parallelism between the Bhagavadgītā and the Scandinavian mythology rather than between the Bhagavadgītā and the Kaṭhopaniṣad. How this change was made from the reality of the Aśvattha to its unreality is hard to comprehend. Nevertheless, the stand-points of the two are different, and just as it is true to say that the World is God, and also in a sense it is true to say that the World is not God, similarly support for the one may be found in the Kaṭhopaniṣad and for the other in the Bhagavadgītā.

Muṇḍakopaniṣad

The Muṇḍakopaniṣad supplies us with a conception which assumes very great importance in the Bhagavadgītā. It is the idea of the Viśvarūpa, which probably first originated with the Puruṣa-Sūkta. The Muṇḍaka Upaniṣad developed it a little more, while it was fully developed later on by the Bhagavadgītā. The Puruṣa-Sūkta talks of

चन्द्रमा मनसो जातश्चक्षोः सूर्योऽजायत ।
पद्भ्यां भूमिर्दिशः श्रोत्रात्तथा लोकाँऽकल्पयन् ॥

while in the Muṇḍaka we read

अग्निर्मूर्धा, चक्षुषी चन्द्रसूर्यौ, दिशः श्रोत्रे, वाग् विवृताश्च वेदाः ।
वायुः प्राणो, हृदयं विश्वमस्य, पद्भ्यां पृथिवी ह्येष सर्वभूतान्तरात्मा ॥

Mu. Up. II, 1. 4.

This, in fact, is in miniature a description of the Viśvarūpa of the Bhagavadgītā. We are told here how the eyes of the Viśvarūpa are the sun and the moon, the ears are the quarters and his speech the Vedas. Further, the head is supplied by fire and the earth supplies the feet. The wind constitutes the Prāṇa of that Viśvarūpa, while its heart is made up by the empyrean. In this way, we have a miniature description of the Viśvarūpa in the Muṇḍaka which we find more fully developed in the Bhagavadgītā.

Secondly, in the Muṇḍaka we have a very fine description of the antinomy between ritualism and non-ritualism, which also we find later in the Bhagavadgītā ; and the most wonderful thing is that the descriptions in the two works are in close proximity to each other. Thus, in the Muṇḍaka we find a passage,

तदेतत्सत्यं मन्त्रेषु कर्माणि कवयो यान्यपश्यंस्तानि त्रेतायां बहुधा सन्ततानि ।
तान्याचरथ नियतं सत्यकामा एष वः पन्थाः सुकृतस्य लोके ॥

Mu. Up. I, 2. 1.

exhorting us to do sacrificial action. In contrast to this and immediately following upon this in the same chapter is the passage :

प्लवा ह्येते अदृढा यज्ञरूपा अष्टादशोक्तमवरं येषु कर्म ।
एतच्छ्रेयो येऽभिनन्दन्ति मूढा जरामृत्युं ते पुनरेवापि यन्ति ॥

Mu. Up. I, 2. 7.

which exhorts non-ritualism and tells us that while a life of sacrifice is destined to lead us from existence to existence, a life of contemplation takes us towards God. The essence of the teaching is that we cannot find reality in the Mantras. They are merely rafts which are likely to sink in the ocean of life. Therefore, we must hold on to the steers-man, namely, God, who will take us to the other shore. In the Bhagavadgītā also we have two similar passages, सहयज्ञाः प्रजाः सृष्ट्वा पुरोवाच प्रजापतिः। B.G.III,10., where sacrificial life is exalted and यामिमां पुष्पितां वाचं प्रवदन्त्यविपश्चितः। B. G. II, 42., where the sacrificial life is condemned, and we are told that the spiritual life is much higher than the sacrificial life. In fact, sacrificial action will lead us nowhere. We must resort to God in order to be able to reach our highest ideal.

Chāndogya Upaniṣad

A striking illustration of the indebtedness of the Bhagavadgītā to the Upaniṣads occurs in the Chāndogya Upaniṣad, in a passage of extreme difficulty which it is not possible to solve satisfactorily. Let us quote the passage from the Chāndogya Upaniṣad we are referring to :

तद्धैतद्घोर आङ्गिरसः कृष्णाय देवकीपुत्रायोक्त्वोवाच ।...तपो दानमार्जवमहिंसा सत्यवचनमिति ।...सोऽन्तवेलायामेतत्त्रयं प्रतिपद्येताक्षितमस्यच्युतमसि प्राणसंशितमसीति । Chā. Up. III, 17. 6 & 4.

Now look at the proper names and expressions that occur in this passage. First comes Ghora Āṅgirasa, then Kṛṣṇa as the son of Devakī; then follows the mention of the five virtues—तपस्, दान, आर्जव, अहिंसा and सत्यवचन ; then the Upaniṣad speaks about the अन्तवेला (the time of death); and finally, about the three ideas involved in अक्षितमसि, अच्युतमसि, प्राणसंशितमसि, to which a man must resort at the time of death.

Now let us see how there is a connecting link between the Chāndogya on the one hand and the Ṛgveda on the other. In fact, the passage from the Chāndogya is so full of mystery that it may not be possible for any one to solve it. If we consider the connection of the Chāndogya with the Ṛgveda, we shall see that Kṛṣṇa is already mentioned twice in the Ṛgveda as a Ṛṣi in a hymn to the Aśvins. Let us quote these verses in full:

अयं वा कृष्णोऽश्विना हवते वाजिनीवसू । मध्वः सोमस्य पीतये ॥
शृणुतं जरितुर्हवं कृष्णस्य स्तुवन्तो नरा । मध्वः सोमस्य पीतये ॥

Ṛg. I, 116. 12.

Then secondly, this Ṛṣi, Kṛṣṇa, is called Āṅgirasa in the Anukramaṇikā of the Ṛgveda. We are not yet told that he had anything to do with Ghora, or how he was related to Ghora Āṅgirasa. But that Kṛṣṇa is called an Āṅgirasa is enough for our present purpose. Finally, the name Ghora Āṅgirasa itself occurs in a passage of the Ṛgveda, in the Hymn to Saramā where Saramā says :

नाहं वेद भ्रातृत्वं नो स्वसृत्वमिन्द्रो विदुरंगिरसश्च घोराः ।
गोकामामेऽच्छदयन्यदायमपात इत पणयो वरियः ॥ Ṛg. X, 108·10.

"It is only Indra and Ghora Āṅgirasa that know; I do not know either brotherhood or sisterhood." So, if we put hese passages together, we shall see that Kṛṣṇa, who was a Ṛṣi, was known at the time of the Ṛgveda and also that he was called an Āṅgirasa in the Anukramaṇikā, while the name Ghora Āṅgirasa has been particularly mentioned in the hymn to Saramā, (नाहं वेद भ्रातृत्वम्). We can also see from these references that Kṛṣṇa and Ghora Āṅgirasa are mentioned in the Ṛgveda, while the Chāndogya puts them together and establishes a relationship of disciple and teacher between Kṛṣṇa on the one hand and Ghora Āṅgirasa on the other. The Chāndogya also adds the word Devakīputra which takes one to the Mahābhārata or the Bhagavadgītā.

We know nothing about Devakīputra Kṛṣṇa in the Ṛgveda and hence arises the liaison of the Chāndogya with the Bhagavadgītā. In this connection there are three important points to be noted. In the first place, the same virtues which have been mentioned in the Chāndogya are also mentioned in the Bhagavadgītā. तपस्, दान, आर्जव, अहिंसा and सत्यवचन of the Chāndogya have been mentioned in the sixteenth chapter of the Bhagavadgītā :—

> दानं दमश्च यज्ञश्च स्वाध्यायस्तप आर्जवम् ।
> अहिंसा सत्यमक्रोधस्त्यागः शान्तिरपैशुनम् ॥ XVI. 1–2.

Now all the five virtues of Chāndogya have been mentioned here, but there is a little difference. The three virtues, Ārjava, Ahiṁsā and Satya, occur exactly in the same order and Dāna and Tapas interchange places. There are certain other virtues mentioned in the Bhagavadgītā, which we do not find in the Chāndogya, such as दम, यज्ञ and स्वाध्याय. But that the five principal virtues of the Chāndogya have been mentioned in two consecutive lines of the Bhagavadgītā is a wonderful resemblance. It is beyond question that the Bhagavadgītā was indebted to the Chāndogya for the conception of these five virtues.

Secondly, the Chāndogya tells us that at the time of death (अन्तवेलायाम्), we should meditate on the three conceptions, अक्षितमसि, अच्युतमसि, प्राणसंशितमसि. In fact, this contemplation is bound to be idealogical. On the other hand, we are told in the Bhagavadgītā that at the time of death we should meditate on OM as a symbol of God (ॐ इत्येकाक्षरं ब्रह्म) VIII, 13. So even though there is no identity between the ideas and the Mantra, the conception of meditation on some symbol of God at the time of death is common to both.

Thirdly, and this is a very important and new point, the Gītā also extends a friendly hand to the Chāndogya. The Bhagavadgītā calls Sāmaveda the highest of the Vedas. This is a very peculiar statement; for, before this and even after this, the Sāmaveda has not been regarded as the highest of the Vedas, and yet the Bhagavadgītā chooses to call it so : वेदानां सामवेदोऽस्मि X, 22. And when we remember that the Chāndogya is an Upaniṣad of the Sāmaveda, and also that the Bhagavadgītā speaks about बृहत्साम तथा साम्नाम् X, 35., it is clear that the author of the Bhagavadgītā had a soft corner for both the Sāmaveda and the Chāndogya, and consequently the perfect liaison of the Bhagavadgītā with the Chāndogya is clearly proved.

Śvetāśvataropaniṣad

Finally, we shall see how much the Bhagavadgītā is indebted to the Śvetāśvatara Upaniṣad for its Yogic teachings. In fact, the Śvetāśvatara Upaniṣad might be regarded as giving us one of the most important descriptions of Yoga that have been made. In about nine or ten verses it describes all the conditions that are required for perfection in Yoga. The Bhagavadgītā has been a popular summary of this description, while the Śvetāśvatara Upaniṣad might be regarded as supplying these ideas even to the great Patañjali. We know in the sixth chapter of the Bhagavadgītā how much and in what terms it describes the practice of Yoga. Let us see how this teaching is indebted to the original teaching of the Śvetāśvatara (II, 8–14). In the first place, the Śvetāśvatara tells us that we must select a proper place for meditation (समे शुचौ शर्करावह्निवालुकाविवर्जिते ।). Then it tells us to hold the body erect, especially its three parts, chest, neck and head (त्रिरुन्नतं स्थाप्य समं शरीरम्). Thirdly, it advises us to control our breath (प्राणान् प्रपीड्य). Not merely this, it tells us further that our senses must be regulated by our mind (हृदीन्द्रियाणि मनसा संनिरुध्य). Further, when this system of Yoga is being practised, there are certain early physiological effects—lightness of body, healthiness (लघुत्वमारोग्यम्), beautiful colour of the body, a sonorous voice (वर्णप्रसादः स्वरसौष्ठवम् च) and so on. Also we are told how the practice of Yoga enables us to conquer both disease and old age (न तस्य रोगो न जरा). It also talks of the conquest of death (न मृत्युः); but this is no simple matter. Further, we are let into the secret of early mystical experiences, such as those of नीहार, धूमार्क and अनल. Two other kinds of early experiences also are mentioned, which are not so well known, namely, Anil or wind, and Aśani or thunderbolt. These experiences make an appeal to senses other than that of vision. Anila, for example, refers to the touch sense, and Aśani to the organ of audition. Further, the acme of spiritual life is obtained by the Yogic process, when the Yogin is able to visualise his own Self (यथैव बिम्बं मृदयोपलिप्तं तेजोमयं भ्राजते तत्सुधौतम् । तद्वात्मतत्त्वं प्रसमीक्ष्य देही एकः कृतार्थो भवते वीतशोकः । Śve. Up. II, 14.). It is a very fine Form, full of lustre, which appears to the vision of the Yogin, and when he has seen this Form, he experiences his ultimate identity with that Form. By the self he is able to reach the Brahman—यदात्मतत्त्वेन तु ब्रह्मतत्त्वम्. He finds an equation between the two as in the expressions तत्त्वमसि and सोऽहम् , and to him it is a matter of experience reached through Yogic process and not intellectually. We see here how all these stages of Yogic development have been mentioned by the Śvetāśvatara : the place, the posture, the breath, the sense-control, the physiological effects, the conquest of disease and old age, the early mystical experiences, the vision of the Self, and the ultimate identity of Self with God. It is needless for us to point out how the Bhagavadgītā takes up many of these ideas and weaves them into its system of Yoga which is known to all the students of that great work.

CHAPTER II

THE RELATION OF THE BHAGAVADGĪTĀ TO SĀṀKHYA AND YOGA

We have hitherto seen the relation in which the Bhagavadgītā stands to the Upaniṣads. We shall now consider how it is related to Sāṁkhya and Yoga on the one hand and to the Brahmasūtras on the other. The Brahmasūtras were later commented on by great commentators. So we shall also have to discuss the relation of the Gītā to the interpretations of the great Vedāntic commentators. In the Upaniṣads, in the Bhagavadgītā and even in later works all the three systems of Sāṁkhya, Yoga and Vedānta were in a state of fusion. The lines separating them were not clearly demarcated. These systems had run into each other and as there had been no definite systematization, there were many overlapping ideas in the three systems. The philosophic development proper of these systems came on later. So when we are dealing with the relation of the Bhagavadgītā to Sāṁkhya, Yoga and Vedānta, we are not only to consider its relation to the systems as then prevalent, but also to devote some attention to their later developments.

Sāṁkhya and Yoga

We have said above that before the time of the Bhagavadgītā and even at the time of the Upaniṣads, Sāṁkhya and Yoga had been fused together. When the Bhagavadgītā speaks of the ultimate identity of Sāṁkhya and Yoga, it is not in the sense of mere identity of linguistic expressions. It is a conceptual identity, which the Bhagavadgītā points out between Sāṁkhya and Yoga. The Bhagavadgītā says that the seer is he who regards Sāṁkhya and Yoga as one and identical.

एकं सांख्यं च योगं च यः पश्यति स पश्यति । V. 5.

Now this doctrine of identity of Sāṁkhya and Yoga is based upon certain conceptions. The word Sāṁkhya itself is derived from the word Saṁkhyā, which means either to enumerate or to reason. When the twenty-five principles were enumerated later, the system came to be called Sāṁkhya. When reason was at the back of these principles, it was also called Sāṁkhya. Reasoning, knowledge, intellect—all were the aspects of Sāṁkhya philosophy as it was later developed. When the author of the Bhagavadgītā talks about Yoga, he has also three different conceptions in his mind. First, Yoga means power (पश्य मे योगमैश्वरम्). Secondly, it means the process of meditation which is its proper meaning (उपविश्यासने युञ्ज्याद् योगमात्मविशुद्धये). Thirdly, the Bhagavadgītā uses the word Yoga in the sense of action (योगः कर्मसु कौशलम्) almost in the sense of Karmayoga. It is their identification which the Bhagavadgītā points out. Sāṁkhya as philosophy and Yoga as activism are reconcilable, if we ultimately find a common basis for them. The basis is as follows: The Bhagavadgītā defines Sāṁkhya as the path of knowledge, which involves renunciation; it defines Yoga as the path of action which involves disinterestedness. Now renunciation and disinterestedness are identical, says the Bhagavadgītā. We must not divorce Sāṁkhya from Yoga or Yoga from Sāṁkhya. The two run into each other. In fact, the relation of Sāṁkhya to Yoga is ultimately like the relation of philosophy to mysticism.

Mahat

One of the fundamental teachings of the later Sāṁkhya philosophy is the doctrine of Mahat. The

Mahat was the first evolute from Prakṛti— महदाद्याः प्रकृति-विकृतयः सप्त. It is also identified with Buddhi, thus involving an identification of the cosmic and psychic principles. In these two principles there is no mere parallelism, as in Spinoza, but a veritable identitate philosophy. This is the fundamental position of the later Sāṁkhya. When the Bhagavadgītā talks about मम योनिर्महद्ब्रह्म XIV, 3., Mahat might be taken either as adjectival to Brahman, or in a substantival sense in apposition to or identical with Brahman. But the Bhagavadgītā also speaks of Puruṣa as sowing seed in Mahat (तस्मिन् गर्भं दधाम्यहम्). Prakṛti refuses to play this part, because she disappears as soon as the Puruṣa looks at her as a spectator. What is of consequence, therefore, in this connection is the Mahat. The Puruṣa sows the seed in the Mahat and from that arises the entire world. This is, of course, the conception of the Bhagavadgītā, which was later developed systematically by the Sāṁkhya philosophers, identifying Mahat with Buddhi, which implied the identification of the cosmic and psychic principles.

Avyakta

The second important principle in the Sāṁkhya is the conception of Avyakta. Of course, this is not technically recognised as such by the Sāṁkhya philosophers ; but it means Prakṛti as we shall see presently. In the first place, this conception of Avyakta is familiar to the Upaniṣads. The Upaniṣads interpose Avyakta between Mahat on the one hand and Puruṣa on the other (महतः परमव्यक्तमव्यक्तात् पुरुषः परः) ; and if Avyakta thus comes to be interposed between Mahat on the one hand and Puruṣa on the other, it evidently means Prakṛti as in later Sāṁkhya philosophy.

The Sāṁkhya philosophy itself, as expounded in the Kārikā, also takes the same view as the Upaniṣads. It also regards Avyakta as equivalent to Prakṛti and, therefore, intermediate between Mahat and Puruṣa. Let us see this from the Sāṁkhya Kārikā :

औत्सुक्य-निवृत्त्यर्थं यथा क्रियासु प्रवर्तते लोकः ।
पुरुषस्य विमोक्षार्थं प्रवर्तते तद्वद्व्यक्तम् ॥ S. K. 8. 58.

The Sāṁkhya Kārikā tells us that the function of the Avyakta is to see that the Puruṣa is released. Now as this is the function which Prakṛti performs, there is no harm in saying that this Avyakta is the same thing as the Sāṁkhya Prakṛti. The Gītā takes a different view from both the Upaniṣads and the Sāṁkhya philosophy. It regards Avyakta as equivalent to Puruṣa, Akṣara, or Paramā gati (अव्यक्तोऽक्षर इत्युक्तः तमाहुः परमां गतिम् VIII, 21.). In this way, the Bhagavadgītā calls Avyakta the Puruṣa, calls him the Paramā gati, and at the same time equates him with Akṣara. We thus see that there is a difference between the views about Avyakta taken by the Upaniṣads and Sāṁkhya on the one hand and the Bhagavadgītā on the other.

Tanmātras

The next important conception in Sāṁkhya philosophy is the conception of Tanmātras. This expression might be compared to the Kantian "thing-in-itself" though it is not identical with it. Tanmātras mean the essences of the five elements, namely, Śabda, Sparśa, Rūpa, Rasa and Gandha. Now the question arises, "Do the Tanmātras exist first or the elements?" And the Sāṁkhya view is that the Tanmātras exist first and that from the essences spring the elements. Aristotle has made us familiar with his famous dictum that there are certain conceptions which exist first, but which are the last to be known. On the other hand, those which are known first, come into existence last. Applying this dictum to the Sāṁkhya conception of the Tanmātras, we may say, the Tanmātras are the first to exist and last to be known, like the logical and universal principles, or the Platonic Forms. They exist first and from them are born elements and objects of the universe. We have to make an important statement here about the Tanmātras in proof of the priority of the Bhagavadgītā to the systematized Sāṁkhya philosophy. That the Tanmātras are not mentioned by the Bhagavadgītā might evidently be taken to be an argument for its priority. That these are developed in Sāṁkhya philosophy later is out of question.

Triguṇas

We have hitherto dealt with the Mahat, Avyakta and Tanmātras, which constitute an essential part of Sāṁkhya philosophy, no doubt; but the most fundamental idea in Sāṁkhya philosophy is the conception of the Triguṇas. Let us see how this conception is developed from its beginnings. In the Upaniṣads the conception of the Triguṇas occurs in an embryonic form. We have two passages where the properties of the Guṇas are given : यदग्ने रोहितं रूपम् । Chā. Up. VI, 4.1. and अजामेकां लोहित-शुक्लकृष्णाम् । Śve. Up. IV, 5. Here the red, black and white colours, which are the properties of the three Guṇas, are mentioned. The Bhagavadgītā, which came later, developed the conception of the Guṇas in its own way; but the conception was not fully systematized as in Sāṁkhya philosophy. We have whole chapters in the Bhagavadgītā devoted to the conception of the Triguṇas.

The conception is mentioned very frequently in the last chapters of the Bhagavadgītā, which fact has been regarded by some as an argument for the later production of these chapters. Among other conceptions, the Bhagavadgītā talks about twelve subjects such as श्रद्धा, आहार, यज्ञ, तपस्, दान, त्याग, ज्ञान, कर्म, कर्ता, बुद्धि, धृति and सुख, as being subject to the Triguṇas. All these are Sāttvika, Rājasa and Tāmasa. Mr. Justice Divatia has made an interesting suggestion that even though these might be regarded by the Bhagavadgītā as subject to the three Guṇas, Bhakti itself is not mentioned therein; therefore, Bhakti remains out of the scope of the Triguṇas. Bhakti, according to this view, would be entirely a *sui generis* category, only of one nature or colour ; neither Sāttvika, nor Rājasa, nor Tāmasa — neither white, nor red, nor black. This is a good view and we prize it for the suggestion it makes, namely, that Bhakti stands above the three Guṇas; but we cannot help equating Bhakti with Śraddhā, which has been already mentioned by the Bhagavadgītā, and Śraddhā is of three different types, showing the influence of the three Gunas. Bhakti might be regarded as subject to the three Guṇas also, because we evidently know that there are Sāttvika Bhaktas, Rājasa Bhaktas and Tāmasa Bhaktas. Of course, it is an ideal devoutly to be wished that our Bhakti should be only of a super-qualitative kind, and neither Sāttvika, nor Rājasa, nor Tāmasa element should enter into it. But social psychology stands, and we must regard Bhakti also as subject to the three Guṇas. When we come later to Sāṁkhya philosophy, we have a fully developed conception of the Triguṇas. In fact, these Guṇas constitute the corner stone of Sāṁkhya philosophy. The ideas, which I shall be suggesting just now, I shall develop in a later work on the "Vedānta as the Culmination of Indian Thought". But there is no harm in suggesting in a few lines here the central ideas underlying the conception of the three Guṇas in Sāṁkhya philosophy. The first question that arises is: " Are the three Guṇas substantival or adjectival? What is their relation to Prakṛti? Does Prakṛti exist first, or do the Triguṇas exist first?" This is a question difficult to answer. Secondly, the Triguṇas become analogues of certain other conceptions — humours as in Mediaeval Physiology, Tridoṣas as in Indian Medicine and colours as in spectroscopy. Thirdly, the Sāṁkhya Kārikās have given a fine description of the reciprocal generation, conquest and concert of these three Guṇas:

> प्रीत्यप्रीतिविषादात्मकाः प्रकाशप्रवृत्तिनियमार्थाः ।
> अन्योन्याभिभवाश्रय-जनन-मिथुन-वृत्तयश्च गुणाः ॥ S. K. 12.

This is as much as to say that the Guṇas are born from each other, they conquer each other and they ultimately merge into one another. Fourthly, the Sāṁkhya philosophy suggests also the supersession of these three Guṇas: त्रिगुणात् विपर्ययात्...अधिष्ठानात्...पुरुषोऽस्ति. What is Puruṣa, if he does not supersede these conceptions? A Being, who supersedes all these three Guṇas, is alone entitled to the name of the Highest Being. And finally, if we apply these Triguṇas to modern conditions and modern sciences, we shall see that our so-called psychological types are based upon these three Guṇas. Hence the Guṇas play a very important part not only in Sāṁkhya philosophy, but even in social and other modern sciences.

Puruṣa

The conception of Puruṣa occurs in Sāṁkhya and Yoga as well as in the Bhagavadgītā. Sāṁkhya maintains a pluralistic atheism. There is no *theos* in Sāṁkhya. It recognises a plurality of "spiritual principles" which are called Puruṣas. In the first Kārikā, however, the author speaks about Puruṣa in the singular and not about Puruṣās ; hence there is a subconscious monism lurking in the mind of the Sāṁkhya philosopher. In Yoga, we have Puruṣa and Puruṣas. It is a sort of a pluralistic theism; but the Puruṣa is related to the Puruṣas as *primus inter pares*. In the Gītā, we have a monistic theism with its doctrine of Uttama Puruṣa. This Uttama Puruṣa is raised above two other kinds of Puruṣas, namely, the Kṣara-Puruṣa meaning the world consisting of the different elements (क्षरः सर्वाणि भूतानि) and the Akṣara Puruṣa meaning the कूटस्थ or the Self. These two latter are only Puruṣas by sufferance. The real Puruṣa is the Supreme Principle, namely, the Uttama Puruṣa, Paramātman, or God. This involves a monistic theism, and it would be an interesting thing to see how this is made compatible with an Absolutism which is also taught in the Bhagavadgītā.

Kaivalya

Finally, we come to the conception of Kaivalya in the three systems, the Sāṁkhya, Yoga and Vedānta. Their different conceptions of Liberation are developed later on, but we must indicate them here in a succinct way. While these systems deal with Kaivalya, by which they mean liberation, they stress different aspects of it. Sāṁkhya stresses the aspect of isolation, aloneness, separation or unitary existence :

तस्माच्च विपर्यासात्सिद्धं साक्षित्वमस्य पुरुषस्य ।
कैवल्यं माध्यस्थं द्रष्टृत्वमकर्तृभावश्च ॥ S. K. 19.

So, by Kaivalya the Sāṁkhya philosophy means a state of liberation, in which the Puruṣa exists alone to himself and for himself, Prakṛti having " long ago vanished ". Yoga stresses another aspect of liberation, the vision of the Self by the Self. In fact, Self-vision constitutes the essence of the teaching of the Yoga so far as liberation is concerned.

तदा द्रष्टुः स्वरूपेऽवस्थानम् । Y. S. I. 3.

When this ideal is attained, we are liberated. Finally, the Gītā itself refers to the Kevala-Puruṣa,

तत्रैवं सति कर्तारमात्मानं केवलं तु यः ।
पश्यत्यकृतबुद्धित्वान्न स पश्यति दुर्मतिः ॥ B. G. XVIII. 16.

The Self is not the doer, is not the sufferer. He remains Kevala, absolutely uncontaminated by anything whatsover. This was later developed by the Vedānta as an aspect of unison, absorption or mergence.

CHAPTER III

THE RELATION OF THE BHAGAVADGĪTA TO THE BRAHMASŪTRAS

Let us now proceed to the consideration of the relation of the Bhagavadgītā to the Brahmasūtras. We are not concerned here with any doctrinal relationship between the Gītā and the Brahmasūtras. That is a big question which need not engage our attention at present. What we are concerned with here is the historical relationship between the Gītā and the Brahmasūtras. Under this head there are three distinctive opinions, and for each opinion we shall cite one prominent authority. The first opinion holds that the Gītā is earlier than the Brahmasūtras; the second maintains that the Brahmasūtras are earlier than the Bhagavadgītā; and the third emphasises inter-reference, inter-dependence and even a co-authorship theory of the Gītā and the Brahmasūtras. The representative of the first might be taken to be the late Justice K. T. Telang, of the second the late Dr. Maxmüller and of the third the late Bal Gangadhar Tilak. Lokamanya Tilak cites a passage from the Śāntiparva of the Mahābhārata, which tells us, वेदान्तं कर्मयोगं च वेदविद् ब्रह्मविद्विभुः । द्वैपायनो निजग्राह ... (212), which means that Dvaipāyana or Vyāsa or Bādarāyaṇa was responsible for the Vedānta and the Karmayoga, Karmayoga meaning the doctrine of the Bhagavadgītā. But Tilak is careful in pointing out that this occurs only in the Southern recensions of the Mahābhārata, and not in the Northern recensions. In any case we are not dependent only upon such a passage from the Śāntiparva from the Southern recensions. Tilak generally was of the opinion that the two did not merely have inter-reference and inter-dependence, but also a possible co-authorship.

Priority of the Bhagavadgītā

Let us begin with the doctrine which holds that the Gītā is earlier than the Brahmasūtras, which involves a presupposition by the Brahmasūtras of the teachings of the Bhagavadgītā. The whole doctrine rests upon one fundamental Sūtra in Bādarāyaṇa,

योगिनः प्रति च स्मर्यते स्मार्ते चैते । IV. 2. 21.

There may be other references in the Brahmasūtras to the Bhagavadgītā; but this is the most important of them which will enable us to clinch the point. By the dual in स्मार्ते चैते Bādarāyaṇa means the two paths, Dakṣiṇāyana and Uttarāyaṇa, which have a reference to the passing away of the Yogin. In regard to these two paths, the path of the gods and the path of the fathers, we have got references first in the Vedas, second in the Upaniṣads and third in the Bhagavadgītā, and later in the Brahmasūtras also. We shall see presently how the first three are identical, while the last is developmental, takes a philosophical view, and might, therefore, be regarded as coming after the first three doctrines. The Vedas talk about Devayāna and Pitṛyāṇa in the two celebrated Ṛcs:

परं मृत्यो अनुपरे हि पन्थां यस्ते स्व इतरो देवयानात् । Ṛg. X. 19. 1.
पन्थामनु प्रविद्वान् पितृयाणं द्युमदग्ने समिधानो विभाहि । Ṛg. X. 2. 7.

where both the paths of the gods and of the fathers have been mentioned. The Upaniṣads refer to the अर्चिर्मार्ग and धूममार्ग.

श्रद्धा तप इत्युपासते तेऽर्चिषमभिसम्भवन्ति.... ।
इष्टापूर्ते दत्तमित्युपासते ते धूममभिसम्भवन्ति ॥ Chā. Up. V.10.

The Bhagavadgītā has a double nomenclature. It talks

about Śuklagati and Kṛṣṇagati as well as Uttarāyaṇa and Dakṣiṇāyana. One celebrated passage from the Bhagavadgītā tells us :

अग्निर्ज्योतिरहः शुक्लः षण्मासा उत्तरायणम् ।
तत्र प्रयाता गच्छन्ति ब्रह्म ब्रह्मविदो जनाः ॥

and

धूमो रात्रिस्तथा कृष्णः षण्मासा दक्षिणायनम् ।
तत्र चान्द्रमसं ज्योतिर्योगी प्राप्य निवर्तते ॥

शुक्लकृष्णे गती ह्येते . . . . VIII. 24–26

Those who die in the Uttarāyaṇa go by the path of अग्निर्ज्योतिः and those who die in the Dakṣiṇāyana go by the path of धूमो रात्रिः and so forth. Now philosophically, the path of the fathers and the path of the gods is an absolute mis-conception. Neither day nor night, neither Dakṣiṇāyana nor Uttarāyaṇa have got anything to do with the destiny of the departed soul, far less is it so in the case of liberation. There are many common-place philosophic ideas which have to be tested by reason. The Brahmasūtras take a more philosophical view than any of the three above references. Bādarāyaṇa speaks of अतश्चायनेऽपि दक्षिणे (B.S. IV. 2–20) including under दक्षिण, उत्तर also by implication. Bādarāyaṇa's doctrine is that it is immaterial whether a man dies in Dakṣiṇāyana or Uttarāyaṇa. His liberation does not depend upon these times and seasons ; it depends upon his own qualifications for liberation. He does neither condemn Dakṣiṇāyana nor extol Uttarāyaṇa for liberation. He says that liberation is attained only on the basis of moral and spiritual development and is not dependent upon times, days and seasons. The same doctrine was later preached by the great Marāthā saint Rāmadāsa :

उत्तरायण तें उत्तम । दक्षिणायन तें अधम ।
हा संदेहीं वसे भ्रम । साधू तो निःसंदेह ॥ Dāsabodha: VII.10-13.

Now Bādarāyaṇa and Rāmadāsa agree and we also agree with them that liberation is a thing which is *sui generis*, and is not dependent either on the Śuklamārga or the Kṛṣṇamārga. As Bādarāyaṇa takes a more philosophically developed view, the Bādarāyaṇa-Sūtras might be regarded as later than the Bhagavadgītā.

Priority of the Brahmasūtras

Let us now try to understand the other point of view, namely, the doctrine that Brahmasūtras are earlier and the Gītā pre-supposes the Brahmasūtras. Here one fundamental verse from the Bhagavadgītā is quoted.

ऋषिभिर्बहुधा गीतं छन्दोभिर्विविधैः पृथक् ।
ब्रह्मसूत्रपदैश्चैव हेतुमद्भिर्विनिश्चितैः ॥ XIII. 4

It is a very important verse and a full interpretation of it has not yet been attempted as it ought to have been. Let us now understand each one of all these words that constitute this verse. In the first line there are three important words, ऋषिभिः, गीतम् and छन्दोभिः. The Ṛṣis evidently are the seers of the Vedas and the Upaniṣads. गीतम् means sung 'in metrical songs' which are to be found both in the Vedas and the Upaniṣads, and छन्दोभिः (by metres or variegated metres) which are to be found in the Vedas and the metrical Upaniṣads. So, on the whole, when the supreme doctrines referred to in the above chapter are said to have been sung by the great seers of old, the reference is undoubtedly to the Vedas and the Upaniṣads.

Let us now go to the second point. What is meant by ब्रह्मसूत्रपदैः ? Śaṁkara, in order to avoid the difficulty, talks about ब्रह्मसूत्रपदैः as involving both the Vedic texts and the Upaniṣadic texts only. Rāmānuja and Madhva disagree with Śaṁkara and say that the Brahmasūtras do indicate Brahmasūtras themselves; while Ānandagiri, though an Advaitic commentator himself, sides with Rāmānuja and Madhva and does not follow Śaṁkara. According to him also the Brahmasūtras mean the Brahmasūtras. What is our opinion on this point? The expression चैव tells us that the Brahmasūtras constitute an addition to what has been spoken of in the first line, namely, the Vedas and Upaniṣads; so something which is additional to the Vedas and the Upaniṣads must necessarily be the Brahmasūtras. The Brahmasūtras preach a doctrine which is additional to the छन्दोगीत of the Vedas and the Upaniṣads.

Let us go to the second word हेतुमद्भिः. हेतु means cause or reason. हेतुमत् means giving reason and this reason is given in the ablative case. This is the most familiar usage of the word in all the systems of Indian thought. In the Nyāyasūtras, for example, we read of प्रतिज्ञाहेतूदाहरणोपनयनिगमनानि. Grammar talks about हेत्वर्थे पंचमी and the Vedānta Sūtras themselves on almost every page point out in the ablative case the reasons for the statements they make, for example, तत्तु समन्वयात्, आनन्दमयोऽभ्यासात् and वैषम्यनैर्घृण्यप्रसंगात्. So हेतुमद्भिः also points to Brahmasūtra literature, bacause it involves giving reasons for the statements they make.

Finally, the word विनिश्चितैः also signifies Sūtra literature. विनिश्चितैः means having a definite meaning, and this definite meaning belongs to the Sūtra literature in Sanskrit and not so much to any other. For example, let us take the definition of Sūtra :—

अल्पाक्षरमसंदिग्धं सारवद्विश्वतोमुखं । अस्तोभ्यमनवद्यं च सूत्रं सूत्रविदो विदुः ॥

It is only the Sūtras which talk aphoristically, and when विनिश्चितैः is the word that is used by the Bhagavadgītā, it designates evidently the Brahmasūtra literature. So, on the whole, the significance of the second line of that verse is that the Brahmasūtras are to be regarded as constituting an additional reason to the Vedas and Upaniṣads for the proof of God.

Now, granted that the Brahmasūtras are referred to, but "what Brahmasūtras?" is the next question. This is a difficult matter to decide. "What is truth?" asked the Jesting Pilate and, we know, would not stay for an answer. Even here the great Bādarāyaṇa himself mentions eight of the Sūtrakāras besides himself. It is not necessary that the Bādarāyaṇa Sūtras themselves might be regarded as being referred to in the Gītā. Any of these Brahmasūtra systems might have been referred to by the Bhagavadgītā. For example, eight great names are mentioned by Bādarāyaṇa himself in his Brahmasūtras: आत्रेय, आश्मरथ्य, औडुलोमि, काशकृत्स्न, कार्ष्णाजिनि, जैमिनि, बादरि and वामदेव. Their sūtras might not have been extant fully or partially; but at least they must have left an impression, so that they have been all incorporated by Bādarāyaṇa in his Sūtras. We do not know which of these Sūtras, which one or many of them, have been in the mind of the author of the Bhagavadgītā. In any case, the implication is that just as the Vedas and Upaniṣads do refer to the Highest Reality, the Brahmasūtras themselves also refer to the Highest Reality, and for three reasons: (i) because they constitute an addition, (ii) because they give reasons and (iii) because they give an aphoristic, cryptic and definite meaning to their utterances.

The Bhagavadgītā : a Sarvaśākhīya Upaniṣad

Apart from the question of inter-reference, inter-dependence or inter-quotation between the Brahmasūtras and the Bhagavadgītā, we have a very interesting parallelism between the Brahmasūtras and the Bhagavadgītā. The Brahmasūtras of Bādarāyaṇa take over into themselves the Sūtras of various schools or Śākhās prevalent before his time; similarly, the Gītā takes into itself the ideas of all the Upaniṣads that prevailed before its time. Dr. Belvalkar has very happily called the Bādarāyaṇa Brahmasūtras a Sarvaśākhīya Brahmasūtra, which incorporates into itself many Prātiśākhīya Brahmasūtras. We may point out analogically that the Bhagavadgītā might well be called a Sarvaśākhīya Upaniṣad, because it incorporates into itself many Prātiśākhīya Upaniṣads. To call the Bhagavadgītā by the name of an Upaniṣad is the highest compliment that can be paid to it. Let us see how this is borne out by certain facts. First, two great European writers on the Bhagavadgītā, Keith and Hopkins, have called Gītā by the name of an Upaniṣad, and they say it is an Upaniṣad of the Śvetāśvatara type. This is not wrong. Secondly, the नृसिंहपूर्वतापनीयोपनिषत् calls each one of its chapters by the name of an Upaniṣad. So there are five Upaniṣads under the general title of the नृसिंहपूर्वतापनीयोपनिषत्. Even the नृसिंहोत्तरतापनीयोपनिषत् does not call its chapters by the name of Upaniṣads, but by the name of Khaṇḍas. This came to my notice while studying those two Upaniṣads in another connection, referred to later on in the present work. Then thirdly, all the colophons in the different Adhyāyas of the Bhagavadgītā include the expression गीतासूपनिषत्सु. So according to the colophons we must understand that the Gītā is the cumulation of the Upaniṣads, which have been sung.

Finally, in the Gītā-Dhyāna, which is a meditational prelude to the Bhagavadgītā, we have a celebrated verse, namely,

सर्वोपनिषदो गावो दोग्धा गोपालनन्दनः ।
पार्थो वत्सः सुधीर्भोक्ता दुग्धं गीतामृतं महत् ॥

But nobody has yet suggested how to draw the essence from this verse itself. Are we not justified by reading this verse as giving the highest compliment to the Bhagavadgītā by calling it उपनिषदमृतम् ?

PART II

VEDĀNTIC AND MYSTICAL INTERPRETATIONS OF THE BHAGAVADGĪTĀ.

CHAPTER IV

VEDĀNTIC INTERPRETATIONS OF THE BHAGAVADGĪTĀ

(*Śaṁkara, Rāmānuja, Madhva and Vallabha*)

The second part of our work deals with two topics, the Vedāntic interpretations of the great commentators and the mystical interpretation of Jñāneśvara. After having seen the relationship of the Bhagavadgītā to the Brahmasūtras, it behoves us to bring the Gītā into relation with the interpretations of the great Vedāntic teachers. It is not possible for us to do justice here to the fullness of their teachings. We are only concerned with showing the relevant points in which they differ from each other, and the way in which many of them make use of the text of the Bhagavadgītā to support their own points of view. This latter procedure very often becomes inconvenient. For example, we shall see that Asat is inconvenient to Madhva, and Aṁśa to Śaṁkara. Nevertheless, in all the points to be discussed here, we shall present the most important contributions which these Vedāntic teachers have made to the interpretation of the Bhagavadgītā. Under this head we shall be concerned with six main points. We shall review the Vedāntic interpretations of the Bhagavadgītā, first in regard to Absolutistic Reality, and then to Personalistic Reality. We shall next deal with the doctrine of Not-Being or Asat. The Gītā doctrine of Māyā however will not be treated here but elsewhere in this work. The next point which we shall take up for consideration is the Nature of the Self in the Bhagavadgītā according to these Vedāntic interpreters. Here it is that we say that Aṁśa presented a difficulty to Śaṁkara, as Asat did to Madhva, as stated above. We shall then discuss the doctrine of Naiṣkarmya or transcendence of actions, and finally, proceed to the consideration of the various views held by the Vedantic commentators about the problem of Liberation as treated by the Bhagavadgītā.

Absolutistic Reality

Let us begin by considering the views about Absolutistic Reality which have been held by the Vedāntic interpreters. There are two contrary statements made about this in the Bhagavadgītā and the Upaniṣads. The Bhagavadgītā talks of सर्वतः पाणिपादं तत्, and the Upaniṣads speak of अपाणिपादो जवनो ग्रहीता. How are these points of view to be reconciled? Is God with hands and feet? Or is He without hands and feet? The Gītā tells us that we have to consider God as सर्वतः पाणिपाद, having his hands and feet everywhere. Are these merely imaginary? That is the important question. Now Śaṁkara tells us that these are illusory. An illusory thing, he tells us, may be the cause of a real thing. Similarly, the पाणिपाद्s which are unreal, according to Śaṁkara, indicate a ज्ञेय which is अपाणिपाद. The Reality is without hands and feet, and when the Bhagavadgītā speaks about hands and feet they are to be supposed as illusory things, which are the cause of a real thing which is अपाणिपाद. A famous utterance from Śaṁkara in his शतश्लोकी might be mentioned here to show how an unreal thing might be the cause of a real thing:

स्वप्ने मन्त्रोपदेशः श्रवणपरिचितः सत्य एष प्रबोधे।
स्वाप्नादेव प्रसादादभिलषितफलं सत्यतां प्रातरेति॥

सत्यप्राप्तिस्त्वसत्यादपि भवति तथा किंच तत्स्वप्रकाशं ।
येनेदं भाति सर्वं चरमचरमथोच्चावचं दृश्यजातम् ॥ 38.

Rāmānuja takes another point of view, God may be अपाणिपाद, he says agreeing with Śaṁkara, and yet He may be the cause of पाणिपाद, in the created world, which is real. So Śaṁkara and Rāmānuja agree in regarding the Reality as अपाणिपाद. Their views, however, regarding पाणिपाद are different. We may submit here that neither Śaṁkara nor Rāmānuja has taken into account the mystical manifestation of God to an aspirant in the process of his realisation. Arjuna saw God with hands and feet and other organs everywhere. We have that celebrated description in the eleventh chapter of the Bhagavadgītā :

अनेकबाहूदरवक्त्रनेत्रं पश्यामि त्वां सर्वतोऽनन्तरूपम् ।
नान्तं न मध्यं न पुनस्तवादिं पश्यामि विश्वेश्वर विश्वरूपम् ॥ XI.16.

These are mystical manifestations, and it is these which the Bhagavadgītā has described, in the above passage.

Personalistic Reality

In regard to Personalistic Reality, we shall see how the Vedantic interpreters differ, particularly Śaṁkara and Rāmānuja. There are two classical passages in the Bhagavadgītā, one in the thirteenth chapter, where there is a discussion about क्षेत्र and क्षेत्रज्ञ, and the other in the fifteenth chapter where there is a discussion about क्षर and अक्षर पुरुष. In the first, both Śaṁkara and Rāmānuja show their great powers of exposition and argument, and if we clinch the difference between Śaṁkara and Rāmānuja on this point, we might say that it consists in a vindication of अविद्या on the one hand, and of चिदचिद्विशिष्ट ईश्वरः on the other. In the second, the same difference in their points of view is seen in their description of क्षर and अक्षर पुरुष. As a matter of fact, the क्षर पुरुष is a misnomer, because it signifies the elements.

क्षरः सर्वाणि भूतानि कूटस्थोऽक्षर उच्यते। XV. 16.

The अक्षर पुरुष is a Puruṣa only by sufference; it is not a Puruṣa at all. It is only the Uttama Puruṣa, who can be called by the title of Puruṣa,

उत्तमः पुरुषस्त्वन्यः परमात्मेत्युदाहृतः। XV. 17.

and it is in this respect that the Gītā describes him as the beginning, the end and the sustenance of the entire world.

पुरुषः स परः पार्थ येन सर्वमिदं ततम्। VIII. 22.

This is in general the relationship between क्षरपुरुष, अक्षरपुरुष and उत्तमपुरुष.:

Let us now see how Śaṁkara and Rāmānuja differ fundamentally on one very important point. Śaṁkara explains Kṣara as 'Sarvāṇi Bhūtani' and he regards them as perishable; but when he comes to discuss अक्षरपुरुष, Śaṁkara understands Jīva by अक्षरपुरुष and calls him कूटस्थ; because to him कूट means Māyā or illusion. We have seen elsewhere how the word is lifted to a high level in कूटस्थो विजितेन्द्रियः, as also to the place which it occupies as Cit in Rāmānuja. It is true that according to Rāmānuja, Kṣara Puruṣa and Akṣara Puruṣa designate the difference between Acit and Cit. In regard to Kṣara–Puruṣa, it indicates all things in the universe, आब्रह्मपिपीलिकापर्यन्तम्. In regard to Akṣara–Puruṣa, Rāmānuja gives an original interpretation. He regards Him as Cit or Kūṭastha, taking an altogether different point of view from that of Śaṁkara. Śaṁkara calls Kūṭastha a Being possessed of Vañcanā; on the other hand Rāmānuja regards him as स्वेन रूपेण अवस्थितः, a Being who lives in his own form, the Highest Reality. In fact, there is a fundamental difference in regard to the Kūṭastha between Śaṁkara and Rāmānuja. In regard to Uttama Puruṣa, however, they do not differ very much. It is God, the Highest Being; and the Uttama Puruṣa is fully equivalent to the Paramātman or the Supreme Self.

Not-Being (Asat)

Let us now proceed to consider the meaning of the word Asat as it occurs in the Bhagavadgītā. The passage in which it occurs is

नासतो विद्यते भावो नाभावो विद्यते सतः ।

This verse, as pointed out above, is a very inconvenient verse for Madhva. Madhva's doctrine is that both Prakṛti and Puruṣa are eternal. He brings out this meaning from the above verse. There is no harm, he tells us, for Asat or Prakṛti and Sat or Brahman both existing eternally. Now in order to interpret the original verse in this manner, Madhva must read an Avagraha between Vidyate and Bhāva, which may or may not exist. Nevertheless, if it does exist, Madhva would be justified; but if it does not, he cannot regard both Asat and Sat as eternal according to the Bhagavadgītā. The passage where Madhva explains his views is as follows :—

नित्यमात्मेत्युक्तम् । किमात्मैव नित्य आहोस्विदन्यदपि । अन्यदपि । तत्किमिति आह । नासत इति । असतः (कारणस्य) प्रकृतेः सतो ब्रह्मणश्चाभावो न विद्यते । 'प्रकृतिः पुरुषश्चैव नित्यौ कालश्च सत्तमः' इति विष्णुपुराणे ।

'प्रकृतिं पुरुषं चैव विद्ध्यनादी उभावपि' इति गीतायाम् ।

So far so good. We might also come to the help of Madhva by interpreting the first part of this line, namely, नासतो विद्यते भावो, as probably implying that Asat or Māyā itself does not exist. Of course, this is not the usual interpretation; but if we want to support Madhva, we can interpret it in that manner. Finally, Vallabha takes an important view in this matter of Asat and Sat. He tells us that Reality is beyond both Sat and Asat. He calls it दुर्ज्ञेय or incomprehensible. That probably is not an unjustifiable statement. Apart from the general question of Asat and Sat, however, there are some very important passages in the Bhagavadgītā which speak about Reality and non–Reality, which we may not discuss here; for example, the two celebrated passages in regard to the reality and non–reality of the world are भूमिरापोऽनलो वायुः on the one hand, and the evanescence of Aśvattha as described in the fifteenth chapter of the Bhagavadgītā on the other, both of which we shall discuss in our chapter on the Antinomies.

Nature of the Self

After this discussion about the reality and unreality and the general doctrine of Not-Being (Asat) or illusion, let us proceed to the consideration of the Gītā doctrine of the Self. There is one very important verse ममैवांशो जीवलोके जीवभूतः सनातनः। This verse is a very inconvenient one to Śaṁkara as we have already pointed out. The doctrine of Aṁśa has become a great handle in the hands of the non-advaitins. Śaṁkara, however, explains this doctrine of Aṁśa as अविद्याकृतोपाधिपरिच्छिन्न. This is a merely philosophic interpretation in contrast with the realistic interpretation of Aṁśa. The word Aṁśa is elsewhere called in the Upaniṣads by the name of विस्फुलिंग. A विस्फुलिंग is both real and unreal. It is real so long as it exists, but as soon as it vanishes it becomes unreal. Similar is the case with Aṁśa, says Śaṁkara, for which in his commentary he gives two illustrations, जलसूर्यक and घटाद्याकाश. These are philosophic conceptions which, according to Śaṁkara, contain exactly the meaning of the word Aṁśa, as used in the Bhagavadgītā.

ननु निरवयवस्य परमात्मनः कुतोऽवयव एकदेशोंऽश इति । सावयवत्वे च विनाशप्रसंगोऽवयवविभागात् । नैष दोषोऽविद्याकृतोपाधिपरिच्छिन्न एकदेशोंऽश इव कल्पितः । यथा जलसूर्यकः सूर्यांशो जलानिमित्तापाये सूर्यमेव गत्वा घटाद्याकाशांश आकाशं प्राप्य ।

Let us see what the Brahmasūtras say on this point. There is a famous Sūtra called

अंशो नानाव्यपदेशात् अन्यथा चापि दाशकितवादित्वमधीयत एके ।

II. 3.43.

In fact, the intention of the Sūtrakāra here is to show that God is not only present in all infinitesimal particles, but also in the whole of the universe, consisting of good and bad, high and low objects, including slaves, servants, fishermen, men, women and insects. All these constitute God दाशकितवादित्वमधीयत एके. So then Bādarāyaṇa's point of view was to show that God is all-comprehensive. He is present in all the atoms as well as in the whole universe, animate and inanimate.

Later Advaitins, however, took a different view in regard to the nature of Aṁśa. There are definitely three conceptions, namely, the conceptions of बिंबप्रतिबिंबवाद, आभासवाद and अवच्छेदकवाद in order to explain the nature of the Self and God. The sources of these conceptions are found in the commentary of Śaṁkara above referred to. When he speaks about the जलसूर्यक, he is referring to बिंबप्रतिबिंबवाद, which latter almost borders upon आभासवाद, and when he speaks of घटाद्याकाश, he speaks of अवच्छेदकवाद. These conceptions became an inspiration to later

Advaitins who founded their theories upon the doctrine originally cryptically enunciated by Śaṁkara in his commentary. We are concerned here with these philosophic developments only in order to explain how Jīva forms a part of God. The Jīva might be either an image or an illusion or else a limitation of God. These are the ideas which we might later examine in a work on the "Vedānta as the Culmination of Indian Thought"

Transcendence of Actions (Naiṣkarmya)

After the consideration of the nature of the Self in the Bhagavadgītā, we shall proceed to discuss a very important conception, namely, its doctrine of Naiṣkarmya. The Mīmāṁsakas advanced the doctrine of Karma which the Vedāntists all refute, even though they differ from one another in some slight respect. We may say, in regard to this doctrine of Naiṣkarmya, that there are three different points of view.

The Karmayogī-Vedāntists tell us that transcendence of actions is to be obtained by non-attachment to the fruits of the actions. The representatives of this doctrine might be taken to be Tilak and Gandhi. The Bhaktiyogī-Vedāntists tell us that all actions are to be surrendered to God, and thus Naiṣkarmya is to be attained. For example, Madhva in his commentary regards कर्मत्याग as equal to फलत्याग. Also the Jñānayogī-Vedāntists, who regard Naiṣkarmya as the end of all actions, equate it with Jñāna. This celebrated doctrine is advocated by Sureśvara. Coming to the origin of these later distinctions, we have to quote two short utterances from Śaṁkara and Rāmānuja on this head. Śaṁkara in his commentary defines नैष्कर्म्य as निष्क्रियब्रह्मात्मसंबोध or निष्क्रियात्मस्वरूपस्थान, either the knowledge of God who is above actions or a station in the आत्मस्वरूप which is निष्क्रिय. Rāmānuja does not differ very much from Śaṁkara. His doctrine is a variant of Śaṁkara's doctrine. He tells us

परमपुरुषकर्तृत्वानुसंधानेनात्मकर्तृत्वे विगतस्पृहः ।

He leaves all attachment to Karmas because he knows God is the real doer, God is the vindicator and when all action is to be attributed to God, man has no business to attribute it to himself.

Let us now proceed to two other conceptions: one indicated in

सर्वकर्माण्यपि सदा कुर्वाणो मद्व्यपाश्रयः । B. G. XVIII. 56.

and the other in

सर्वधर्मान् परित्यज्य मामेकं शरणं व्रज । B. G. XVIII. 66.

We are told by Śaṁkara in his interpretation of सर्वकर्माण्यपि that Karmas include प्रतिषिद्धान्यपि कर्माणि, which is tantamount to saying that there is no distinction between actions which are ordained and actions which are disdained. Rāmānuja tells us that Naiṣkarmya is to be obtained by leaving away all Kāmya Karmas. In any case, they agree with each other in the idea of Naiṣkarmya, which was left to Sureśvara to develop later as equivalent to Jñāna. Finally, in the passage सर्वधर्मान् परित्यज्य, Śaṁkara advises us to transcend both Dharma and Adharma धर्मशब्देन अत्र अधर्मोऽपि गृह्यते । नैष्कर्म्यविवक्षितत्वात्, and he quotes a passage where we are told त्यज धर्ममधर्मं च. What about duties and non-duties, what about religion and non-religion, what about actions which are ordained and about actions which are disdained? One should, says Śaṁkara, rise above all these. Vallabha goes to the Texts and defines सर्वधर्मान् as those which are ordained by the Sāstras, and tells us that we should leave away all the ordinances of the so-called philosophic and ethical

Śāstras and ultimately go in submission to one God, सर्वधर्मान् चोदनालक्षणात्, परित्यज्य मां एकं मुख्यं पुरुषोत्तमं शरणं व्रज । What Vallabha's doctrine comes to is that ordinances and non-ordinances have no significance before God. This is probably a point of view with which Aurobindo Ghosh entirely agrees. He does speak about the abandonment of all standards of duty to take refuge in the Supreme alone.

Liberation

Let us now proceed to the question of Liberation in the Bhagavadgītā and see how it is tackled by the great Vedāntic commentators. Under this head we shall consider three expressions – साधर्म्य, ब्रह्मभूयाय and विशते. The classical passage for साधर्म्य is इदं ज्ञानमुपाश्रित्य मम साधर्म्यमागताः । We shall consider its explanations as offered by Śaṁkara, Rāmānuja, Vallabha and Nīlakaṇṭha. Śaṁkara explains साधर्म्य as स्वरूपता, मत्स्वरूपमागताः। But the question arises whether स्वरूपता is the same as सरूपता. In any case, Śaṁkara negates समानधर्मता as an explanation of साधर्म्य. Rāmānuja understands साधर्म्य as साम्य counting upon the Upaniṣadic passage like निरंजनः परमं साम्यमुपैति। Vallabha takes cudgels against Śaṁkara and posits समानधर्मता as the explanation of साधर्म्य. He waxes eloquent over the explanation of साधर्म्य in terms of the philosophical categories, such as लीलायोग्यत्वम्, षड्गुणैश्वर्यत्वम्, सलोकता (वैकुंठ) and (मुक्तानां) बाहुल्यम्. All these he enumerates. Of course, it is evident that he does not include सायुज्यता in the scheme of साधर्म्य. In a similar manner, Nīlakaṇṭha includes under साधर्म्य, सर्वात्मत्वं, सर्वनियंतृत्वं, सर्वभावाधिष्ठातृत्वम्, because, he says, a Sruti passage tells us सर्वस्य वशी सर्वस्येशानः सर्वस्याधिपतिः । A man must be supposed to have attained साधर्म्य when all things are under his governance, when he becomes the over-lord and the king of all.

The Second conception of Liberation is ब्रह्मभूय. It occurs in the eighteenth chapter in the verse,

अहंकारं बलं दर्पं कामं क्रोधं परिग्रहम् । ...... ब्रह्मभूयाय कल्पते ।
XVIII. 53.

Śaṁkara understands ब्रह्मभूयाय as ब्रह्मभवनाय and Ānandagiri explains ब्रह्मणो भवनं as अनुसंधानपरिपाकपर्यंतं साक्षात्करणं इत्यावत् ।. In fact, ब्रह्मभवन includes the whole process of spiritual realisation according to Ānandagiri's interpretation of Śaṁkara. Rāmānuja understands by ब्रह्मभूय as आत्मानुभव and Madhva as ब्रह्मणि स्थितिः सर्वदा तन्मनस्कता. So these are the explanations of these Vedāntic commentators. Vallabha expatiates upon the conception of ब्रह्मभूय. He tells us that ब्रह्मभूय is to be interpreted as ब्रह्मात्मकस्वरूपे अवस्थानम्, taking his station in the form of Brahman, and relying upon two Sūtras from Bādarāyaṇa ब्राह्मेण अनन्तादि सूत्रोक्तरीत्या. What are those two Sūtras ? (1) ब्राह्मेण जैमिनिः IV. 45. (2) अतोऽनन्तेन III. 26. It is obvious that this Sūtra does contain an idea of liberation according to Bādarāyaṇa, and Vallabha follows Bādarāyaṇa in this respect and tells us that the highest form of ब्रह्मभूय is to take our station in God.

The third conception of liberation according to the Bhagavadgītā is that of Praveśa. There is a celebrated passage in the eighteenth chapter, where we are told:

ब्रह्मभूतः प्रसन्नात्मा न शोचति न कांक्षति ।
समः सर्वेषु भूतेषु मद्भक्तिं लभते पराम् ॥ 54
भक्त्या मामभिजानाति यावान्यश्चास्मि तत्त्वतः ।
ततो मां तत्त्वतो ज्ञात्वा विशते तदनन्तरम् ॥ 55

Let us understand the stages of this process. According to the Bhagavadgītā, there is first ब्रह्मभूय or ब्रह्मभवन; then the obtainment of Bhakti; then the knowledge of God, a perfect knowledge according to its full lineaments and finally, after this knowledge, entry into Brahman. Now the first stage seems to be absolutely unnecessary. Where is the necessity of attaining to Bhakti or Jñāna after there is a Brahmabhavana? If the devotee began with Bhakti (भक्त्या मामभिजानाति), it would have been quite understandable. From Bhakti a man goes to knowledge and from true knowledge he enters into the being of God. But once Brahmabhavana is attained there is no necessity of Bhakti or Jñāna or even Praveśa. Śaṁkara tells us that we need not make a difference between Jñāna on the one hand and Praveśa on the other. In fact, the two are identical:

नात्र ज्ञानानन्तरप्रवेशक्रिये भिन्ने विवक्षिते।

To obtain knowledge of God is to enter into Him. Rāmānuja is more literary:

स्वरूपतः स्वभावतश्च योऽहं गुणते। विभूतितो यावांश्चाहं तं मां एवं रूपया भक्त्या तत्त्वतो विजानाति। मां तत्त्वतो ज्ञात्वा तदनन्तरं मां विशते प्रविशाति इत्यर्थः।

Of course, he explains the meanings of all the words, योऽहम्, यावांश्चाहम्, भक्ति, ज्ञान and प्रवेश; but he does not bring this whole series of facts into relation with an earlier Brahmabhavana. Vallabha, following his usual scheme of Līlā and Ānanda as the chief constituents of his philosophy, tells us,

भक्त्या अगणितानन्दलीलारूपो योऽहमस्मि तादृशं मां तत्त्वतः अभिजानाति। तदनन्तरं मां लीलाकर्तारं विशते, आनन्दरूपो भवति इत्यर्थः।

God, according to him, is evidently the source of all Līlā. A devotee of God being in Him attains a share in his Līlā. Līlā produces Ānanda. Therefore, a devotee has a share in God's Ānanda also. This, according to Vallabha, constitutes liberation. But even this view fails to connect the conceptions of Līlā and Ānanda with the earlier Brahmabhavana, about which the Bhagavadgītā speaks.

CHAPTER V

A MYSTICAL INTERPRETATION OF THE BHAGAVADGĪTĀ (JÑĀNEŚVARA)

After a review of the doctrines of the great Vedāntic interpreters about the Bhagavadgītā, let us now pass on to the mystical interpretation of Jñāneśvara. Jñāneśvara is not far removed even in time from the "last of the Romans", the great Vedāntic commentators, and his interpretation is absolutely mystical and in a way super-Vedāntic. Jñāneśvara was not merely one of the greatest saints of Mahārāṣṭra, but also certainly one of the greatest interpreters of the Bhagavadgītā that have ever lived. The most distinguishing feature of his interpretation of the Bhagavadgītā is his unique combination of philosophy, poetry and mysticism. Its philosophy is of a high order no doubt, but its poetry is of a still higher order. And when mysticism is combined with philosophical insight and poetical imagination, one can easily see how Jñāneśvara's interpretation of the Bhagavadgītā stands supreme.

The eight original points of interpretation which we have selected from Jñāneśvara are these: In the first place, we shall speak of what he terms the Sun of Absolute Reality, अद्वैतसूर्य or चित्सूर्य, a very sustained metaphor in poetico-mystical terminology. We shall then go to the cosmological argument which has been advanced by Jñāneśvara for the existence of God. This occupies a peculiar position in Indian philosophy, because other philosophers have not touched this aspect of the question. In fact, it can very well be compared with the cosmological argument as is advanced by the

Western philosophers. Thirdly, we shall see how he takes up the scheme of illusion from interpreters like Śaṁkarācārya, and speaks of the Flood of Illusion or Māyānadī, which he describes in a very beautiful manner in a sustained metaphor. We shall next see how Jñāneśvara tells us the way of search for God through miseries. It is probably miseries themselves which take us towards God. This will be followed by our account of his excellent psychological analysis of the eight mystical emotions which a mystic experiences in his onward journey on the spiritual path. This compares well with the description of mystical emotions in classical Sanskrit Rhetoric, as well as with that given by a powerful Marathi poet-saint belonging to the line of Jñāneśvara, namely, Ekanātha. We shall thereafter proceed to a very important point in Jñāneśvara, namely, the doctrine of unison which he unfolds at great length and in powerful terms. In fact, this might be regarded as one of his chief contributions to the interpretation of the Bhagavadgītā, and even more than this is his original doctrine of asymptotism, for which it would be difficult to find a parallel. No other Indian philosopher has thought of positing such a doctrine of asymptotism, and it is this doctrine which crowns Jñāneśvara's mystical interpretation of the Bhagavadgītā. Finally, we come to a very graphic poetical description of spiritual victory, which is obtained by a mystic towards the end of his spiritual career.

The Sun of Absolute Reality

Let us begin with the sublime description of the Sun of Absolute Reality given by Jñāneśvara. We are reminded of a similar description, though not in such poetical and powerful terms, by Plato in his Republic, when he speaks of his highest Idea, the Idea of the Good, as the Sun of the world of Ideas. Jñāneśvara has developed his conception of the Sun of Absolute Reality in mystical terms in his Jñāneśvarī. There is a great difference between the spiritual sun and the physical sun, he says. While the physical sun makes the phenomenal world rise into view, the spiritual sun makes it disappear altogether. As the physical Sun eats up the celestial stars when he rises above the horizon, the spiritual sun eats up the stars both of knowledge and of ignorance. Jñāneśvara proceeds to point out further resemblances as well as differences in the working of the spiritual sun and the physical sun. When the spiritual sun dawns, the individual souls leave their nests, like birds, at dawn of day and go on their spiritual pilgrimage. Varying the metaphor, Jñāneśvara tells us that the souls are like bees, which have been hitherto pent up inside the flowers of the subtle bodies, but as soon as the day dawns they rush out of the petals and fly into the open air. Further, intellect and illumination have been compared by Jñāneśvara to a pair of Cakravāka birds who love each other but who are divided at night by the river of difference. They are crying out for each other but they cannot meet. It is only when the day dawns that they come together and there is great rejoicing. This is as much as to say that when mystical realisation arises, intellect and illumination meet. The intellectual faculty and the mystical faculty, which had hitherto been separated, now meet and there is great consonance between them. Jñāneśvara further goes on to tell us that as the spiritual sun comes above the horizon, and as he gathers light and power and throws his rays upon the double convex lens of our consciousness, the rays meet in a focus which burns the forests of worldly life. Also taking another physical metaphor, Jñāneśvara tells us that as the rays of the spiritual sun pass obliquely through various strata to the surface of the earth, a mirage of occult powers is produced on account of the refraction of the rays. Let us not be tempted by these occult powers, says Jñāneśvara, in the course of our spiritual illumination. He gives us a further happy metaphor when he tells us that when the spiritual sun reaches the zenith, the shadow of the body hides itself altogether beneath one's feet and one feels one's identity with the spiritual sun. Finally, Jñāneśvara asks us " Who is there, let me know, who has visualised this spiritual sun ? " The spiritual sun shines so miraculously that he alone is the ultimate Reality and there is nothing left for him to illuminate. The subject-object relation comes to an end, he alone remains, the unity of the subject and object, the Absolute, the Sun of Spiritual Reality.

Apart from the philosophical and mystical import of this passage, we have to notice what great powers Jñāneśvara had in the observation of nature. The disappearance of the stars when the sun rises, the birds flying out of their nests at dawn of day, the bees rushing hastily out of the blown-up flowers, the meeting of the pair of Cakravāka birds at daylight, and the disappearance of the shadow of the body beneath the feet when the sun comes to the zenith are observations clever enough. But the two observations of nature which Jñāneśvara makes may be regarded as of extraordinary value, considering the times in which he lived, namely, the rays of light passing through a double convex lens producing a flame of fire and the refraction of the sun's rays through different strata producing a mirage, observations which do not make mysticism incompatible with scientific insight.

The Cosmological Argument for the Existence of God.

Let us now proceed to the cosmological argument for the existence of God, which has been very well developed by Jñāneśvara. As we have said, this argument has hardly been used by other Indian philosophers, and we must compliment Jñāneśvara upon having advanced this argument for the existence of God. In fact, the cosmological argument has had a great history, as students of philosophy know. The so-called arguments for the existence of God, the ontological, the cosmological and the physico-theological, have all been criticised by Kant, and he comes to the conclusion that these do not prove God; but that God can be proved only by the moral argument which he advances in the Critique of Practical Reason, or by the teleological argument which he advances in the Critique of Judgment The ontological argument has had an excellent exponent in Descartes, which Kant mentions with respect; but there was no necessity for him to make a disjunction between the cosmological argument and the physico-theological argument. The two really are connected and not merely this, but the teleological argument about which Kant speaks in his last critique, is also connected with both. So, on the whole, the cosmological argument is a very important one in trying to prove the existence of God from the order in nature. It is exactly this order in nature which Jñāneśvara stresses here. In the first place, he tells us that God is the mover of the world. The forces of nature are merely his bond-servants. We are reminded of Aristotle's dictum that God is the unmoved mover of the whole universe. We are also put in mind of the famous passage in the Upaniṣad अहं वृक्षस्य रेरिवा ।... "I am the mover of the tree" and so on. And the tree goes on in its individual and universal aspects to be regulated by the mover of the body and the mover of the world who are ultimately one. Jñāneśvara also gives us some illustrations in which God's cosmological power is exhibited. It is God who commands the sun to follow a particular order every day during all months and seasons. Canute, the great king, rebuked his flattering courtiers by pointing out to them that the order of God in nature was superior to his own. God orders the wind to move ceaselessly on ; He orders the earth to bear the burden of all the creatures upon her surface. Unfortunately, sometimes there are earthquakes also, but even they are due to the Will of God. He orders the mountains not to move from their places, and he tells the ocean not to overstep its boundaries. So God's power pervades all these natural forces. Also we will not be far wrong if we say that God is the sum-total of all the forces of nature. When we look at nature, we see that the Order which governs it is nothing else except the Will of God. Also if we look at the matter even physiologically, we see that our exhalations and inhalations are themselves due to the Order of God, and when God desires that we should have final exhalation, we do finally exhale and there is no further inhalation. Death is thus itself due to the Will and Order of God. All these things show that God's omnipotence is every where and this omnipotence is, according to Jñāneśvara, one supreme cosmological argument for the existence of God.

The Flood of Illusion (Māyānadī)

Jñāneśvara's description of the flood of illusion is a very wonderful one. The concept of Māyā, which Śaṁkara had inaugurated, finds its best poetic expression in Jñāneśvara. He speaks of the course of Māyānadī which starts from the precipice of Brahman, which he calls Brahmācala or Brahmagiri. Who will not be reminded of the Brahmagiri mountain at Tryambakeśvara around which Jñāneśvara's father with his four children used to make peregrinations? The reference to the Brahmagiri seems to be a definite personal one. Issuing from the precipice of Brahman, therefore, Jñāneśvara tells us, as the river moves on, it produces bubbles in the shape of the elements which appear on its surface. It is further augmented by the rain of the qualities. The qualities send showers of rain into the flood and increase its flow. In this flood, as it moves on, there are whirlpools of hatred and windings of jealousy, and huge fishes in the shape of moral aberrations (Pramādas) swim inside the flood. The flood in its motion carries off the small hamlets of restraint and self-control which are situated on its two banks; it breaks its waters upon the island of sexual enjoyment which is a resort of a number of creatures, so that all these creatures ultimately are destined to be drowned in that great flood. Jñāneśvara very intelligently refers to the different kinds of Pramāṇas. One does not know how far he had studied Nyāya philosophy, but certainly here he makes mention of two important Pramāṇas, namely, reason and scriptures (बुद्धिप्रामाण्य and शब्दप्रामाण्य). Of those who are dependent upon their reason trying to swim across the river, no trace is left in the course of their swimming, and they sink in the abyss of self-conceit. The sacred scriptures are merely huge pieces of stone which a man fastens to his chest and thus being heavily laden, he falls into the mouth of the whale of arrogance. बुद्धिप्रामाण्य and शब्दप्रामाण्य having been thus disposed of, Jñāneśvara tells us in a general way that other means of swimming across the river, that is, other criteria or Pramāṇas are only sure ways of destruction. Ultimately no intellectual criterion enables us to escape the Māyānadī. Finally, if we want to cross such a terrific stream, we must have a steersman in the shape of a spiritual teacher. We must have a rudder in the shape of devotion, which conception we take the liberty of introducing in the description. We must travel on the sure raft of mystical experience. It is only when these three things meet, namely, the spiritual teacher, devotion and mystical experience, that we have the possibility of crossing that great flood of illusion. But one very extraordinary phenomenon takes place in the course of this flood. It disappears as soon as we begin to cross it. As we have noticed before that when the Sun of Absolute Reality rises, there is nothing left for him to illuminate; similarly here, in the case of the flood of illusion, it so happens that as soon as we have begun to cross it, no water remains to cross.

The Search of God through Miseries.

Jñāneśvara's description of the search of God through miseries can hardly be paralleled by similar descriptions, reminding us as it does, at two different places of certain Hindi songs, especially the poems of Kabīra, the parallelism of which we have discussed elsewhere. Jñāneśvara tells us that our life might be regarded as a boat with a hundred holes. Kabīra had spoken of टूटी नाव ऊपर जा बैठा, which we have discussed elsewhere in our explanation of the song रे दिल गाफ़िल गफ़लत मत कर एक दिन जम आवेगा. Who can keep his body bare, asks Jñāneśvara, when missiles are being hurled at him every moment? When a conflagration is raging all round, as happened once in the Khāṇḍava-vana, who can hope to remain enclosed inside it? Our best endeavour should be to get ourselves out of that conflagration as early as possible. Then Jñāneśvara tells us that life indeed might be regarded as a fair. Here again we are reminded of another line of Kabīra's song सौदा करने या जग आया. In this fair what we see is that wares of miseries are being spread out by the sellers, and Death, who is one of the principal sellers, is measuring the years and the destinies of men; he is rationing life's years to people. Making an appeal to the heavens, Jñāneśvara asks "Is not the moon proverbially consumptive? Do not the stars rise only in order to set"? If this happens to the heavens, why should this not happen to men upon the earth? In a very important discussion upon the nature of death, Jñāneśvara further tells us that at the very beginning, death is encircling the foetus in the mother's womb. Perhaps, when a child is born the parents hoist auspicious flags. But in the midst of happiness comes misery. The child is really approaching death every day as it grows, and yet people rejoice and hoist flags. People cannot afford even to hear the word 'death'. As Spinoza has said, in the course of the life-history of man, when he begins to watch the track of those that have gone by, he sees no returning footprints. All steps point towards the den of death and none returns. Histories and mythologies consequently, says Jñāneśvara, are merely collections of death-stories. Who will not be reminded of taking ourselves away from the purview of death when all these things are taking place round about us? Finally, taking a beautiful metaphor from animal life, Jñāneśvara tells us that a frog, which is attempting to catch at flies, is itself at the same time being swallowed by a big boa. We in this mortal world try to aspire after many objects, unmindful of the fact that we ourselves are at the same time being devoured by death. The present writer had an opportunity of witnessing (under a microscope) an analogous phenomenon in the region of the microbes, when he saw one medium-sized microbe catching hold of another, while at the same time it was itself being caught up inside the circle set up by the tentacles of a rotifera. Such is the life of creatures from protozoa upwards to the life of the highest creatures. Wherever we look, death is encircling us and it behoves all of us, therefore, to return to God and to think about Him unmindful of the power of death. On a contemplation of the various kinds of miseries enumerated above, we shall see that there is no way of escape from them except by devotion to God. Jñāneśvara asks:

> "Upon what power do these people count, that they do not try to worship Me?...... Who has ever heard a tale of happiness in this world of mortals? Can one sleep with comfort on a bed of scorpions or of burning coals?...... Alas, born in this mortal world, Oh Arjuna, get thyself away from it; go by the path of Bhakti, so that thou mayest reach My immaculate home."
>
> —Jñā. IX. 493...516.

The Eight Mystical Emotions

As a man advances in his mystical experience, he exhibits various kinds of physiological, physio-psychological reactions, which have been classified by writers on Alaṅkāra Śāstra as well as on mysticism into a number of prominent emotional features. They are generally regarded to be eight Sāttvika Bhāvas; but it is not necessary that there should be only eight. There might be many more; and even in regard to the eight there is no consensus of opinion among the various writers on the science of emotions. On the whole, therefore, we may say that the following are the chief mystical emotions that a man exhibits in his spiritual development. Physiologically, we might say, the symptoms which a mystic develops are horripilation, perspiration and lachrymation, this last being particularly due to feelings inside the mind. Then there are physio-psychological reactions such as tremor and paresis. These two are opposed to each other and yet the mystic develops them both and exhibits them at different times. As regards the psychological reactions, we have *epoche*, peace and joy. Paresis physiologically produces *epoche* psychologically. Consequently, *epoche* is equivalent and conducive to peace, while opposed to peace is joy, and the great beauty of psychological reaction to mystical experience is that antithetical qualities become mingled together. On the whole, therefore, the eight different mystical emotions which a man enjoys on his spiritual march are horripilation, perspiration, lachrymation, tremor, paresis, *epoche*, peace and joy. Jñāneśvara has given a graphic description of these emotions in a classical passage which we quote below :

"The duality that so long existed between the self and the world, now ceased to exist. The mind became immediately composed. Internally there was a feeling of joy. Externally there was a fading of the power of the limbs. From top to toe, the aspirant became full of horripilation, as at the beginning of the rainy season the body of a mountain becomes overspread with grass. Drops of sweat crept over his body, as drops of water creep on the moonstone, when it is touched by the rays of the moon. As an unblown lotus swings to and fro on the surface of the water on account of the bee which is pent up inside its petals, similarly the body of the devotee began to shake on account of the feelings of internal bliss. As drops of camphor fall down when the core of the camphor plant opens out, similarly tears of joy trickled down from his eyes. As the sea experiences tide after tide when the moon arises, similarly his mind experienced surge after surge of emotions. Thus all the eight Sāttvika emotions began to compete in the mind of the mystic, and he sat on the Throne of Beatific Joy."

—Jñā. XI. 245–252

Unison

Jñāneśvara has given an excellent account of the unison of a devotee with God. He gives a good philosophical interpretation of it which shows what great powers of reasoning he had. In the first place, he tells us that the chief condition of unison is surrender.

Surrender philosophically interpreted means identification. "Be submissive unto Me", says the Lord, "so that thou mayest become united with Me." Unless, therefore, we surrender to God, no unison can ultimately take place. Secondly, we have to see how Jñāneśvara discusses the complete annihilation of individuality which leads to a mystical unison. He gives various illustrations to express what he means. These illustrations might be classified as scientific, material, psychological and moral. The mystic becomes identified with God, as space inside a pitcher becomes identified with the space outside when the pitcher breaks. When iron and fuel, which are material objects, come in contact with the touch-stone and the fire respectively, they are transformed into gold and conflagration. Dreams pass into wakefulness and lose their individuality. Sin and merit likewise, which are moral conceptions, says Jñāneśvara, are ultimately transformed into God's Being, so that from all these points of view there is annihilation of individuality and unison with God.

> "To say that, when God is seen, the separate individuality of a person remains, is this not a piece of foolish gibbering ?...Iron in its ironness may rust, but when it has become gold by contact with the philosopher's stone, no impurities can continue to spoil it. When fire is churned out of sticks, the sticks will no longer remain as sticks. When the Sun has arisen, shall darkness reappear? Or when wakefulness comes, shall the illusion of a dream continue to give trouble? Take no thought, therefore, Oh Arjuna, for thy sin and merit shall both be transformed into My Being...From

this time onwards thou hast become free. Entertain no anxiety, therefore, and resign thyself to Me in being united with Me."

—Jñā. XVIII. 1398–1416.

After having discussed the philosophical conception of unison, Jñāneśvara next proceeds to a further one, namely, the annihilation of difference. Is there any difference between Eastern and Western waters, he asks. The Eastern sea and the Western sea are only different in name. The ocean and the river cease to be separate when the river flows into the ocean. If a piece of salt, says Jñāneśvara, tries to separate two different kinds of water, it becomes mingled with both. Jñāneśvara gives an excellent illustration referring to Sañjaya, who says that when he was hearing the sublime mystical conversation between Arjuna and Kṛṣṇa, he was so enraptured that he became mingled with both. In this way, in a state of unison all difference is annihilated. Further, Jñāneśvara tells us that in such a state, the self and God may be related to each other as quality and substance. Rāmānuja has already said so. Jñāneśvara points out that as camphor and its fragrance are not different, or a jewel and its lustre are not different, so there is no difference left between the individual soul and God in such a state. One becomes the quality of the other, which is the substance, *causa sui*, that which exists in itself and for itself.

Jñāneśvara goes on to his favourite metaphor of the mirror and tells us that in the case either of single reflection or of infinite reflection, the difference between the devotee and God vanishes. Taking the case of single reflection in a mirror, the original and the image lose their difference. Patañjali has spoken of तदा द्रष्टुः स्वरूपेऽवस्थानम्. The Gītā speaks of आत्मना आत्मानं पश्यन् आत्मनि तुष्यति. In any case, the devotee sees God in his own image. The Bible says that God created man in His image, and we may say man is paying back the debt by creating God in his. Further, there is that sublime conception of infinite reflection which Jñāneśvara now puts forth. When two mirrors are placed, one in front of the other, which, shall we say, reflects which ? There are infinite reflections between the two. As a student of physics in the year 1904 at the Deccan College, I used to perform this experiment in our room. Two mirrors with two differently coloured borders, when placed against each other, show themselves in alternately coloured infinite reflections, one into the other. Similarly Jñāneśvara tells us that there is no limit to the number of reflections that take place between the devotee and God. Arjuna, he tells us, saw himself along with God in God, and God saw himself along with Arjuna in Arjuna. This is a state of infinite reflection to which the devotee is ultimately led.

We now go on to two final points under this head of unison : First, devotional unison and then mystical unison. Under devotional unison, we have two extracts from Jñāneśvara, which tell us that God says whatever His devotee utters is His praise, whatever he sees is His vision, whatever he touches is His worship, whatever he contemplates is the chanting of His prayer, while his sleep constitues ecstasy. Then again, being pleased with the great devotion of the aspirant, God says ultimately "I am he". We are accustomed to hear in Vedānta of the expression 'I am he' as uttered by the realiser ; सोऽहं or तत्त्वमसि is that expression. In the present case, however, it is God who says : 'I am he', that He is the devotee. The tables are turned. Whether I am He or He is I, it does not matter. It only means there is absolute devotional unison between the devotee and God. Finally, we find one very significent remark in the Jñāneśvarī, where Jñāneśvara speaks of the identification of the aspiring mystic with the object of his vision :

हा गां जीवांपैलीकडिली खुणे । जो पावोनि वावरोंह जाणें ।
तो देहाचेनि वेगळेपणें । काय वेगळा होय ॥

—Jñā. VII. 118

Now, it has been the usual teaching of the great mystics that the forms which they see in mystical experience are ultimately identical with themselves, and a man has to sit in judgment upon the quality of his own mind and his own experience by taking into account the different forms of mystical realisation which he experiences. There is also a graded development in these forms. The mystics teach also that such a rising devotee must ultimately feel his identity with his own Self. It is only then that there is perfect unison; but the point is that whatever a devotee mystically experiences is always an index of his own spiritual achievement.

Asymptotic Realisation

Jñāneśvara next makes a very original contribution to the philosophy of mysticism. This is what might be called his doctrine of asymptotism. Under this we shall discuss two points: (1) asymptotic realisation and (2) the doctrine that perfection can be attained only gradually. We are familiar with the word 'asymptote' in mathematics. A curve and an axis approaching each other infinitely and meeting at infinity is the essence of asymptotic approximation. What we find in the case of an aspiring mystic is that he goes on asymptotically approaching God. That is Jñāneśvara's doctrine. Instead of there being a final and perfect identity between the mystic and God, the mystic moves towards God and so we may say that he meets God at infinity. There is just a little difference beween them. Just as there is difference between the moon of the fourteenth day and the full-moon of the fifteenth day, or just as gold of fifteen carats just falls short of gold of sixteen carats, to that extent only does the devotee fall short of full divine attainment. As one can distinguish between the sea and the river by the stillness and the motion of the waters, similarly in the case of God and devotee also we can make a slight distinction. " The devotee attains to the Godhead, falling just short of His entire Being" (Jñā. XVIII. 1087–90). The reason for this approximation or asymptotic realisation is the physical, the mental and other limitations of the mystic. So long as he has a body and a mind and has to live in the world, to that extent and till that time he must fall short of complete divine attainment.

> " Even though the devotee may reach unison with God, yet he remains a devotee. The saint remains a saint so long as he has to discharge his bodily functions. "
>
> —Jñā. VII. 114, 117.

जैसा वारा कां गगनीं विरे । मग वारेपण वेगळें नुरे ।
तेवीं भक्त हे पैज न सरे । जरी ऐक्या आला ॥ ११४ ॥

आणि ज्ञानाचेनि उजिडलेपणें । मी आत्मा ऐसें तो जाणे ।
म्हणऊनि मीही तैसेंचि म्हणे । उचंबळला सांता ॥ ११७ ॥

Jñāneśvara further proceeds to talk of the gradual and graduated perfection in the mystic. It is the time factor that counts. A man who starts on his journey must not expect to reach the end at once. There is bound to be a time interval between initiation and realisation. A Sādhaka who gets himself initiated by a teacher must work and wait for attaining realisation and therefore liberation. It will require a good deal of time before he conquers his mind and intellect, devotes himself entirely to God, makes possible some definite attainment in that line and ultimately achieves divine realisation. So, initiation and realisation should not be spoken of in the same breath. Perfection is only gradual. साधु कि संगत गुरुजी की सेवा, बनत बनत बनि आई रे, says Mīrābāī. A gardener might sprinkle water upon the trees and the plants, but it is only after the spring sets in that the trees and plants bear fruit. Also Jñāneśvara here makes a fine remark that the great God Śaṁkara Himself is only a pilgrim journeying on the spiritual path, जये मार्गींचा कापडी महेश अजुनी. He has just made an approximation to the infinitude of God; and if this happens in the case of God Śaṁkara, far more must it happen in the case of us small mortals.

> "Granted that all the preparation is made for the realisation of God, that one meets the Guru, that the Guru imparts to him the knowledge of the true path; granted that the seed that is sown is the best of its kind, yet it is only in course of time that a rich harvest can be reaped."
>
> —Jñā. XVIII. 996–1008.

The Spiritual Victory

Jñāneśvara closes his account of the message of the Gītā in a passage which it would be hard to surpass. In that passage he summarises the whole mystical teaching of the Bhagavadgītā; and as this would be a fitting sequel not merely to our discussion of the mystical philosophy of Jñāneśvara but also to our present part of the work, we shall end it by an account of Jñāneśvara's powerful mystical description of the ultimate victory of a spiritual warrior. This victory could be looked at in four stages of development. First, the accoutrements of the warrior; second, the battlefield of life; third, the imperial procession after conquest and the last, the coronation of the mystic on the Throne of Unitive Life. As regards the accoutrements, Jñāneśvara tells us that such a developing mystic mounts the steed of Rājayoga, puts on the armour of dispassion and holds the sword of concentration in his hand. Equipped with these accoutrements, he proceeds to the battlefield of life. Into the battlefield itself he moves like the Sun into darkness, and cuts to pieces all the different eneimes, such as अहंकार, बल, दर्प, काम, क्रोध and परिग्रह which Jñāneśvara mentions by name. All this is done ultimately for the sake of winning the bride of liberation;

तुका म्हणे मुक्ति परिणिली नोवरी । आतां दिवस चारी खेळी मेळी ॥

Similarly a great Kannada poet-saint has spoken of the mystic as marrying the Maid of Liberation, मुक्तांगिन मद्वियागी. So when the battle is won, liberation is attained. Then we go on to see how Jñāneśvara describes the mystic's procession on the imperial road. Virtues such as अमानित्व, अदंभित्व, अहिंसा, क्षांति and the rest, which have been enumerated in the Bhagavadgītā, all now act as vassals and move along with the victorious warrior as his retinue. The socalled Yoga-Bhūmikās, the different stages of Yogic development and all the powers and prosperities, ऋद्धि सिद्धिs, assemble in thousands in order to see the spectacle and shower flowers on the mystic who is now soon to be crowned king. Ultimately, the coronation takes place, the drum of victory is beaten, attainment of Swarājya, which word has been specially mentioned by Jñāneśvara, is proclaimed. All the three worlds become filled with joy. In such a state of beatification, the banner of self-identity is unfurled, as is seen in the case of all victorious achievements. In the present case, it must be remembered, the banner is of self-identity, identity of self with God. And finally, when all this has been accomplished by the mystic, he is crowned king on the Throne of Spiritual Experience.

PART III

THE LABYRINTH OF MODERN INTERPRETATIONS

CHAPTER VI

INTERPOLATIONISM

Hitherto we have seen how the Bhagavadgītā stands in relation to the Upaniṣads, Sāṁkhya-Yoga and the Brahmasūtras, and how the great Vedāntic commentators have interpreted the Bhagavadgītā, each in his own way. We have also seen the original points in the mystical interpretation of the Bhagavadgītā by the great poet-saint of Mahārāṣṭra, Jñāneśvara. We shall now pass on to modern interpretations of the Bhagavadgītā. There is a very large number of such interpretations, but we shall select only eight of them for our purpose, namely those of Garbe and Bhandarkar, Farquhar and Buddhiraja, Tilak and Gandhi, Otto and Aurobindo. The opinions of these we shall consider under the following philosophical heads: Interpolationism and Bhāgavatism, Christianism and Buddhism, Activism and Detachment, Numenism and Divinisation. A student who undertakes a study of the Bhagavadgītā will really find his head turned when he goes into the depths of all these different interpretations and he may well find himself in a labyrinth. Is there a way of rescue for him from this labyrinth? Yes. The only line of rescue for him, according to us, would be the path of God-realisation.

Let us begin by discussing the theories of interpolationism in regard to the interpretation of the Bhagavadgītā. On the whole, there might be said to be five such theories, the first being the most important. The names that can be mentioned here in connection with these theories of interpolationism are Garbe, Holtzmann, Oldenberg, Schrader and Otto. Garbe's theory of interpolationism is intertwined with the doctrine of theism; Holtzmann's with the interests of pantheism; Schrader's is really an exterpolationism more than an interpolationism; Oldenberg stands as an apostle of a twelve-chapter work of the Bhagavadgītā and Otto introduces eight external tracts in the original form of the Bhagavadgītā. We shall see that even though there is this incidence of a pluralistic interpolationism in Otto, still the total summing up of the meaning of the Bhagavadgītā is a numenistic, mystical ideal for which he stands, as we shall see at the close of this chapter.

Garbe

(*a*) *Exclusion of Mīmāṁsic and Vedānta Passages* :— Before we go on to Garbe, we must mention that the theory of interpolationism was first suspected by Humboldt in the year 1826, and that Garbe might be regarded as one of the great modern apostles of interpolationism. We may say that just as there is a large collection of works on Biblical criticism, so even here the Gītā criticism was started by Garbe. We shall consider the following points under Garbe's interpolationistic theory about the Bhagavadgītā. We shall begin by considering the reasons why he excludes the Vedāntic and Mīmāṁsic passages from his text. Then we shall deal with the criticism that has been made upon this procedure particularly by Edgerton and Winternitz. Next we shall examine the significance of the capital which Garbe makes out of the occurrence of the word Māyā six times in the Bhagavadgītā. Then comes a very important point and a point to the great credit of Garbe, namely, his interpretation of उपद्रष्टा and

अनुमन्ता, God, the all-seer and the all-knower, as common to the नृसिंहोत्तरतापनियोपनिषत् and the Bhagavadgītā. Finally, following his philosophic bent of mind, we see Garbe speaking about Kṛṣṇa as rising from the conception of a man through the conception of a man-God to the conception of God in the course of progressive development. This, in short, is a brief outline of Garbe's account of his interpolationist theory about the Bhagavadgītā.

We have said above that Garbe excludes the Mīmāṁsic and Vedāntic passages from his text of the Bhagavadgītā. On a general review of all the passages that have been excluded by Garbe, we do find that his two chief enemies are Mīmāṁsā and Vedānta, Advaitism in particular. But there are many other points also on account of which Garbe tries to exclude a number of verses from the original Bhagavadgītā. For example, all considerations of super-moralism or transcendence of the three qualities involved in the conception of Nistraiguṇya, all essences such as the great luminosity in the Sun as in the XV chapter, the conception of the Vibhūtis in the X chapter, all considerations or references to Brahman, all schemes of absorption in Brahman, Yogic effects like the equanimity to be obtained in the process of Yoga, all these have been excluded by Garbe. On the other hand, all those passages have been retained which promote theism, which promote moralism as ancillary to theism, and particularly philosophic devotion. It would take a long time to go into the details of all these exclusions and preferences; but we have mentioned these because, of all these exclusions, Advaitism is the chief enemy whom Garbe wants to fight. Dr. Bhandarkar liked his procedure very much, though he would have preferred to interpret the whole of the Bhagavadgītā theistically, regarding even the pantheistic passages, as theistic. That of course is going even a little further than Garbe. Garbe is endowed with great powers of linguistic interpretation, of philology and of philosophic analysis. So, his opinion became the most respectable during the early years of the present century.

Garbe himself mentions that the two sets of passages which he wants to exclude are the Mīmāṁsic and the Vedāntic. We shall take two typical specimens of these very shortly. In the meanwhile, we might mention that Garbe suggests that it was a slowly gathering and accumulating conviction that he was able to exclude these passages not as a matter of chance nor as a fit of fancy, with the result that out of 700 verses 170 fall out. He says :

> "I have ventured to carry into practical execution the idea of separating certain portions of the Bhagavadgītā not as a result of any abrupt conceit but on the basis of a slowly accumulating conviction. (He takes the credit for having read the Gītā six times !); thus decidedly by removing passages from most of the chapters of the Gītā with the result that out of 700 verses, 170 fall out."
>
> —Introduction to the Bhagavadgītā, p. 31.

These according to Garbe do not belong to the original Bhagavadgītā. In this procedure Garbe has given a rude shock for the first time to the traditional interpreters of the Bhagavadgītā. He takes theism for granted and everything that goes against it is an interpolation. His method involves a *petitio principii*, taking a thing for granted and then working out from it, in fact taking for granted what one wants to prove. The outcome of such a procedure ultimately, Garbe tells us, is that no real gap is left anywhere in the whole of the Bhagavadgītā. We shall see presently what other scholars have said in regard to this real gap or unreal gap. We cannot help noticing here the words of Garbe, " putting into execution his scheme of exclusions ". We must indeed give him the credit for having carried out his scheme of exclusions! For, was it not he who first sundered the Bhagavadgītā into two parts, the theistic and the pantheistic, under the impression that the pantheistic doctrine did not belong to the time of the Bhagavadgītā? If, however, we were to interpret the Bhagavadgītā in a mystical manner, we might well see how the theistic and the pantheistic portions could be reconciled.

We might take two typical passages of exclusion in order to justify what we mean. The first is a passage from Chapter III, verses 10 to 15, where a defence of Yajña is made, which Garbe wants to exclude; the second is a passage from Chapter II, verses 42 to 46, which is of anti-Mīmāṁsic and Vedāntic content and which defends self-realisation. If we just bring out, in a very terse form, the meanings of these two passages, we shall see the reason why Garbe was tempted to exclude both. He wants neither the Pūrva Mīmāṁsā, nor the Uttara Mīmāṁsā to interfere in his theistic interpretation of the Bhagavadgītā. If we take the first passage, Chapter III, 10–15 (सह यज्ञाः प्रजाः सृष्ट्वा), we shall see that that passage makes the following points: (i) It was God who created the institution of sacrifice which is indeed the fulfiller of all desires. (ii) We are asked to propitiate the gods with the result that the gods will propitiate us. (iii) The highest ideal, therefore, to be achieved is such a mutual propitiation by gods of men and by men of gods. (iv) He who does not perform a sacrifice and who does not make an oblation, or an offering, in fact, he who does not give, as we shall see later on, a spiritual income-tax, should be regarded as a thief. (v) Finally, all sins will be removed in the case of a man who lives on the remnants of a sacrifice. He must first offer everything to others, and what remains as residue with him, with that alone he should remain content. He who thus partakes and lives merely on the remnants of a sacrifice is the greatest of those who lead a sacrificial life. This is a passage which Garbe wants to exclude, because it defends ritualism.

Another passage which he wants to exclude on the ground of its defence of the Vedāntic attitude consists of the verses, 42 to 46 in Chapter II (यामिमां पुष्पितां वाचम् … ब्राह्मणस्य विजानतः). Let us note the points which this passage makes: (i) The passage condemns sacrifice because the ideals of a sacrifice are merely enjoyment and power. (ii) It involves no aspiration towards stability in God. (iii) The Vedas, the author tells us, are subject to the suzerainty of the three guṇas and hence of no avail. (iv) It is only life in Ātman which can take one beyond considerations of Yoga and Kṣema, acquisition and security. (v) Finally, the Vedas are like a pond in an all-enveloping sea of spiritual experience and are of no consequence when we take into account spiritual realisation as a whole. These are the points which the Vedāntic passage makes and on that account Garbe wants to exclude this Vedāntic passage also. So on the whole, both ritualism and non-ritualism seem to be his enemies. In a similar way, if we just carry our imagination back, we shall find that the same antinomy of ritualism and non-ritualism as in the Bhagavadgītā is mentioned in the Muṇḍaka Upaniṣad also. What the Bhagavadgītā has done is merely to copy the antinomy from the Muṇḍaka. As the writer has observed in his " Creative Period of Indian Philosophy " (Bombay University, 1927) : "It is evident from a consideration of the halting attitude of the philosopher of the Muṇḍaka that while in one breath he extols ritualism (I. ii. 1.6) and in another condemns it outright (I. ii. 7–12), that even in this respect the Muṇḍaka has been the prototype of the Bhagavadgītā " (p. 279). This conception of the battle of ritualism and non-ritualism, which was started by the Muṇḍaka, has been taken over bodily by the Bhagavadgītā from the Muṇḍaka, but it rises beyond both ritualism and non-ritualism.

Garbe's procedure has been subjected to criticism from different points of view and by different scholars. We shall not enter here into many linguistic or philological criticisms which have been made but mention only a few points of philosophic importance. (1) Edgerton tells us that Garbe contents himself by saying that when we have removed the excised passages, the two ends meet and there is no real gap created anywhere. This is exactly the point with which Edgerton disagrees. According to him, the excised passages, even as they are, can in many cases be shown to be connected both ways to the preceding and the following portions. (2) Again, Edgerton relies upon the authority of an old scholar like Oldenberg, who believed in the unitary teaching of the

Bhagavadgītā, and entirely agrees with him in regarding the spirit of the Bhagavadgītā as completely unitary. Edgerton says :

> "Garbe is mistaken in thinking that the elimination of certain passages reunites verses which evidently belong together but have been separated by the alleged interpolations. I believe that just the opposite is the case. That is, a verse immediately following a passage excised by Garbe can in many cases be shown to be connected with the excised passage."
>
> The Bhagavadgītā, P. 98.

> "I am glad to find that so high an authority as Oldenberg felt as I do that the general spirit of the Gītā is no less unitary than that of similar works of its class, and that it is an error to see in it a mixture of different schools of philosophy."
>
> Ibid, P. 99, Footnote.

(3) Winternitz tells us that a reconciliation of different points of view or of different aspects of philosophic thought which has been effected by the Bhagavadgītā, and which, in fact, is the essence of its teaching, has been falsely represented as involving a theory of interpolation. (4) Bhandarkar's point of view instead of being merely theistic may be regarded as even super-theistic, which we may call by the name of Bhāgavatism or Prapattism. He would go even a little further than Garbe so far as the theistic aspect of the Bhagavadgītā is concerned, and not allow anything to be understood in a pantheistic sense. Instead of dividing the Gītā into the theistic and pantheistic

portions, he would like to regard the whole of the Bhagavadgītā as theistic or even as super-theistic involving the doctrine of Bhāgavatism or Prapattism.

(b) *Occurrence of the word Māyā in the Bhagavadgītā* :– Taking his stand on the theistic interpretation of the Bhagavadgītā, it is no wonder that Garbe should fight shy of the word Māyā, and particularly of its significance which involves the conception of unreality or illusion. The word Māyā has occurred six times in the Bhagavad-gītā, twice in the sense in which Garbe would like to have it, thrice in the sense to which Garbe is opposed, and once in the sense which Garbe would try to enlist along with those who support Vedāntism, but which is really Janus-faced pointing both ways. Garbe's contention is that the earlier passages are theistic in character and the word Māyā occurring in those passages means miraculous power. For example, take the two quotations : (1) संभवाम्यात्ममायया (IV. 6) and (2) यंत्रारूढानि मायया (XVIII. 61), where Māyā means miraculous power, the power of God who wields a magical weapon in his hand. Later passages according to Garbe involve pantheism, and therefore Māyā is introduced there, according to him, in the sense of illusion. These passages are : मम माया दुरत्यया...... मायामेतां तरन्ति ते । VII. 14. and माययाऽपहृतज्ञाना । VII. 15. In these cases, the word Māyā means illusion and the passages must therefore be excluded, says Garbe, from the orthodox scheme. Finally, the word Māyā also occurs in the expression, योगमायासमावृतः । VII. 25. Garbe would like to understand Māyā here in the sense of illusion, but we may point out that it may mean power also. Hence even though Garbe would try to include it in the later passages, we feel that it cannot be so included. The reason for such inclusion by Garbe, in our opinion, seems to be that he approaches the question from a preconceived notion.

(*c*) *God as All-Seer and All-Knower in Nṛsiṁha Tāpanīya Upaniṣad*:—We must, however, compliment Garbe upon having in fact made a discovery in regard to the expression उपद्रष्टाऽनुमन्ता 9. 1. showing the connections between the नृसिंहोत्तरतापनीयोपनिषद् and the Bhagavadgītā. Garbe contends, and contends correctly, that the word Anumantā in this sense is of rare occurrence, and if the नृसिंहोत्तरतापनीयोपनिषद् has used that expression उपद्रष्टाऽनुमन्ता and if that expression occurs in the Bhagavadgītā also, it would follow that the Bhagavadgītā is the borrowing party provided the Upaniṣad could be proved to be earlier. In any case, this is a remarkable coincidence about उपद्रष्टाऽनुमन्ता, God the all-seer and God the all-knower, that these words should occur both in the नृसिंहोत्तरतापनीयोपनिषद् and the Bhagavadgītā. Garbe contends for the value of the present reference only so far as the age of the Bhagavadgītā is concerned as being later than that of the नृसिंहोत्तरतापनीयोपनिषद्. But he should have also contended for this expression उपद्रष्टाऽनुमन्ता as having a particularly theistic significance, and should therefore have included this under his own scheme of a theistic interpretation of the Bhagavadgītā. It has been observed above that उपद्रष्टाऽनुमन्ता is an expression of rare occurrence; but another analogue for the word Anumantā in the नृसिंहोत्तरतापनीयोपनिषद् is अनुज्ञाता which occurs many times in that Upaniṣad. In one case it links itself up with उपद्रष्टा. For example, in the verse :

ओतमोतेन जानीयादनुज्ञातारमान्तरम् ।
अनुज्ञामद्वयं लब्ध्वा उपद्रष्टारमाव्रजेत् ॥ IX.

Also we have in the same Upaniṣad that famous expression रहस्यमनुज्ञाता–VIII, one who penetrates the secret of things. Hence even though अनुज्ञाता is a more familiar expression than अनुमन्ता and both mean the same thing, the expression उपद्रष्टाऽनुमन्ता occurring even once in the Bhagavadgītā as in the नृसिंहोत्तरतापनीयोपनिषत् might well lead us to suppose that the Bhagavadgītā relies upon that Upaniṣad for its authority for the expression. Let us see what Garbe says :

> "The words उपद्रष्टा "spectator" and अनुमन्ता "assurer" here stand side by side, of which the latter is of such rare occurrence that the historical connection of the two passages is not open to doubt. As in the case of other references to Upaniṣadic literature, the नृसिंहोत्तरतापनीयोपनिषत् must here be regarded as the original and the Bhagavadgītā (XIII. 22) the copy, because the word Anumantā, as the designation of a form of the highest spirit, has its originality absolutely guaranteed in the नृसिंहोत्तरतापनीयोपनिषत् by the whole content of the text."
>
> Introduction to the B. G., p. 46

In this connection the present writer feels that the पूर्वतापनीय and उत्तरतापनीय Upaniṣads have not received their due recognition from Upaniṣadic scholars. Both the Upaniṣads are of high poetico-mystical value and replete with quotations. This might itself have served as an incentive to the Bhagavadgītā. Further, the नृसिंहपूर्वतापनीयोपनिषत् particularly calls its chapters by the name of Upaniṣads, not Khaṇḍas, Prapāṭhakas, Vallis or Adhyāyas. The Bhagavadgītā also consciously or unconsciously calls its chapters by the title of Upaniṣads, भगवद्गीतासूपनिषत्सु. Keith points out in this connection that the Gītā might itself be regarded as an Upaniṣad of the Śvetāśvatara type. As the present writer has said in a previous chapter, he would himself like to give to the Bhagavadgītā the status of an Upaniṣad. The determination of the age of the नृसिंहतापनीय Upaniṣad would go a long way in the determination of the age of the Bhagavadgītā and would be of greater service than the older Upaniṣads such as Kaṭha, Muṇḍaka, and the rest from which the Bhagavadgītā has definitely borrowed. In any case it stands to reason that the Bhagavadgītā was deeply influenced by the expression उपद्रष्टाऽनुमन्ता as occurring in the नृसिंह उत्तर तापनीय Upaniṣad in the following passage : देवा ह वै प्रजापतिमब्रुवन्निममेव नो भगवन्नोंकारमात्मानमुपादिशेति । तथेत्युपद्रष्टानुमन्तैष आत्मा नृसिंहश्चिद्रूप एवाविकारो ह्युपलब्धः। IX. 1. which has certainly a theistico-mystic significance.

(*d*) *Doctrine of Kṛṣṇa as Man, Man-God and God*:— Finally, we come to the interpretation of the personality of Kṛṣṇa by Garbe. With his deep insight into philosophy he does not find it difficult to point out that the conception of Kṛṣṇa rises from the status of a mere man through that of a demi-god to that of God himself. It was when Kṛṣṇa helped the Pāṇḍavas to secure victory in the great war that he was veritably raised from manhood to demi-godhood and then to God-hood itself. In a similar vein Hopkins has told us that exceptional personages may first be raised to the status of a demi-god and then to the status of God. Edgerton tells us the same story:

> " In the greater part of the Mahābhārata, Kṛṣṇa appears in a strictly human guise. In the narrative of the Gītā he is still both god and man, an incarnation of the Deity in human form. In the philosophical teaching of the Gītā, Kṛṣṇa has all the attributes of a full-fledged mono-theistic deity and at the same time the attributes of the Upaniṣadic Absolute. " The Bhagavadgītā, P. 31.

Other Interpolative Theories

(*a*) *Holtzmann.* Let us go on now to the four other interpolative theories. These are not so important as that of Garbe, and yet there are some points in them which are worth noticing, especially in the case of Otto whom we shall treat last in this section. As Garbe stands for theism, Holtzmann stands for a pantheistic interpretation of Bhagavadgītā. If Garbe said that theism was the original portion and pantheism the added one, Holtzmann says that pantheism was the original portion and theism was added later. Winternitz tries to reconcile these two extremes. He stands between Garbe and Holtzmann. He tells us that "after repeated readings of the Gītā and the most thorough investigation of the passages cut out by Garbe, he has come to the conclusion that even the original poem did not teach pure theism but theism tinged with pantheism." The points on which Holtzmann relies about the pantheistic interpretation of the Bhagavadgītā are the conception of the world-soul and the illusory nature of the fear of death. When these two are combined together, we have a pantheistic poem like the Bhagavadgītā. Very peculiarly, however, Droṇa is made by Holtzmann the speaker of the older portion, while Kṛṣṇa's character as speaker has been retained in the later one. We cannot call such an utterance by any other name except that of a rambling statement. What Droṇa had got to do with the pantheistic basis of the original Bhagavadgītā is hard to imagine. Kṛṣṇa, of course, had got something to do with the theistic portion; but his name is mentioned by commentators more in connection with pantheism than even with theism. Finally, Holtzmann tells us that "the theological idea underlying the Bhagavadgītā is at war with itself. On the one hand, we have the pantheistic world-soul which is impersonal, and on the other, a personalistic and realistic Kṛṣṇa-Viṣṇu, and we are asked to believe that the two are one." In trying to reconcile, therefore, the pantheistic conception of the world-soul with the theistic conception of a personal God, we find the present Bhagavadgītā to be a peculiar mixture of both these doctrines.

(*b*) *Oldenberg*. When we come to Oldenberg, we find him to be more level-minded than Holtzmann. He is a great Sanskrit scholar. His idea is that out of the eighteen chapters of the Bhagavadgītā, the first twelve only constitute the original text, while the last six may be regarded as addenda. Such suggestions have been made by other writers also, especially in view of the fact that a particular chapter of the Bhagavadgītā like the XVI finds a place in these last six chapters, as well as a chapter like the XVII. The XV, of course, is alright, and a major portion of the XVIII. But the fact that the group of the last six chapters contains some Adhyāyas, which do not stand on a level with the other parts of the Bhagavadgītā, might well tempt a scholar like Oldenberg to suppose that only the first twelve chapters constitute the original Bhagavadgītā. Also a suggestion has been made by other scholars that if the Mahābhārata is to be supposed to contain interpolations, as it grew from its early beginnings to its later fully developed form, from Jaya to Bhārata and from Bhārata to Mahābhārata, why should not a suggestion like this also have tempted Oldenberg to consider that the original Bhagavadgītā consisted only of twelve Adhyāyas while the later Adhyāyas were added in course of time?

(c) *Schrader*. The theory of Schrader might be regarded as a theory of exterpolationism more than that of interpolationism : the former, because according to the Kāśmīrian text there are 714½ verses in the Bhagavadgītā which figure is greater than the orthodox number of 700 ; the latter, because the Kāśmīrian text introduces 282 new readings of the orthodox text. For these reasons the Kāśmīrian recension may be regarded as a peculiar combination of exterpolationism and interpolationism. The grounds for constituting a distinct Kāśmīrian recension on account of these readings, says Dr. Belvalkar, are not of any more compelling character than those for constituting a Bengali or a Malyalam recension. Out of the 282 new readings in the Kāśmīrian text, Dr. Schrader claims greater intrinsic importance for thirty-seven. Dr. Belvalkar has examined carefully all these thirty-seven cases and has come to the conclusion that most of them are not of any particular significance, except a dozen minor variants. Out of these we select only three for our purpose. (i) In the Bhagavadgītā II. 5, the classical reading is, अर्थकामान् भुञ्जीय. While Schrader reads अर्थकामः, for grammatical purposes we have to append भुञ्जीत to अर्थकामः instead of भुञ्जीय ; (ii) In the Bhagavadgītā II. 11, the classical reading is प्रज्ञावादांश्च भाषसे which has been the cause of much controversy. In the first place, Schrader who seems to be too much influenced by socio-democratic doctrine reads 'प्रजावादांश्च भाषसे' and translates : "as the people speaketh" which has no significance for the context in the Bhagavadgītā. Madhusūdan Sarasvati interprets it as प्राज्ञैः वक्तुं अनुचितान् शब्दान् (probably combining प्राज्ञ and अवाद), words not fit to be uttered by intelligent men." Ānandatīrtha interprets प्रज्ञावाद as "words of thy own understanding and not sanctioned by Śāstras," which seems to be a good interpretation. Finally, Schrader tells us that the Kāśmīrian reading is प्राज्ञवत् नाभिभाषसे which has some significance, but is not so good as the orthodox reading itself, प्रज्ञावादांश्च भाषसे. (iii) Lastly, in regard to the Bhagavadgītā, VI. 7, the classical reading is परमात्मा समाहितः. We are told by Schrader that the Kāśmīrian recension is परात्मसु समामतिः "We must have in mind the treatment of others like our own selves." This is not a bad reading, but there is no reason why the original reading परमात्मा समाहितः should be dispensed with. On the whole, therefore, the value of the efforts undertaken by Dr. Schrader for the establishment of the Kāśmīrian recension of the Bhagavadgītā hardly bears any comparison with that of the efforts undertaken by either Garbe or Otto for the establishment of their own theories of interpolation.

(*d*) *Otto.* In the discussion of the theories of interpolation Otto stands on a much higher level than the previous scholars. He was a pupil of Dr. Garbe, but there were certain points of difference between their theories of interpolation; (1) While Garbe advocated a dualistic hypothesis, Otto advocated a pluralistic one; and (2) while Garbe remained content with theism, Otto came very near to mysticism. According to Otto, the original Bhagavadgītā consisted only of 133 stanzas, all the other stanzas being later interpolated either individually or in groups. "The original Bhagavadgītā, according to Otto", says Radhakrishnan, "was a splendid epic fragment and did not include any doctrinal literature." Eight tracts consisting of 450 stanzas, says Otto, were later on interpolated; and 117 were either glosses or marginalia. These together with the original 133 stanzas make up the total figure of 700 verses. We shall see towards the close of the present part of our work that Otto's doctrine is concerned more with a philosophico-theological interpretation of the Bhagavadgītā than with a mere theory of interpolation. The four fundamental points that he raises in the teaching of the Bhagavadgītā are the immortality of the soul, the Viśvarūpa Darśana, the doctrine of pre-destination and the theory of divine instrumentalism. All these must be covered in the original 133 stanzas of the Bhagavadgītā. The eight different tracts, which were interpolated later, were introduced by different writers and at different times. Otto does not fight shy of saying that the Prapatti-Bhakti tract has thus been introduced, a Seśvara Yoga has been introduced, a Vibhūti Yoga has been introduced and so on; so that he does not confine himself, as Garbe did, to the division of the Bhagavadgītā into mere theistic and pantheistic portions. There are, he tells us, eight such tracts. We shall make a slight re-arrangement of these tracts and mention them as follows :—

(1) Prapatti-Bhakti Tract (XI-XII), in the manner of the Nārada Sūtras.

(2) Moral Theism (XVI-XVIII).

(3) Seśvara Sāṁkhya (XIII).

(4) A Combination of Sāṁkhya and Yoga (V).

(5) Seśvara Yoga—Psycho-technical Yoga (VI).

(6) Seśvara Yoga—Character Yoga (II). God in the Bhagavadgītā, not अपरामृष्ट as in Patañjali.

(7) Advaita Bhakti (VII). There is neither mere Advaita nor mere Bhakti, but a combination of the two.

(8) Vibhūti Yoga (X). God is here the optimum in the omnibus song of praise and is present in all excellence.

These are very fine names. Otto was a master of philosophy and a master of language; hence he could use such beautiful expressions. A full discussion of these tracts is beyond the scope of a philosophical work like the present. It is really a tempting work for any linguist who might undertake it for finding out the original text of the Bhagavadgītā. We ourselves think that Otto has gone beyond his own limitations. While he should have contented himself with interpreting the fundamental ideas of the Bhagavadgītā philosophically and theologically, he has entered too much into a linguistic discussion of these tracts and their justification in which, we think that he has not succeeded. A philosopher should deal with philosophic problems and not with merely linguistic or textual questions. These to him ought to be secondary, and should remain secondary. We are glad, however, to find that a full discussion of these eight tracts which Otto has made does not come in the way of his numenistic interpretation of the Bhagavadgītā, as we shall see later on. That is a fine interpretation and he has earned a great place among the interpreters of the Bhagavadgītā by his doctrine of holyism and numenism.

CHAPTER VII

DEVOTIONALISM : BHANDARKAR

Aikāntika Bhakti in the Nārāyaṇīya

Now we come to Dr. Bhandarkar, who is the most important representative of the Bhakti interpretation of the Bhagavadgītā. I do not think there has been another person in the whole of India who has stood for the importance of Bhakti (called by him also as Aikāntika Bhakti or Aikāntika Dharma, or Nārāyaṇīya Dharma) as he finds it in the Bhagavadgītā. In fact, Dr. Bhandarkar's contribution to the interpretation of the Bhagavadgītā is two-fold. First, the assertion that the Aikāntika Bhakti of the Bhagavadgītā has descended from the Aikāntika Dharma or the Nārāyaṇīya Dharma, and that it was from the Aikāntika Bhakti of the Bhagavadgītā that all the later developments of Bhakti took place. Second, Dr. Bhandarkar was the greatest representative of the school which demolished the doctrine of Christian influence on the Bhagavadgītā. Among the many critics who have contended that the Bhagavadgītā was a product of Christian influence we might particularly mention three, Lorinser, Weber and Lassen. A few others also might be mentioned, but they are more or less inclined to take a little more rational view of things, for example, Barth, Edgerton, Garbe and Farquhar. On the whole, the antiquarian researches of Dr. Bhandarkar, and his interpretation of the researches that had been already made in regard to Vāsudeva-Kṛṣṇa worship have firmly established that the Bhagavadgītā was not influenced by Christianity at all. Christianity was a very late product. This is then the two-fold importance of Dr. Bhandarkar for the interpretation of the Bhagavadgītā.

(*a*) *Vivasvān, Manu and Ikṣvāku in the Nārāyaṇīya and the Bhagavadgītā*:—One very significant verse of the fourth chapter of the Bhagavadgītā

इमं विवस्वते योगं प्रोक्तवानहमव्ययम् ।
विवस्वान्मनवे प्राह मनुरिक्ष्वाकवेऽब्रवीत् । IV. 1.

Which is rather a difficult knot to unloose for an ordinary student of literature or philosophy, has supplied the basis for Bhandarkar's historical interpretation of the foundation of the Bhakti of the Bhagavadgītā in the Nārāyaṇīya Dharma of the Mahābhārata. Let us see how this happens. We are told in the famous verse of the Bhagavadgītā that it was Kṛshṇa in a former incarnation (probably that of Nārāyaṇa), who communicated the secret of Aikāntika Bhakti to these three, Vivasvat, Manu and Ikṣvāku. Now if we go back to the source, we find that these names occur in the Nārāyaṇīya section of the Śāntiparva of the Mahābhārata. There Nārāyaṇa has been described as having communicated the secret of spiritual life, the Aikāntika Dharma as it might be called, to Prajāpati, and then it gradually descended to the three great representatives of Aikāntika Bhakti, Vivasvat, Manu and Ikṣvāku, exactly the persons whom the Bhagavadgītā mentions. We are also told in the Nārāyaṇīya that the secret of spiritual life which had descended from Nārāyaṇa to these three representatives, when it had run its course, would at the end of time return to Nārāyaṇa. तत्रैष धर्मः कथितः स्वयं नारायणेन ह ।..... गमिष्यति क्षयान्ते च पुनर्नारायणं नृप-Nārāyaṇīya, 48... 52. Exactly in the same manner we are told in the Bhagavadgītā that the river of spiritual experience hides itself at intervals like the Phalgu river in the sands of time.

स कालेनेह महता योगो नष्टः परंतप ।
स एवायं मया तेऽद्य योगः प्रोक्तः पुरातनः ॥ IV. 2-3.

All things have an end. Even good things have an end. And good things have an end because God intends it. He does not desire that the secret of spiritual life should lie open before humanity for all time. After the secret of the spiritual doctrine has played its part, it pleases God to hide its course for a while.

(b) *Nārada's visit to Nārāyaṇa*:—The beginnings of Aikāntika Bhakti or the Nārāyaṇīya Dharma might be found, according to Dr. Bhandarkar, in a very celebrated passage in the Mahābhārata where Nārada meets Nārāyaṇa and asks him the way for development in spiritual life. Nārada was a novice according to Nārāyaṇa. Nārada asked him "the whole of humanity is worshipping you, Oh Nārāyaṇa; whom are you worshipping", because he had seen Nārāyaṇa wrapt in meditation: यजन्ते त्वामहरहर्नानामूर्तिसमास्थितं कं त्वय यजसे देवम् । Nārāyaṇa was not surprised and told Nārada that it was not possible for him to explain by word of mouth the way of meditation for the realisation of God:

अवाच्यमेतद्वक्तव्यमात्मगुह्यं सनातनम् ।
तव भक्तिमतो ब्रह्मन् वक्ष्यामि तु यथातथम् ॥ २८ ॥
....
स ह्यन्तरात्मा भूतानां क्षेत्रज्ञश्चेति कथ्यते ।
त्रिगुणव्यतिरिक्तो वै पुरुषश्चेति कल्पितः ॥ ३० ॥

After having told Nārada in a general way that the way of spiritual life is very difficult to obtain, he told him to go to the mountain Meru and to श्वेतद्वीप and there to observe five seekers after the spiritual life, Bṛhaspati, Ekata, Dwita, Trita and Vasu-Uparicara, and after full observation to return to him. The expression which Nārāyaṇa uses is गच्छेति तं नारदमुक्तवान् सः. Nārāyaṇa's only business was to say to people गच्छ or गच्छध्वम् । You have no business here. You go and mind your own work, fulfil your part of the mission and then return to me. Then we shall see whether you deserve to be told the secret of spiritual life.

(c) *Vasu-Uparicara* :—Nārada went to श्वेतद्वीप which has been interpreted differently by Dr. Bhandarkar and by European scholars. European scholars regard the श्वेतद्वीप as the fountain source of the influence of Christianity on Hinduism and on the Bhagavadgītā. Dr. Bhandarkar regards it as the seat of spiritual devotion. In the श्वेतद्वीप a sacrifice was going on and five persons were engaged in it. Bṛhaspati was the chief priest; Ekata, Dvita, and Trita were the Sadasyas, and king Vasu-Uparicara was the Yajamāna. We are told an interesting story from which we know how Bṛhaspati could not have a vision of God, because his mind was fixed on the Saṁhitās and Brāhmaṇas and was given to Hiṁsā and sacrifice. Secondly, Ekata, Dvita and Trita, even though the Mahābhārata calls them as the sons of Brahmā and महर्षयः, could not reach God, because they had delivered themselves over only to mortificatory penances for hundreds of years. It is not mere penance; it is not bodily tormentation that wins God for the seeker; hence they failed to see God. Third, Vasu-Uparicara, whose mind was fixed on Āraṇyakas and Upaniṣads, who was more devoted than any of the others, in fact, who was the only man of real devotion in the entire sacrifice, could see God, because he had not given himself over to Hiṁsā. He did not regard mortificatory penance as capable of enabling one to reach God, but it was Bhāva or internal devotion that enabled one to see God. In that way God being pleased showed himself to Vasu-Uparicara. प्रीतस्ततोऽस्य भगवान् देवदेवः पुरातनः। साक्षात्तं दर्शयामास सोऽदृश्योऽन्येन केनचित्. It was in fact a sort of a miniature Viśvarūpa which Nārāyaṇa unfolded to Vasu-Uparicara, and when Vasu-Uparicara had seen this, he was satisfied and we know from history that Vasu-Uparicara was an earlier disciple of Nārāyaṇa in spiritual life than even Nārada himself.

(*d*) *The supremacy of Aikāntika Bhakti*:—When Nārada returned to Nārāyaṇa, Nārāyaṇa found that the Aikāntika Bhakti had germinated in him. Nārāyaṇa told Nārada a short history of the way in which he had dispensed with Ekata, Dvita, and Trita, who had come to meet him at that place, telling them that they were not capable of getting the secret of spiritual life from him, because in fact their mind was centered only upon mortificatory penances. He had only told them गच्छध्वं; but now that Nārada had returned with the requisites of spiritual life, Nārāyaṇa was satisfied. He went to the length of calling Nārada ऐकान्तिकोत्तम and therefore, had no difficulty in imparting to him the secret of spiritual life. The way in which Nārāyaṇa tells Nārada the whole story of the spiritual life is expressed in a passage to which there are very few parallels even in the Mahābhārata itself, so far as devotional life is concerned. We quote it below in extenso:

श्रीभगवानुवाच :—

एकतश्च द्वितश्चैव त्रितश्चैव महर्षयः।
इमं देशमनुप्राप्ता मम दर्शनलालसाः॥

गच्छध्वं मुनयः सर्वे यथागतमितोऽचिरात्।
न स शक्यस्त्वभक्तेन द्रष्टुं देवः कथंचन॥

कामं कालेन महता एकान्तिकत्वमुपागतैः ।
शक्यो द्रष्टुं स भगवान् प्रभामण्डलदुर्दृशः ॥

न च मां ते ददृशिरे न च द्रक्ष्यति कश्चन ।
ऋते ह्येकान्तिकश्रेष्ठत्वं चैवैकान्तिकोत्तम ॥

(*e*) *Nārada's Vision of God* :—When Nārāyaṇa had imparted to Nārada the secret of spiritual life, he progressed in that life according to his own intense spiritual abilities, and we are told in the Mahābhārata that Nārada had a vision of the Viśvarūpa of God, manifesting itself in different forms and colours, in hundreds of faces and eyes and feet, almost a replica, and earlier replica of the Viśvarūpa which Kṛṣṇa later showed to Arjuna. We also quote this passage in extenso, because nobody has stressed the significance of this vision of Nārada as it should have been :

एवं स्तुतः स भगवान्गुह्यैस्तथ्यैश्च नामभिः ।
तं मुनिं दर्शयामास नारदं विश्वरूपधृक् ॥ १ ॥

किंचिच्चन्द्राद्विशुद्धात्मा किंचिच्चन्द्राद्विशेषवान् ।
कृशानुवर्णः किंचित्किंचिद्धिष्ण्याकृतिः प्रभुः ॥ २ ॥

शुकपत्रनिभः किंचित्किंचित्स्फटिकसंनिभः ।
नीलाञ्जनचयप्रख्यो जातरूपप्रभः क्वचित् ॥ ३ ॥

प्रवालांकुरवर्णश्च श्वेतवर्णस्तथा क्वचित् ।
क्वचित्सुवर्णवर्णाभो वैडूर्यसदृशः क्वचित् ॥ ४ ॥

नीलवैडूर्यसदृश इन्द्रनीलनिभः क्वचित् ।
मयूरग्रीववर्णाभो मुक्ताहारनिभः क्वचित् ॥ ५ ॥

एतान् बहुविधान् वर्णान् रूपैर्बिभ्रत् सनातनः ।
सहस्रनयनः श्रीमान् शतशीर्षः सहस्रपात् ॥ ६ ॥

(*f*) *Nārada's Gratification* :—When Nārada had seen that Viśvarūpa, he was absolutely gratified and he expressed his gratification in the following two verses :

नारद उवाच—

अथ मे तपसो देव यमस्य नियमस्य च ।
सद्यः फलमवाप्तं वै दृष्टो यद्भगवान् मया ॥ १६ ॥
वर एष ममात्यन्तं दृष्टस्त्वं यत्सनातनः ।
भगवान् विश्वदृक् सिंहः सर्वमूर्तिर्महाप्रभुः ॥ १७ ॥

He ends with the words सिंहः सर्वमूर्तिः, telling Nārāyaṇa that he had seen God-lion, and that that form was the source of all other forms of God and that it was the supreme spiritual principle governing the world.

Aikāntika Bhakti in the Bhagavadgītā

Dr. Bhandarkar finds this Aikāntika Dharma in the Bhagavadgītā and not without justification. The Bhakti principle in the Bhagavadgītā is necessarily founded upon such a conception of Nārāyaṇīya Dharma as we find in the Mahābhārata. We may say that after Nārāyaṇīya, the Bhagavadgītā is the earliest exposition of this doctrine of Parābhakti. In a famous verse in the Bhagavadgītā we are told: शाश्वतस्य च धर्मस्य सुखस्यैकान्तिकस्य च XIV·27. In this verse occurs the germ of that Aikāntika Dharma. If we just transpose the expressions शाश्वतधर्म and ऐकान्तिक सुख, we shall have ऐकान्तिक धर्म and शाश्वत सुख, implying that it is this Aikāntika Dharma which leads to शाश्वत सुख. It is thus that the Bhagavadgītā stands for Aikāntika Dharma, the principle of supreme Bhakti. This is the first point to be noticed in the development of the Bhakti doctrine from the Nārāyaṇīya to the Bhagavadgītā.

We have two further points to narrate about the Bhagavadgītā so far as the Bhakti-doctrine is concerned and its fructification. Kṛṣṇa, we are told, was both a warrior and a mystic. As a mystic, we know from the Mahābhārata and from other Purāṇas how Kṛṣṇa had meditated long in the Gandha-Mādan forest, on the

Puṣkara lake, and on the Badarī mountain. This aspect of Kṛṣṇa's mystical achievement has not been noticed by many, because like La Place in his famous reply to Napoleon "they have not felt the necessity for the hypothesis." It was due to the spiritual power that Kṛṣṇa gathered in his meditations at these three places of natural scenery, a forest, a lake and a mountain, devoted himself to God, and having ultimately succeeded in realising Him, that he became later on what the Gītā calls Yogeśvara and as Yogeśvara he was responsible for the victory of the Pāṇḍavas. It is due to the spiritual power which a man gets through his meditation that he is enabled to spread the spiritual influence far and wide. It was thus, therefore, that the presence of Kṛṣṇa himself, even though he acted merely as a charioteer, was responsible for securing victory to Arjuna and the Pāṇḍavas in their war with the Kauravas.

Finally, the Viśvarūpa, which Kṛṣṇa had shown to Arjuna in the eleventh chapter of the Bhagavadgītā, had its germ, as we have already pointed out, in the miniature Viśvarūpa revealed to Vasu-Uparicara and then in a more extended form to Nārada. Of course, it finds its fullest expression in the Bhagavadgītā. We are told how Kṛṣṇa was at the same time Vāsudeva, Bhagavān and Viṣṇu, Vāsudeva implying that God was Omnipresent, Bhagavān that God was omnipotent, and Viṣṇu that God was omnilustrous. Presence, power and lustre, therefore, constitute the essence of God's being. We are reminded of another such occasion when as described in the Śiva Gītā, Rāma saw the Viśvarūpa which Śiva had revealed to him. On the whole, it does not seem possible that unless man's will and power are conquered by God's Will and Power that a man can humble himself before God and do as he is bidden by God to do.

The later developments of the Aikāntika doctrine are to be found in a system like that of the Pāñcarātra. The Pāñcarātra makes mention of the four Vyūhas of which there is no mention in the Bhagavadgītā at all. According to Dr. Bhandarkar, therefore, the Pāñcarātra, which belongs to the 3rd century B. C., is evidently later than the Bhagavadgītā. Also from among the Vyūhas about which the Pāñcarātra speaks, two, namely, Vāsudeva and Saṁkarṣaṇa, are mentioned in some important inscriptions of the 2nd century B. C. If Vāsudeva had risen to the position of a deity even in the 2nd century B. C., says Dr. Bhandarkar, it is impossible that the Bhagavadgīta should have been, in any way, influenced by Christianity and we think that it is absolutely correct. We know also how this Pāñcarātra doctrine influenced the Bhāgavata, and later the Rāmānuja school and then Dr. Bhandarkar himself. He was not satisfied with calling himself a Prapanna but was content with calling himself a mere Prapitsu, one who is not a Prapanna at all, but who only desires to be so.

No Christian Influence on the Bhagavadgītā

The greatest service which Dr. Bhandarkar has rendered to Gītā scholarship, is the way in which he has, relying upon antiquarian researches, refuted the doctrine of the influence of Christianity on the Bhagavadgītā. The antiquarian researches centre round three kinds of evidence : inscriptional, historical and philological. On this threefold evidence we see how the Bhagavadgītā must be definitely regarded as being earlier than Christianity.

(*a*) *Inscriptional evidence*:—In regard to the inscriptional evidence, we have first the Nāṇāghāta inscription of the 2nd century B. C., where the names of Saṁkarṣaṇa and Vāsudeva are seen inscribed in a Dvandva compound in the inscription. A second piece of evidence, in this case architectural, comes from Ghosundi which shows that there was the construction of a wall round the worship-hall of Vāsudeva and Saṁkarṣaṇa, who are mentioned by name. Thirdly, there is another evidence, this time in an artistic production in the shape of the erection of a Garuḍa-Dhvaja at Basenagar, in honour of Vāsudeva, by Heliodora, Indian ambassador at the court of Bhāgabhadra, ruler of Mālavā. From all these evidences we see that Vāsudeva was established as a deity in the 2nd century B. C. at least.

(*b*) *Historical evidence*:—In the account which has been left to us by Megasthenes, the Macedonian ambassador at the court of King Chandragupta, in the 4th century B. C., we have got a definite historical reference to the places where Kṛṣṇa's life was spent. Megasthenes among other things makes a definite reference to Sourasenoi, meaning thereby the Sourasena community, Mathura, Methora and Jobares and the Jamuna river. A definite historical reference to these, which are connected with the early life of Kṛṣṇa in the 4th century B. C., is sufficient to show that Kṛṣṇa was regarded as a deity even in those old days.

(*c*) *Philological evidence*:—Finally, when we come to the philological evidence, we have the authority of Pāṇini, who is supposed to have lived in the 6th century B. C., and who has given us a sūtra वासुदेवार्जुनाभ्यां वुन् in his अष्टाध्यायी, which implies that Vāsudeva was regarded as a deity even in those old days. According to Pāṇini,

Vāsudevaka means worshipper of Vāsudeva, and Arjunaka means an admirer of Arjuna. Vāsudeva was a great God and Arjuna was a great warrior. This is evidence enough to show that the name Vāsudeva was famous even so far back as the 6th century B. C. We have thus accumulating evidence from inscriptional records of the 2nd century B. C., historical documents of the 4th century B. C. and philological evidence of the 6th century B. C. almost in a graded order like that of an arithmetical progression, which proves that Christianity did not influence the Bhagavadgītā at all.

We do not think that Prof. V. K. Rajwade was justified in applying the canons of Pāṇiniyan grammar to the Bhagavadgītā. He has written an able, interesting and accurate essay, no doubt, in which he points out the grammatical defects of the Bhagavadgītā according to the rules of Pāṇini. But when Pāṇini's grammar itself makes mention of Vāsudeva, Arjuna and Kṛṣṇa, it would be impossible to judge of the grammatical merits or defects of the Bhagavadgītā according to the rules of Pāṇini. It would be like placing the cart before the horse. What, therefore, constitutes grammatical defects in the Bhagavadgītā according to V. K. Rajwade is in our opinion a historical asset to prove that the Bhagavadgītā was a pre-Pāṇiniyan composition. In no case, therefore it stands to reason that we can, in any way, regard the Bhagavadgītā as having been influenced by Christianity which actually came into existence six centuries after Pāṇini.

CHAPTER VIII

CHRISTIANISM

Of the Christian interpreters of the Bhagavadgītā, and their name is legion, we shall select only six as being somewhat typical. Even from among them we shall select four for special consideration. These four are Weber, Garbe, Farquhar and Edgerton. We classify them under four heads: (*a*) Dogmatic and highly prejudiced, (*b*) Prejudiced but partly rational, (*c*) Mostly rational and (*d*) Philosophical. Weber, Farquhar, Garbe and Edgerton belong to these four types respectively. We shall briefly refer to the views of Lorinser and Lassen, but they are not of much consequence.

Lorinser

Lorinser published his metrical translation of the Bhagavadgītā in the year 1869. It was rather courageous on his part to publish it in as much as he did not know Sanskrit, as we shall see presently. But he is a good theologian and his contention is that the author of the Bhagavadgītā utilised the Christian scriptures, particularly the epistles of St. Paul, excepting the epistles to Thessalonians and Philemon. In general, says Lorinser, the author of the Bhagavadgītā knew Christianity, and has woven Christian ideas and conceptions into his system. Garbe in his criticism of Lorinser tells us that he himself takes a standpoint precisely opposed to that of Lorinser. He admits that Lorinser was a good theologian, but accuses him of false orthography. He further finds fault with Lorinser for not being equipped with the requisite philological knowledge. As Garbe says :—

"Lorinser was certainly a good theologian; but here he betook himself to a region with which he was not sufficiently conversant. That Indian words often appear in his work with a false orthography is not a mere externality, but a symptom of the fact that he was not equipped with the requisite philological knowledge which would entitle him to form a judgment in regard to things Indian."

—Introduction to the Bhagavadgītā, p. 22.

Weber

In the beginning he was not so highly prejudiced as he later on turned out to be. For example, while reviewing Lorinser he tells us that the idea of the Christian influence on the Bhagavadgītā, which Lorinser had introduced, must still be regarded as subjudice, because no sound information, no documents were available in that connection. Later, he himself became the forerunner of the extremely biassed Christian interpreters of the Bhagavadgītā. It was he practically who suggested that the idea of Kṛṣṇa was borrowed from that of Christ. He points out four analogues in the stories connected with them. Christ was born in a manger, and Kṛṣṇa was born in a prison. Christ was born from the Divine Virgin Mary and Kṛṣṇa from Devakī the Divine. There were shepherds round about in the first case and cowherds in the other; and the killing of children at Bethlehem and Gokul respectively was common to the two stories. From this point of view, Weber argues that the story of Kṛṣṇa was taken over literally from the story of Christ.

When Weber read the account of the Śvetadvīpa from Mahābhārata, he thought that he had made a great discovery. Śvetadvīpa, he tells us, literally means the island of white men, or the white island, and as there are many white islands, and as the men also are white in the western part of the world, Weber thought probably that the Mahābhārata and, therefore, also the Bhagavadgītā were influenced by the doctrines and teachings of these white men. Now as Bhakti was the central teaching of the Bible, Weber had no hesitation, nor any difficulty in saying that the Bhakti-doctrine in the Bhagavadgītā was borrowed from Christianity. The journeys of the Brāhmaṇas, Ekata, Dvita, Trita and Nārada to the Śvetadvīpa, he interpreted as the journeys of the Brāhmaṇas from India to the Western World. Particularly such a journey was made to Alexandria, which was at that time the connecting link between the Eastern and the Western worlds. These Brāhmaṇas brought back to India two central conceptions, namely, the worship of the invisible God, which is a fundamental thing in Christianity, and the gently murmured prayers. Weber did not know that the उपांशुजप or the gently murmured prayers were the characteristic of Hinduism from the times of the Vedas downwards. Fair-minded people like Garbe are not impressed by such an interpretation from Weber. Garbe allows that the gently murmured prayers look "extraordinarily Christian," but later he goes on to point out that he does, in no way, agree with what Weber and others like him have said in this connection.

Lassen

The next interpreter that we have to deal with is Lassen. Lassen criticises Weber's theory in regard to the influence of Christianity on the Pāñcarātra system. But he welcomes his idea of Christian influence on the Bhagavadgītā and the Mahābhārata through the Śvetadvīpa. He agrees that Śvetadvīpa must be interpreted as the island of white men, but he says that by Śvetadvīpa we must mean Parthia, and for one particular reason, namely, that the Apostle Thomas preached the Christian doctrine there. It was probably there in Parthia, says Lassen, that the Brāhmaṇa travellers got this information about Christianity, and brought it to their own country. Lassen's account, however, of the whole procedure is full of conjecture, hesitancy and imagination, as may be seen from the following quotation :

> " Some Brāhmaṇas had become acquainted with Christianity in some country lying to the North-West of their own land, and had brought some Christian doctrines to India. One may conjecture that this country may have been Parthia, because the tradition that the Apostle Thomas preached the gospel in this country is an ancient tradition. "

—Introduction to the Bhagavadgītā, p. 22.

Garbe

Garbe criticises both Lorinser and Lassen in their view of the influence of Christian doctrines on the Bhagavadgītā through the Śvetadvīpa and does not believe that there is any historical kernel in that story. The story is so fantastic, says Garbe, that we must consider the Śvetadvīpa as a purely mythical country of " blessed creatures ". He quotes Barth with whom he fully agrees and who regards the story as a product of mere poetical fancy. Garbe goes on to tell us that instead of Bhakti being borrowed from Christianity, it was of genuine Indian origin and growth, and here also he quotes Barth in his support. Both these scholars, Garbe and Barth, tell us that the Bhakti–doctrine of the Bhagavadgītā must be regarded as entirely independent of any Christian influence. Garbe says :

> " I have not been able to convince myself in reading these remarkable passages that there lies in that legend the historical kernel which Weber and Lassen believe they find in it. The story is so fantastic that I can see in it only the description of a purely mythical country of blessed creatures. The view of Barth (Religions de l' Inde, p. 132) that here we have before us merely a product of poetic fancy seems to me to be thoroughly to the point.
>
> —Introduction to the Bhagavadgītā, pp. 22–23.

Garbe advances three arguments against Weberism and says that the account of Śvetadvīpa and the " blessed creatures " there must be regarded as purely fanciful. In the first place, he says, that the so-called blessed creatures of the Śvetadvīpa have been described as having no senses ; they are supposed to live without nourishment and their brilliance is so great that they blind the eyes of the sinful by their lustre. Secondly, the sages Ekata, Dvita and Trita, says Garbe, must not be regarded as historical. They are described as the sons of Brahmā who is a mythological deity. Nārada also is always regarded in India as a proverbial traveller and as an intermediary between gods and men. But the connection between gods and men is not so easy to establish. For these reasons Ekata, Dvita, Trita and Nārada must all be regarded as products of a purely poetic mythology. Lastly Garbe tells us that the Indians need not have gone either to Alexandria or Parthia or Asia Minor to receive Christian influence. They had already had abundent contact with the Greeks in their own land even before the days of Alexander and hence it was not necessary for them to go to any of these countries later on to receive Christian influence.

So far so good. We have already treated Garbe at some length in a previous chapter and have pointed out that he divides the Bhagavadgītā into two portions, the earlier and the later, the theistic and the pantheistic. The theistic portion, he maintains elsewhere, has been influenced by Christianity while the pantheistic is not. In a contradictory strain he also maintains that the earlier portion of the Bhagavadgītā belongs to the 2nd century B. C. and the later to the 2nd century A. D. This is as much as to say that Christianity existed two centuries before Christ! Such a fantastic statement could be avoided only by accepting that there are no two parts of the Bhagavadgītā at all, but that it is a unitary work.

Farquhar

As a Christian theologian, he was interested in proving the superiority of Christianity over Hinduism and particularly of Christ over Kṛṣṇa. But his philosophical aspirations and literary abilities made him give the Gītā a philosophic and devotional status which it deserves. Hence we find two strands in the account which Farquhar gives of the Bhagavadgītā. Before his time Kṛṣṇa was proved to be a historical figure. Weber had taken advantage of the absence of that proof in his time to say that Kṛṣṇa was not a historical person, but

Bhandarkar and a number of other scholars later proved that Kṛṣṇa was a truly historical person. Farquhar, therefore, adopted a different kind of procedure. Instead of saying that Kṛṣṇa was not historical, he said that the portrait of Kṛṣṇa had many imaginative features about it. Jesus of Nazareth, on the other hand, according to him, was a perfectly historical being. Let us see what Farquhar says :

> " On the one hand, we have the imaginative portrait of Kṛṣṇa, surrounded by millions of adoring worshippers — touching spectacle ! On the other, stands the historical Jesus of Nazareth, Son of Man and Son of God, stretching out his nail-pierced hands to India (Why to India only and why to India at all ? We might ask), as He says ' Come unto me, all ye that labour and are heavy laden, and I will give you rest. ' Rightly read, the Gītā is a clear-tongued prophecy of Christ and the hearts that bow down to the idea of Kṛṣṇa are really seeking the incarnate son of God. "
>
> —Gītā and Gospel, p. 84.

That Kṛṣṇa was a merely imaginative portrait has been disproved by the important researches which scholars like Dr. Bhandarkar as well as many European antiquarians have made, as we have pointed out in the previous chapter. That Kṛṣṇa was a perfectly historical person has been established beyond doubt from different kinds of evidences such as grammatical, historical and inscriptional, supplied by Pāṇini, Megasthenes, Besanagar, Heliodora, Ghosundi and Nāṇāghāt. All these point to the true historical existence of Kṛṣṇa who was also regarded as a divine being even before the days of Pāṇini.

As we have said above, the devotee in Farquhar now stands out and he showers praise upon the Bhagavadgītā instead of criticism. That great work, he tells us, has been very successful in intertwining "speculative thought with fervid devotion", and it might, therefore, be easily regarded as the "noblest and purest expression of modern Hinduism." This is what Farquhar says:

> "The author of the Gītā was catholic rather than critical, more inclined to piece things together than to worry over the differences between them. He was as fully in sympathy with Kṛṣṇa worship as with the philosophy of the Ātman. Indeed, it was the union of these qualities in him that fitted him to produce the noblest and purest expression of modern Hinduism."
>
> Gītā and Gospel. p.28.

Edgerton

We have said at the beginning of this chapter that Edgerton belongs to the philosophic type. In fact, some of his judgments on the Bhagavadgītā are so good that they can hardly be equalled by many of those who boast of Hinduism. In the first place, Edgerton tells us that the essence of the teaching of the Bhagavadgītā is anti-rational and mystical as is also the essence of the teaching of Christ. This is his opinion with which other Christian interpreters may not agree. Still philosophical-minded as he is, Edgerton has no difficulty in telling us that reason is an uncertain factor and that the Bhagavadgītā speaks of intuitive perception as any great work on mysticism would. Edgerton further tells us that there is no difficulty felt by the author of the Bhagavadgītā in combining this mysticism with personal devotional theism. Secondly, the Bhagavadgītā speaks of the focussing of our attention within, suggesting the process of introspective meditation. Lastly, he tells us that the final goal of the Bhagavadgītā is the attainment of complete union with God, supreme joy and peace. In this connection we can do no better than quote Edgerton's words in the original :

> " To the Gītā as to the Christian mystics reason is an uncertain and flickering light.
>
> What it calls knowledge is really intiuitional perception which is not based on rational analysis.
>
> It recalls Christian teachings in its mystical anti-rational point of view, in its ardent personal devotional theism, its focussing of the attention within, and its conception of the final goal as complete union with God, a state of supernal and indescribable bliss and peace. "
>
> The Bhagavadgītā. p. 96.

CHAPTER IX

BUDDHISM : BUDDHIRĀJA

Question of Parallelism and Borrowal

After having reviewed the Christian interpretation of the Bhagavadgītā, let us proceed to a Buddhistic interpretation. There are not many Buddhistic interpreters of that kind; but Buddhirāja stands prominent among them. He was a Judge of the Kashmir High Court and published a book on "The Bhagavadgītā: A study" about a quarter of a century ago. His principal aim was to show the influence which Buddhism exercised on the Bhagavadgītā. This influence he tells us, was exercised in two ways, one by way of parallelisms and the other by way of borrowals. His whole interpretation is concerned with the list of virtues and vices in the Bhagavadgītā. Buddhirāja's contention is that though in some cases there are to be noted parallelisms between Buddhism and the Bhagavadgītā, in certain others there are definite borrowals by the Bhagavadgītā from Buddhism. In respect of parallelisms, he cites passages from two chapters of the Bhagavadgītā, chapters II and XII. Any word from the Bhagavadgītā which suggests to Buddhirāja even a distant parallelism with some Buddhistic conception is to him very tempting. For example, the words समाधि, प्रज्ञा and स्मृति, even though they occur at long intervals between verses 44 and 63 of the II chapter of the Bhagavadgītā, remind him of a passage in the महापरिनिब्बानसुत्त in which the three virtues are mentioned सतिस्मृति, समाधि and प्रज्ञा. Then again he points out that these same virtues have been elaborated in Patañjali in the Sūtra I. 20, श्रद्धावीर्यस्मृतिसमाधिप्रज्ञापूर्वक इतरेषाम्।

Secondly, the 13th verse of the XII chapter of the Bhagavadgītā, which contains the words मैत्रः करुण एव च, reminds him at once of महासुदस्सनसुत्त where the four virtues have been mentioned, मेत्ता, करुणा, मुदिता and उपेक्खा which that Sutta along with Tevijjasutta calls Brahmavihāras. Even in this case another Sūtra from Patañjali 1·33 (मैत्रीकरुणामुदितोपेक्षाणां...भावनातश्चित्तप्रसादनम्) reminds him of a parallelism in regard to the same virtues. True that the Brahmavihāras have played an important part in Buddhistic scriptures. The idea was that the Buddhist monks were to be advised to let their minds roam in the whole universe contemplating all these virtues in respect of the universe. "Let them feel *friendship* with all creatures in the universe, let them feel *compassion*, let them feel *happy* and let them be *indifferent* wherever they are required to be so." Even though Buddhirāja does not say it in so many words, the idea at the back of his mind is that the Bhagavadgītā has borrowed the conceptions of its virtues from the Buddhist scriptures. The very fact that these virtues are so elaborately treated in the Buddhist scriptures is itself an indication of their later development. So far about the question of parallelism.

Now in regard to the question of borrowals. Buddhirāja finds this question of the borrowals illustrated in the XVI chapter of the Bhagavadgītā which discusses the Daivī Sampat and the Āsurī Sampat. We know the very famous verses 3 and 4 in the XVI chapter in the Bhagavadgītā, wherein are mentioned the virtues, तेजः क्षमा धृतिः शौचम् and the vices दंभो दर्पोऽतिमानः and so on; these together constitute Daivāsura-Sampat. Now Buddhirāja's contention is that so far as the virtues constituting the Daivī Sampat are concerned, they are based definitely on the Dhammapada. Now the Dhammapada may be credited with having set forth, sustained and developed high ethical ideals, no doubt, but in fact, there is no central principle in the list of virtues in the Dhammapada which may be paralleled to that in the Bhagavadgītā. Hence even though in a way the general teaching might be similar, the Bhagavadgītā has expressed the virtues so aphoristically that it is impossible for these to have been summarised or borrowed from Buddhism at all. The Dhammapada is an extensive work, and the virtues enumerated in the XVI chapter of the Bhagavadgītā find a full exposition in the Dhammapada.

In regard to the vices in the Āsurī Sampat, Buddhirāja points out two verses in the Bhagavadgītā, क्षिपाम्यजस्रमशुभानासुरीष्वेव योनिषु। XVI.19 and पतन्ति नरकेऽशुचौ XVI. 16. Here he definitely says that the Bhagavadgītā has been influenced by the Amagandhasutta. " Hostile, offending, always bent upon evil, when dead, they go to the darkness and fall with their heads downwards into hell." This is how Buddhirāja translates one of the passages from the Amagandhasutta and he says that this must be the source from which the Bhagavadgītā has derived its idea of the evil-doers falling into hell. This is a large conclusion, and no supporting arguments have been given in its favour.

In fact, Buddhirāja commits a sublime *petitio principii.* He takes for granted what he wants to prove. In regard to the division of the divine and the demoniac in the Bhagavadgītā, as in Buddhism, we might say that if the Bhagavadgītā might be regarded as having borrowed this division of divine and demoniac from Buddhism, why should we not suppose that it has so borrowed from the Iranian sources, where the divine and the demoniac play a very fundamental part. To say that the Bhagavadgītā has borrowed from either Buddhism or Iranian sources would be equally unjustifiable. There is, however, one clinching argument which finally disposes of Buddhirāja's contention in the matter of the borrowal of the conception of the Daivāsura-Sampat by the Bhagavadgītā from Buddhism. In a famous verse in the XVI chapter, the Bhagavadgītā speaks of असत्यमप्रतिष्ठं ते जगदाहुरनीश्वरम्। XVI. 8. This verse tells us definitely that we must condemn unreservedly all those who regard the world as "unreal, or as unstable, or who preach the doctrine of the negation of God." It was indeed this platform upon which the Buddhistic edifice was later built and the Bhagavadgītā has no sympathy for it. Buddhirāja does say that he holds no brief for Buddhism, being no Buddhist himself. We are prepared to give him all credit for that. We must also give him a compliment for pointing out the parallelisms between the conceptions in the Bhagavadgītā and Buddhism; but his argument for borrowals is an absolute failure. Even such a high authority as Garbe had been led to believe that the so-called influence of Buddhism on the Bhagavadgītā might be regarded as "absolutely far-fetched and extremely doubtful."

We have hitherto seen what one prominent modern interpreter of Buddhism, namely, Bhuddhirāja, has said in regard to the relationship between Buddhism and the Bhagavadgītā. This is not all. Many scholars have spoken about the relationship between them in other matters also. Of course, they cannot lay their finger upon the relationship exactly, because they do not find any reliable evidence to say that Buddhism is earlier than the Bhagavadgītā. But three important matters in which the relationship has been sought to be discussed pertain to the three conceptions, namely, those of Nirvāṇa, Karma and Pessimism, the first being the most important.

Nirvāṇa, Karma and Pessimism

In regard to Nirvāṇa, we know what a variegated panorama has been exhibited to our view by Buddhism in its development from the earliest stages to its culmination. Through one thousand years and more, it might naturally be expected that the conception of Nirvāṇa might have undergone a number of different interpretations. The most fundamental of these is, of course, its ethical meaning, namely, tranquillity, calmness or peace. This is what the Buddhists aimed at when they spoke about Nirvāṇa. Now this conception comes from the so-called extinguishment of the "three fires", namely, राग, द्वेष and मोह. Pāṇini has spoken about the difference between Nirvāṇa and Nirvāta, Nirvāṇa referring to fire and Nirvāta referring to wind. Mrs. Rhys Davids has pointed out that these three fires of राग, द्वेष and मोह must suffer a Kṣaya or extinguishment before the final state of peace, calmness or tranquillity is attained, and it is this ideal, therefore, which Buddhism primarily held before itself. There are also, we may point out, two other aspects connected with this conception, namely, the psychological and the axiological, which describe Nirvāṇa as freedom from desire and freedom from suffering. In these three ways Buddhism has principally worked through all its developmental stages. A fourth important point of interpretation in regard to Nirvāṇa is the epistemological. Buddhism has spoken about twelve Nidānas and the Bhāvacakra and the whole chain consisting of links of which the first link is Avijjā or

Avidyā. Break this first link of ignorance or Avijjā and the whole chain snaps. Avidyā or ignorance is the principal cause of suffering, and it ought to be the aim of the seekers to remove this first link. This constitutes the epistemological aspect of the Buddhistic doctrine of Nirvāṇa. Further, there is the logical aspect which, of course, comes in the development of Buddhistic literature. Nirvāṇa might be interpreted as Predicateless Being, that is, beyond 'Is' and 'Is not'. Interpreters like De La Ville Poussin have taken delight in such absolutistic interpretations. Of course, to read Contemporary European Philosophy too much in Buddhism would not be justifiable; but that the Nirvāṇa is a Predicateless Existence might be regarded as its logical characterisation. The final interpretation of Nirvāṇa which we meet with in Buddhistic literature is the ontological. Annihilation of being is what Buddhism aims at; it also aims at annihilation of evil, annihilation of suffering, annihilation of desire and annihilation of the fires of vices. But a very important point here is to see how in the development of Buddhism the whole gamut of conceptions from annihilation to perpetuation of being is exhibited. It starts, no doubt, with the annihilation of being, but towards the end of Mahāyāna philosophy we find that it becomes equivalent to perpetuation of being. In fact, living in Dharmakāya was to them the principal ideal to be aimed at. Also one might not even fail to include the element of felicity in the conception of Nirvāṇa, as Mrs. Rhys Davids has pointed out. But it was too late a growth, not until a few centuries of the Christian era had elapsed, to have had any influence on the Bhagavadgītā.

Let us see now how these compare with the conception of Nirvāṇa in the Bhagavadgītā. The word Nirvāṇa occurs five times in the Bhagavadgītā, and if we analyse its meanings we find that there are three different senses in which the word Nirvāṇa has been used. In the first place, when the Bhagavadgītā uses the words एषा ब्राह्मी स्थितिः ...... ब्रह्मनिर्वाणमृच्छति । II. 72, it wants to speak about unison. When it tells us योऽन्तः सुखोऽन्तरारामः .... ब्रह्मनिर्वाणं ब्रह्मभूतोऽधिगच्छति । V. 24, it wants to speak about the Supreme Bliss. When it speaks of युञ्जन्नेवं......शान्तिं निर्वाणपरमां......अधिगच्छति VI. 15, it intends to convey the meaning of peace. So, on the whole, there are three different meanings in which the word Nirvāṇa has been used in the Bhagavadgītā: first in the sense of unison, second in the sense of bliss, and third in the sense of peace, and of all these bliss stands highest. There is, however, a noteworthy point in the expression शान्तिं निर्वाणपरमां in the last verse. Now निर्वाणपरमां might be taken either as a Tatpuruṣa compound or even as a Bahuvrīhi compound. If it is regarded as a Tatpuruṣa compound, then peace becomes the end of bliss; if it is taken as a Bahuvrīhi compound, then bliss becomes the end of peace. In fact, peace and bliss are so intertwined, as we have pointed out elsewhere, that it is difficult to say which is prior and which is posterior, which is the means and which is the end. Bliss does lead to peace and peace does lead to bliss. In fact, the two ought to become coeval and co-extensive. So when the Bhagavadgītā makes bliss the supreme ideal at which all human effort is to aim, it differs fundamentally from the conception of Nirvāṇa in Buddhism which speaks of annihilation of desire or annihilation of being itself.

After this question of Nirvāṇa, let us treat briefly two other conceptions, regarding which the Bhagavadgītā and Buddhism have been sought to be compared. First in regard to Karman, we might say that it does play a very fundamental part in Buddhism. It is the Law of Causation, governing both nature and man. In the Bhagavadgītā, Karman assumes more or less an ethical aspect. While in Buddhism, Karman is to be absolutely annihilated, in the Bhagavadgītā it is to be sublimated, surrendered and consecrated to God. Our Karmas are like flowers which should be placed at the feet of God, says Jñāneśvara, in his exposition of the Bhagavadgītā. Finally, as Dr. Radhakrishnan has pointed out, while Buddhism aims at a life of contemplation, the Bhagavadgītā aims at a life of action. This, of course, we shall consider when we come to Tilak's doctrine of activism.

Finally, in regard to Pessimism, we have known that the fundamental platform of Buddhistic philosophy is the famous utterance, सर्वं दुःखं दुःखं, क्षणिकं क्षणिकं; all things are full of misery, all things are momentary. The Bhagavadgītā does not uphold pessimism in any way in that sense. Of course, in all philosophy and in all spiritual effort there is a little element of pessimism. Even the Bhagavadgītā speaks of जन्ममृत्युजराव्याधिदुःखदोषानुदर्शनम् । XIII.8; also it speaks of the end of this grief on a pessimistic-optimistic level दुःखान्तं च निगच्छति । XVII. 36, where we are told that it is possible for man to go beyond the reach of sorrow. But if the Bhagavadgītā stands for anything in particular, it stands for optimism, particularly spiritual optimism. We might quote three utterances from the Bhagavadgītā on this head : (१) सुखमात्यन्तिकं यत् तद् बुद्धि-

ग्राह्यमतीन्द्रियम् । VI.21, which speaks of the supreme happiness as beyond the reach of senses; (२) यं लब्ध्वा चापरं लाभं मन्यते नाधिकं ततः । VI.22, which describes the happiness as so superb that there is nothing in the world that may be compared to it; and (३) ...योगिनं सुखमुत्तमम् । उपैति शान्तरजसं ब्रह्मभूतमकल्मषम् । XI.27, which equates the happiness enjoyed by a Yogin with Brahman itself.

CHAPTER X

ACTIVISM : TILAK

We shall proceed next to two very important interpretations of the Bhagavadgītā in recent times, one by Lokamanya Tilak and the other by Mahatma Gandhi. We may call one a philosophy of activism and the other a philosophy of detachment. It is after a long time that I have been able to say anything about the great work of Lokamanya Tilak. When his Gītā-Rahasya was published about forty years ago, I was Professor of Philosophy at the Fergusson College. When Mr. N. C. Kelkar asked me at the instance of Lokamanya Tilak to write a series of three articles on Gītā-Rahasya for the Kesari, I said I was a small man, I had just started my philosophic career and it would be very rash for me to say anything at that stage about such an important work like the Gītā-Rahasya. So I excused myself and Mr. N. C. Kelkar also excused me. It is today, after the lapse of forty years, that I have been able to speak a few words about the great Gītā-Rahasya.

Tilak on European Moralists

One of the chief contributions which Lok. Tilak has made to the interpretation of the Bhagavadgītā and which has not received the attention of scholars as it deserves, is his scholarly exposition of the ethical doctrines of the Bhagavadgītā in relation to those of the European moralists. In fact, Lok. Tilak's knowledge of the European moralists seems to be a little wonderful, considering that it was not his profession to teach either ethics or philosophy. I have specially selected eight

European moralists about whom Lok. Tilak's expositions are worth while considering as well as developing. The first group of moralists consists of Aristotle and Kant, the second of Schopenhaeur and Nietzsche, the third of Martineau and Green and the fourth of Spencer and Sidgwick. Other moralists are comparatively minor when we are concerned with the doctrines of the Bhagavadgītā. For example, the utilitarianism of Bentham and Mill which stands for पुष्कळांचें पुष्कळ सुख has not much value for us in regard to the Bhagavadgītā except for the criticisms which Lok. Tilak brings to bear upon it. Their writings have no spiritual value; so we restrict our attention to the eight European moralists we have mentioned above. We shall profit by their opinions, and we shall briefly develop them in such a way that the relation in which they stand to the doctrines of the Bhagavadgītā might be brought into greater relief.

(*a*) *Aristotle and Kant.* In regard to Aristotle, his great contribution as found towards the end of his Metaphysics as well as his Ethics is the concept of the theoria, the beatificatory contemplation, which, according to him, is one of the characteristics of God, and which a man has to imbibe to a certain extent at least. In fact, Aristotle regards this as his ideal. It may be paralleled by what Spinoza later on called *Amor intellectualis Dei* (Intellectual love of God). The theoria need not necessarily be Godly, it may be human. Human theoria is a part and parcel, or a fraction, of that great Divine theoria, and that is the ideal at which our metaphysical or ethical life must aim. When we come to Aristotle's politics, we find him discussing two chief vocations for a man, the vocation of a statesman and the vocation of a philosopher and he says it is not possible to fuse them both. These two are different sides of human nature, and both of them are respected, and therefore even though in his politics Aristotle would like to place the life of activity above the life of contemplation, he ultimately inclines to the view that Divine theoria might in any case be regarded as an ideal. It is true, he says, that none but God can live in mere contemplation alone, but it would behove man in his highest state to imitate that kind of theoria. Finally, he makes a very important statement. It is only when we are contemplating scientifically, philosophically, intuitionally, and on a higher level, that our mind can go up to theoria. It is in such cases that we can dispense with the society of others, and our ultimate ideal then would be to live the life of God alone. According to Aristotle, therefore, when we are engaged in such an impersonal pursuit like that of scientific or philosophic contemplation, our aim is to imitate the Divine theoria to a certain extent at least in all our activities.

When we come to Kant, we come to a philosopher of not less importance than Aristotle. In fact, we have devoted a good deal of attention to Kant's ethical teachings in our later chapters and so it is not necessary for us to go into their details here, except briefly to indicate some main points in which his ethical teaching might be considered in relation to that of the Bhagavadgītā. In the first place, Kant tells us that the Categorical Imperative is the supreme rule which ought to guide our conduct. This exactly corresponds to what the Bhagavadgītā has called "duty for duty's sake". (कार्यमित्येव यत्कर्म नियतं क्रियतेऽर्जुन). Secondly, Kant gives us three modifications of the Categorical Imperative, one rising above the other. In a similar fashion, we shall see that the

Gītā also makes three modifications of that original principle, " Duty for duty's sake ", and places them for consideration and imitation before humanity. Finally, we have the opinion of Kant in respect of the Categorical Imperative as having no value for either the Holy Will or the Divine Will. This corresponds closely to what Śaṁkara said later that you cannot dictate rules about activity or inactivity for the life of the highest realiser.

(*b*) *Schopenhaeur and Nietzsche.* We next proceed to the second batch of moralists, Schopenhaeur and Nietzsche, who might be regarded as typical representatives of the संन्यासमार्ग and the कर्ममार्ग respectively in their extreme forms. We are conversant with an expression in Greek philosophy which brings out the distinction between a weeping philosopher and a laughing philosopher. In the present case we can talk about Schopenhaeur and Nietzsche as a weeping philosopher and a fire-breathing philosopher respectively. Schopenhaeur's great work " The World as Will and Idea " is only the negation of the World as Idea, and the affirmation of the World as Will. His is a great voluntarism as against the idealism of his contemporary philosophers. The Will is the unconscious force which governs the development of the whole of nature, inorganic and organic. When we come to its ethical aspect, we find that true morality consists only in the negation of Will. We must accustom ourselves to a sort of an ascetic self-mortification in order that this supreme unconscious force of Will might be negated. The result would be that there will be suffering and misery all round, the misery rising to a climax in man. This leads to the doctrine of pessimism from which Schopenhaeur could extricate himself only by his insistence upon the value of art. If according to Schopenhauer we can escape from suffering by recognition of art, we are sorry that he should not have seen the possibility of escaping from misery by contemplation upon Reality, especially as he was a believer in the Upaniṣads. We are thankful to him for his great utterance which is known to almost every Indian scholar: " The Upaniṣads have been the solace of my life, the Upaniṣads would be the solace of my death." Had the meaning of the Upaniṣads really penetrated the mind of Schopenhaeur, he would have become an optimistic philosopher instead of a pessimistic one.

Nietzsche's great attack was upon the ethics of Christianity, which he called a docile ethics, an ethics of humility, submission and surrender. Nietzsche stood for force. In the socio-political aspect this force manifests itself in the elimination of the weak and the survival of the strong. When the scales are turned, when the weak survive and the strong are eliminated, we get to what he calls a dysgenic spectacle which leads to the destruction of the world. He discusses the nature of two moralities, the slave-morality and the master-morality, and it is the master-morality for which he stands. On reading the details of the master-morality in Nietzsche, who will not be reminded of the आसुरी संपत् of the XVI chapter of the Bhagavadgītā ? In fact, as an advocate of doctrines such as these, he became the morning star of German ascendency at the close of the last century and it was not a little due to him that the idea of German domination became supreme with persons like Kaiser and Hitler. Nietzsche is the founder of this idea of domination in the German race. He talks about the Superman who rises beyond good and bad.

We are, of course, conversant with such an expression so far as ethics and metaphysics are concerned. But when we see its application to the socio-political sphere, it only means that nothing could be said by way either of praise or blame about the actions of a great political and social worker. Such a one transcends all judgments of good and bad, just as a philosopher might transcend them when he reaches the highest stage of Reality. It is strange that even when he talked about a Godless world, or daringly went to the length of declaring that "God is dead", he still believed in the possibility of re-birth. These are, of course, the philosophical sides of Nietzsche's ethico–political theory, and even though Nietzsche did not believe in God like the Sāṁkhya philosopher, he still believed in the soul.

(c) *Martineau and Green.* We proceed to the next batch of modern moralists, namely Martineau and Green. Martineau, on account of his contribution to religious philosophy, was supposed in India to have something in common with the teaching of the Bhagavadgītā; but his teaching, in fact, falls far short of it. Green's teaching, however, comes very near to that of the Bhagavadgītā. Martineau is famous for having introduced the idea of 'springs of action' in his ethics. He arranges these springs of action in a graded order, beginning with appetites and ending with sentiments like reverence; and he tells us that it is conscience which enables us to select any one of these in preference to the other. But conscience according to him is neither a moral nor a spiritual concept but only a psycho–ethical concept. He had led the life of an engineer and it was for that reason that he could speak about conscience in that manner. On mature thought, however, he found that when conscience becomes more fully developed among men, they come almost to the same conclusions. It is for this reason that Martineau speaks of all the consciences as being the aspects of one Supreme Conscience. It is unfortunate that Martineau could not rise to the notion of the Self, or at least he fought shy of it. As a Doctor of Divinity, he had a right to speak about the Self in preference to conscience but he did not choose to do so. On the other hand, he wrote a great work on the Philosophy of Religion, which was almost one of the earliest works written on the subject during the latter half of the last century.

Green rises to a superior concept. He stands for nothing but the idea of the Self. There is a spiritual principle in man as there is a spiritual principle in nature and the one is the reproduction of the other. This great idea he develops in the first chapter of his work, 'The Prolegomena to Ethics' and comes very near to the doctrine of the Self in Indian thought in general and in the Bhagavadgītā in particular. Secondly, who does not know the great pains which Green has taken in analysing and developing the concept of moral consciousness and its application to social welfare? The urge for social development comes through the presence of the spiritual principle in man. It is the spiritual principle in man which enables him to find the spiritual principle in society; and hence perfection in the one involves perfection in the other. In fact, Green's doctrine thus becomes a comprehensive doctrine of perfectionism, both individual and social; but Green does not stop here. The idea of the presence of spirit both in nature and in man leads him to posit a divine consciousness which he regards as transcending the limits of time. What else can we have from a spiritual philosophy like that of the Bhagavadgītā in regard to such statements as the nature of man, the nature of society and the nature of God? In fact, Green makes the nearest approach to the philosophy of the Bhagavadgītā so far as its metaphysical side is concerned, and if his ethics had been developed on appropriate lines, his treatment of the ethical problems would have been exactly similar to that of the Bhagavadgītā. It is interesting to note that when at the time of his passing away he asked the people who were sitting by his bedside to read out to him a passage from the Bible which spoke about the life after death, he was unconsciously reiterating by his own example the supreme teaching of the Bhagavadgītā in this matter:

ओमित्येकाक्षरं ब्रह्म व्याहरन् मामनुस्मरन् ।
यः प्रयाति त्यजन् देहं स याति परमां गतिम् ।। VIII.13.

(*d*) *Spencer and Sidgwick.* We proceed to our last batch of European moralists, namely Spencer and Sidgwick. Sidgwick particularly has made so many points worthy of consideration, as far as ethical philosophy is concerned, that it is impossible to do full justice to them all. We shall select only one item out of his ethical discussions, that is where Spencer and Sidgwick meet and where Indian thinkers either agree with them or criticise them. Spencer speaks about relative ethics and absolute ethics. We are always living in the domain of relative ethics, he says. Absolute ethics transcends us altogether and our practical life should be a combination of these two aspects, namely the relative and the absolute. As a consequence, Spencer tells us that no truth-speaking is desirable in a community of cannibals, the treacherous and the unscrupulous. Truth-speaking has no value at all in these bad surroundings, although in itself it deserves to be regarded as a great ethical virtue. Sidgwick follows suit. We shall restrict our attention, as we have already said, only to this point in Sidgwick's ethical philosophy. No truth-speaking, he says, should be allowed with children, madmen, invalids, people in a mortal condition, enemies, robbers or even with advocates who ask questions which they have no right to ask.

Anāsakti, the Connecting Bond between Tilak and Gandhi

This denial of truth-speaking as a virtue under such circumstances was hotly debated among Indian politicians and statesmen about forty years ago, Lok. Tilak standing for the doctrine of शठं प्रति शाठ्यम् and Mahatma Gandhi standing for the doctrine of शठं प्रति सत्यम्. Tilak's justification was founded upon such utterances as those of Spencer and Sidgwick. शक्यतों शांतीनें, नाहींतर बलानें was what Tilak said about the way of the removal of difficulties. आततायिनमायान्तं हन्यादेवाविचारयन्। has been a doctrine known to the Indian scholars from the times of Manu downwards. If a man lifts his sword against you, it is your duty to lift your sword against him. That was the doctrine of Tilak. On the other hand, Mahatma Gandhi taught the doctrine of शठं प्रति सत्यम्. If an enemy smites you on the right cheek, says the Bible, turn to him the left cheek also. Your self-sacrifice, your self-negation, your assertion and recognition of the presence of the self in others will stand you in good stead in removing the presence of bad ideas from the minds of those who stand against you. We should always speak the truth, says Kant, even though people might come to deceive you. In this way, we find this controversy between शठं प्रति शाठ्यम् and शठं प्रति सत्यम् illustrated finely in the history of two great schools of ethical thought, the one represented by Spencer and Sidgwick, and Tilak agreeing with them, and the other represented by Christianity and Kant, and Mahatma Gandhi following them. We have discussed this topic at some length in a later chapter, and even though it would be difficult to pronounce a judgment upon matters of such high controversy like this, we have pointed out that psychologically there are temperamental differences among men, which enable them either to follow the path of force and retribution or the path of truth and peace. In any case, it is most important to remember that even though there was this difference between Tilak and Gandhi in their doctrines of शठं प्रति शाठ्यम् and शठं प्रति सत्यम्, Anāsakti was the connecting bond between them. Even though, therefore, so far as particulars are concerned, there might be differences between these two great men, it is highly commendable that both of them stand for Anāsakti as the central teaching of the Bhagavadgītā.

A Few Outstanding Points in Tilak's Gītā-Rahasya

(*a*) *Jñāna, Bhakti and Yoga in Relation to Karma.* After having considered the doctrines of the great moralists to whom Lokamanya Tilak has referred in his work and after bringing out the relationship in which Tilak stands to them, let us now proceed to consider a few significant points in Tilak's original contribution to the interpretation of the Bhagavadgītā. In fact, this subject has been so elaborately studied and commented on that it would now be hazardous or impossible to add anything to what has been already said. Yet we feel justified in bringing to the notice of our readers five points which may be regarded as the great contribution of Tilak to the interpretation of the Bhagavadgītā. In fact, he wants to prove that Karma-

Yoga is the essence of the Bhagavadgītā. That is the pole star of his teaching. All procedures of his interpretation are directed towards that end. Jñāna points to it, Bhakti points to it, (Dhyāna) Yoga points to it, so that all these procedures of attainment point to Karma as the ultimate goal of life. What lies at the bottom of this assertion is that the intellectual scheme of oneness, the devotional scheme of love and the meditational scheme of mental equipoise are all directed to the achievement of the ultimate end of human life, namely action. Oneness, love and equanimity, in short, all point to activism as being the goal of them all. After considering these, we shall proceed to two further points: (1) Tilak's admission of realisation as being of greater value than service and (2) the question of the supreme criterion for the interpretation of the teaching of any great work. As is well-known, there are six such criteria according to मीमांसा philosophy but we shall stress अपूर्वता in particular for our purpose.

Jñāna. Let us now proceed to Tilak's doctrine of Jñāna, which according to him, is a means to the achievement of Karma. In the first place, Jñāna may be looked at from two points of view, intellectual and mystical. Very many people have misunderstood or not understood at all this distinction, and by Jñāna they very often mean merely philosophical or intellectual knowledge. But Jñāna also means mystical knowledge. ज्ञान, for example, in उपदेक्ष्यन्ति ते ज्ञानं ज्ञानिनस्तत्त्वदर्शिनः does not refer to mere intellectual knowledge. यज्ज्ञात्वा नेह भूयोऽन्यत् ज्ञातव्यमवशिष्यते । points to that mystical knowledge beyond which there is nothing else to be known. This fact must first be borne in mind. Secondly, there is one very important controversy that has raged between

Śaṁkara and Tilak and this particularly centers round two points : (a) whether ज्ञानोत्तरकर्म is possible and (b) whether ज्ञानकर्मसमुच्चय is possible. These are two important foci round which the controversy turns. According to Śaṁkara, Karma after Jñāna is an impossibility. In one very significant remark he points out गीताशास्त्रं संसारस्य अत्यन्तोपरमलक्षणम्. There is an end to all Karma after Jñāna. This is just the point which Lok. Tilak wants to contradict. Karma must be done even after Jñāna, says Tilak. Secondly, in regard to the combination of Jñāna and Karma, Śaṁkarācārya tells us that it is impossible for us to combine the two. ज्ञानकर्मसमुच्चय is impossible, says Śaṁkara. केवलादेव ज्ञानात्* मोक्षप्राप्तिः । न कर्मसमुच्चितात् । On the other hand, to Tilak ज्ञानकर्मसमुच्चय is not only possible but absolutely real. Of course, Karma in itself would be higher even than ज्ञानकर्म-समुच्चय, but if we descend to a little lower level, ज्ञानकर्म-समुच्चय becomes very essential. The two fundamental passages on which Tilak relies are विद्यां च अविद्यां च यस्तद्वेदोभयं सह and उभाभ्यामेव पक्षाभ्याम्, which tell us that it is essential that Jñāna and Karma should be combined together. We have considered this point in a later chapter ; so, we do not want to enter into it here. (c) We may, however, take the liberty of suggesting the solution pointed out

---

* A recent writer has pointed out that even the great king Janaka about whose activism the Bhagavadgītā has spoken so much कर्मणैवहि संसिद्धिमास्थिता जनकादयः । (III. 20) has been described in the Śānti Parva of the Mahābbārata as having taken Saṁnyāsa towards the end of his life in order that he might attain liberation. He left off his kingdom, handed it over to his sons, parted with everything that he had got and took Saṁnyāsa in order to attain Jñāna. The same thing is repeated in another passage in Mahābhārata.

(Śānti Parva, Adhyāya 318, Śloka 94–95 p. 108. Gītā Marma-Darśana by Khare).

there, namely that this controversy cannot be resolved except on the ground of temperamental differences between men and men. "Ought has no meaning in such a case," as Kant has said. Śaṁkarācārya, who fought for the uniqueness of Jñāna, uncontaminated by Karma, was himself one of the greatest intellectual activists the world has ever seen. Having travelled throughout the length and breadth of India, having established his monasteries at different places and having devoted his life to the fulfilment of his philosophical and spiritual mission, Śaṁkarācārya set himself on a pedestal to which people can only point, but which they can scarcely reach. One has only to remember that it becomes the mission of such a realiser to spread the gospel of God whenever and wherever it becomes possible for him to do so. One God, One World, One Humanity should be his maxim, theo-polity his doctrine. Whosoever realises the unity or the presence of God can never but direct his life in such a way that the greatness of God becomes not merely understood but also achievable. So far then about the true meaning of Jñāna.

Bhakti. What about Bhakti ? Bhakti is also essential for the achievement of any great Karma. (a) Tukārāma and Purandaradāsa devoted their entire life to the spiritual upliftment of humanity. (b) Rāmānuja and Ekanātha gave themselves over to social reform. (c) Political achievement redounded to the credit of two great devotees of God, Nānaka and Rāmadāsa. (d) Finally, Jñāneśvara and Kabīra spent their life in utilising their devotional temperament for the mystical upliftment of the world. In that way, the devotees of God might also be regarded as greatly contributing to the life of action in this world.

Yoga. Lok. Tilak makes a significant point in telling us that the requirements of Pātañjala Yoga as well as its achievements are all to be utilised for the sake of Karma : व्यवसायात्मिक बुद्धि शुद्ध ठेवण्याचें साधन म्हणून गीतेंत पातंजल योग सांगितला आहे (Gītā-Rahasya, pp. 136–137). That, of course, is an extreme point of view. It cannot be said that the only aim of Yoga is to maintain a moral equipoise for the achievement of action. A point of greater significance would be the realisation of God Himself. Lok. Tilak, however, contends that the utility of Pātañjala Yoga, so far as at least the Bhagavadgītā is concerned, is for the achievement of that moral equipoise which is essential for the accomplishment of any great work.

(*b*) *Tilak's Admission of Superiority of Realisation over Service.* After these three points we come to a very significant admission of Lok. Tilak regarding realisation as being higher than service. It could be hardly expected from a great activist like Lok. Tilak that he would recognise this value of self-realisation, but that he has done it is beyond doubt. He says समाजधारणा घ्या किंवा सर्वभूतहित घ्या. हीं बाह्योपयोगी तत्त्वें जर आमच्या आत्मकल्याणाच्या मार्गांच्या आड येत असतील, तर तीं आम्हांस नकोत—(Gītā-Rahasya, p. 67). Tilak, therefore, would prefer आत्मकल्याण or the realisation of the Ātman as of higher consequence than either समाजधारणा or सर्वभूतहित. This, of course, is not the point of view which he always maintains. We are glad that the sub-conscious in Lok. Tilak has come out at least once.

(*c*) *Apūrvatā.* Finally, Lok. Tilak has devoted a great amount of attention to pointing out the significance of the six-fold Mīmāṁsā criterion for the interpretation of the inner meaning of any great work like the Bhagavadgītā.

उपक्रमोपसंहारौ अभ्यासोऽपूर्वताफलम् ।
अर्थवादोपपत्ती च लिंगं तात्पर्यनिर्णये ॥

Jaiminī Sūtra. I.2.

All these criteria, according to Lok. Tilak, point to the real meaning of the Bhagavadgītā as consisting in spreading the gospel of Karma Yoga, Karma Yoga being the be-all and the end-all of its teaching. With Karmayoga the Bhagavadgītā begins, with Karmayoga the Bhagavadgītā ends, and it is Karmayoga which pervades the Bhagavadgītā. From our point of view, we do not stress this six-fold criterion at all. We stress only one out of these, namely Apūrvatā. Apūrvatā means novelty or originality. What is the novelty or the original contribution of the Bhagavadgītā? That ought to be our chief question. It is not whether Arjuna has been advised to fight at the beginning of the work or at the end of the work, or whether the advice is repeated from time to time, that constitutes its supreme teaching. What is the novelty or the originality which the Bhagavadgītā has to offer to the world? In our opinion, as the title of the present work may show, God-realisation constitutes the Apūrvatā, the novelty or the supreme contribution of the Bhagavadgītā. The Bhagavadgītā is one of the greatest works on mysticism that the world has ever seen and when God-realisation has been duly stressed, everything else will follow in its wake.

CHAPTER XI

DETACHMENT : GANDHI

The Nature of Anāsakti and its Relation to Ahiṁsā

In the last chapter we considered Lokamanya Tilak's doctrine of activism. This chapter will be devoted to the discussion of another very important interpretation which Mahatma Gandhi has put upon the Bhagavadgītā. Many years ago when he first translated this Sanskrit work into Gujarati, he called it Anāsakti Yoga. Later, translations of this Anāsakti Yoga appeared in other languages like Marathi, Kannada and Bengali. But it was reserved for Mahadeva Desai to carry into effect his scheme of the English translation of Mahatma Gandhi's Anāsakti Yoga with a profound introduction. Mahadeva Desai was one of the very few disciples of Mahatma Gandhi who loved him from the very bottom of his heart, and he was intellectually very well equipped for carrying out that kind of work. I had correspondence with him since 1920, as an old friend of mine, Mr. Y. N. Yadwadkar, whom Mahadeva Desai called Sarkar, was his friend and worked as co-secretary of Mahatma Gandhi at the time of the Nagpur Congress. On account of his sound knowledge of Sanskrit and philosophy, Mahadeva Desai was well qualified to undertake this great work. Unfortunately, he did not live to see it published. It was published posthumously. Nevertheless, the work reflects the freshness and originality of the writer.

In this chapter, we shall discuss five chief points in regard to Mahatma Gandhi's interpretation of the

Bhagavadgītā : First, his doctrine of Anāsakti; second, his allegorism ; third, his doctrine of incarnation; fourth, his description of what constitutes a real devotee (one of the best descriptions that may be found in the Gandhian literature); finally, we shall discuss Mahadeva Desai's description of what he calls an ideal sage. He probably had in mind Mahatma Gandhi himself.

The word Anāsakti might be interpreted either as non-attachment or detachment or renunciation. Non-attachment is the negative form of it, detachment is its positive form and renunciation, not in the sense of Saṁnyāsa as we understand it, but renunciation of the fruits of action as Mahatma Gandhi calls it. In fact, the title of Mahadeva Desai's English translation of his work on Anāsakti Yoga is the "Doctrine of Renunciation". In the introduction we find the following important statements of Mahatma Gandhi. To quote the very words of Mahatma Gandhi himself: (1) " Anāsakti is the central Sun round which revolve the three planets of devotion, knowledge and works" (Anāsakti Yoga, p. 125). This is as much as to say that Bhakti, Jñāna and Karma are entirely dependent on and governed by the doctrine of Anāsakti. (2) A question may now be asked as to the relation in which Anāsakti stands to Ahiṁsā. Ahiṁsā is the doctrine for which Mahatma Gandhi lived and died. (a) Swami Ananda wrote to Mahatma Gandhi : "I do not think it is just on your part to deduce from stray verses that the Gītā was written to establish Ahiṁsā" (Ibid p. 121). Gandhiji grants that Gītā was not written to establish Ahiṁsā. He says "it was a long accepted principle even before the Gītā age" (Ibid. p. 129). (b) Mahatma Gandhi goes on to say: "After forty years of unremitting endeavour, however, I have felt that perfect renunciation is impossible without perfect observation of Ahiṁsā in every shape and form" (Ibid. p. 130). Mahatma Gandhi tells us further that Anāsakti may be regarded as a coin of which Ahiṁsā and Satya are the obverse and reverse sides. He always spoke not merely about Ahiṁsā but also about Satya. (3) If we analyse the conception of Anāsakti, we see that it consists of three points: (i) desireless action, (ii) the dedication of all actions to God and (iii) surrendering oneself to God, body and soul. In this way only, says Mahatma Gandhi, could the body of man be made the temple of God. All these three points are expressed in one single beautiful sentence by Mahatma Gandhi: "That great matchless remedy consists in desireless action, in dedicating all activities to God, that is, by surrendering oneself to Him, body and soul" (Ibid. p. 125). Mahatma Gandhi further goes on to tell us that really speaking he who renounces, gains a thousandfold (p. 128). There is a very famous Hindi maxim, रामनामके कारन सब धन डाला खोय। मूरख जाने गिर गया दिन दिन दूना होय। This Dohā implies that renunciation may apparently involve us in every possible loss, but really it gives us every possible merit, enabling us to reap a thousandfold the fruits of the seeds which we have sown.

Is Mahābhārata Historical or Allegorical ?

We next proceed to discuss Mahatma Gandhi's doctrine of allegorism. The great question is: Is Mahābhārata historical or allegorical? Mahatma Gandhi tells us on this point that ever since he was first acquainted with Sir Edwin Arnold's translation of the Bhagavadgītā, called the 'Song Celestial', in 1888–89, he had felt that it was not a historical work. "I do not regard Mahābhārata ", he tells us, " as a historical work in the accepted sense of the term " (pp. 123-24). This does not mean that the persons in the Mahābhārata are not historical ; but the many situations, speeches, dialogues, interpretations, conclusions and so forth need not necessarily be regarded as historical. They are what the great Vyāsa has put into the mouths of the great actors. Mahatma Gandhi advances three arguments for regarding the Mahābhārata as allegorical rather than historical: (1) In the first place, he tells us that the Ādiparva contains a very powerful evidence in support of his statement. Vyāsa ascribes to many of the heroes of the Mahābhārata either sub-human or super-human origins. These cannot be regarded as historical in any sense. For example, Bhīṣma, he tells us, was born from the Gaṅgā, Karṇa from the Sun, Dharma from the God of Death, Bhīma from wind and Agastya from a pitcher. Who can say that these actors or anything connected with them may be regarded in any sense as historical? (2) Secondly, as Mahadeva Desai has put it, it is permissible to poets, dramatists and historians to ascribe imaginary characters to historical persons. For example, we may see how the great Shakespeare painted Richard III as a diabolical being.

" So misshapen and sent before my time into the world, that dogs bark at me when I halt by them. "

Thucydides, the great historian, who has by general consent been regardad as a very conscientious historian, has not hesitated to introduce imaginary dialogues or to invent speeches for his characters in order to elucidate the different situations. Thucydides has himself told us that he has deliberately done so in order that the lesson might be well impressed upon the minds of his readers.

(3) Thirdly, Mahatma Gandhi tells us, if we interpret the Mahābhārata more in an allegorical than in a historical sense, then the Bhagavadgītā itself might be taken to represent the moral duel that is perpetually going on inside us. Historical names have been introduced by the author of the great epic only to drive home ethical and religious principles. For example, the Pāṇḍavas were regarded as forces of light, Kauravas as forces of darkness and the Kurukṣetra as the human body in which they played their part. Arjuna and Kṛṣṇa might themselves allegorically be taken to represent the "individual ego and the great In-dweller." In this way, according to Mahatma Gandhi, we have to interpret both the Mahābhārata and the Bhagavadgītā more in an allegorical than in a historical sense.

Meanings of Incarnation

Lastly, we come to Mahatma Gandhi's doctrine of incarnation. (1) Every embodied being, he tells us, is an incarnation, though to be regarded as a perfect incarnation some extra-ordinary service to mankind is necessary. This is an important statement. It is in this way that those who have been called Avatāras are so called, because they have performed great works for the benefit of humanity. Elsewhere in this book we may notice how Garbe, Hopkins and Edgerton have spoken almost in the same strain. Being born men, according to them, people first become men-gods and then gods. Mahatma Gandhi's criterion for incarnation is, in a similar strain, the great service that a man does to humanity. (2) We can approach the doctrine of incarnation from another point of view also. The Bhagavadgītā itself tells us :

> यद्यद्विभूतिमत्सत्त्वं श्रीमदूर्जितमेव वा ।
> तत्तदेवावगच्छ त्वं मम तेजोंऽशसंभवम् ॥ X·41.

Wherever there is excellence, wherever there is pre-eminence, wherever there is a portion of the great power and lustre of God, there we might regard that God is present as an incarnation. The great Vibhūtis, therefore, are themselves embodiments or incarnations of God. Let us select only ten Vibhūtis here for our purpose : Meru and Himālaya among the mountains; Janhavi among the rivers, Mṛgendra and Vainateya among the animals and birds, Sāmaveda among the sacred books, Mārgaśīrṣa and Kusumākara among the months and seasons, Oṁkāra among syllables and Vāsudeva among Divine heroes. (3) Finally, it is wonderful to see how the great German philosopher, Hegel, who evidently seems to have read the Bhagavadgītā, has said that it is the substantial or the universal, which constitutes the essence of things and which we might understand as equivalent to an incarnation. Hegel says :—

> " When God says, ' in the metal I am brightness of its shining, among the rivers I am the Ganges, I am the life of all that lives', he thereby suppresses the individual. He does not say I am the metal, the rivers, the individual things of various kinds as such. The brightness is not the metal itself but is the universal, elevated above any individual form. What is expressed here is no longer pantheism ; the idea expressed is rather that of the essence of things. "
>
> Hegel's Philosophy of Religion. p. 42.3.

This raises the conception of the essence or incarnation to a philosophic level.

Description of an Ideal Devotee and an Ideal Saint

We now proceed to discuss the last two points. We shall first deal with Mahatma Gandhi's sublime description of a devotee. Neither in his work on the Bhagavadgītā nor probably anywhere else has Mahatma Gandhi described the qualifications of a devotee in the manner in which he has done here. It is a superb illustration of what a devotee ought to be. Not merely does he gather together utterances from the Bhagavadgītā, but inserts some of his own reflections in order to present a full picture of a devotee. According to Mahatma Gandhi :—

> " He is a real devotee who is jealous of none, who is a fount of mercy, who is without egoism, who treats alike cold and heat, happiness and misery, who is ever forgiving, who is always contented, whose resolutions are firm, who has dedicated mind and soul to God, who causes no dread, who is not afraid of others, who is free from exultation, sorrow and fear, who is pure, who is versed in action and yet remains unaffected by it, who renounces all fruit, good or bad, who treats friend and foe alike, who is untouched by respect or disrespect, who is not puffed up by praise, who does not go under when people speak ill of him, who loves silence and solitude, who has a disciplined reason."

Anāsakti Yoga. p. 126.

I am tempted to feel that Mahatma Gondhi having thought deeply about the qualifications of a devotee has given almost an autobiographical account in this description.

Finally, when we come to Mahadeva Desai's commentary on Mahatma Gandhi's work, we see that he excels himself in describing what an ideal sage ought to be. Probably, he has got his teacher Mahatma Gandhi in his mind. The description is wonderful and we quote it as it is :—

> " The Yogin is therefore one who reflects all these attributes in his life, who, in the midst of raging storm and blinding spray, will keep his vision of the Sun undisturbed, who will look difficulties and death in the face, who goes with the same mind to the shambles and the scaffold and whose mind is so serene that thunder rocks him to sleep. "
>
> The Gospel of Selfless Action. p. 51.

We are accustomed to read descriptions of the ideal sage according to the Stoics and the Epicureans. Here are descriptions of the ideal sage of the Bhagavadgītā according to Mahatma Gandhi and Mahadeva Desai. We leave it to our readers to judge between the two.

CHAPTER XII

OTHER MODERN PROMINENT INTERPRETERS

After having studied the remarks made by Mahatma Gandhi and Mr. Mahadeva Desai on the Bhagavadgītā, we shall proceed to see the spot-lights thrown on the Bhagavadgītā in the works of some recent eminent Indian scholars. What they have to say we shall give in their own words; but we shall preface their remarks with a short account of what they are going to say. We shall classify these scholars under three groups from the view-points which they particularly want to stress. In the first group will come Mrs. Besant, Munshi, Aldous Huxley and Belvalkar; in the second group come Katju and Divatia; and in the third come Divatia, Hill, Rajagopalachari, Radhakrishnan and Mrs. Besant. Under these three groups we shall consider (1) the unity of the three paths in the Bhagavadgītā, (2) the social application of the teachings of the Bhagavadgītā, and (3) some brilliant modern estimates of the teaching of the Bhagavadgītā.

Group (i) : Unity of the Three Paths

(*a*) *Mrs. Annie Besant.* Let us begin by noticing what Mrs. Besant says in regard to the Bhagavadgītā. She teaches us that the so-called three paths are really one. The paths that are known as knowledge, devotion and action, all ultimately tend to the realisation of God.

> "We see the three paths within the one and according to the dominant temperament will be the path that is chosen." (Four Lectures on the

Bhagavadgītā, Adyar, p. 79). "For him who is full of emotion, the best way is the way of devotion; for him who is by temperament inclined to wisdom, the way of knowledge is the best; and for him who is temperamentally inclined to action, the path of action will be the best. 'For the path men take from every side is Mine.'" Ibid. (p. 96.).

(*b*) *Shri K. M. Munshi.* Shri Munshi tells us that men have trodden the path of God from various sides. Some of them have stumbled and some few have reached the goal. Among those who have reached the goal are: Śaṁkarācārya who stresses the path of knowledge; Calvin who stresses the path of action, and as such is the Father of the Christian Reformation, who made Protestantism a living force; and St. Augustine, the second great founder of Christianity, known for his great devotion and passionate ardour for surrender to God:

> "Shining examples of greatness throughout history have followed this path in all lands. Many have stumbled. Some have reached the goal. A scrutiny of their lives discloses how perfection has been practised and attained."
>
> Bhagavadgītā and Modern Life. p. 35.

> "Śaṁkarācārya leads the world's thought in laying emphasis on knowledge and renunciation. By reason of this emphasis, the human Gospel of Gītā has come to be understood as the message of knowledge and renunciation."
>
> Ibid. p. 35.

"John Calvin was a man of action. He organised the European Reformation and laid the foundation of the broad and liberal movement which the Protestant Church represented in Europe. He made Protestantism a living force in Europe."

Ibid. p. 37.

"St. Augustine, one of the four great fathers of the Latin Church, was a man of love and devotion. He was passionate by nature and an ardent lover. His God called to him. He ran out of his house, flung himself under a fig tree. A voice bade him to surrender himself to God and he did so. What we find in his Confessions is the enthusiasm and passionate ardour to surrender himself to God which is Bhakti Yoga."

Ibid. p. 40.

"The study of these great characters shows that Knowledge, Action and Devotion are the inalienable aspects of the fundamental unity of human nature."

Ibid. p. 41.

(c) *Dr. Aldous Huxley and Dr. Belvalkar.* Dr. Aldous Huxley in his Perennial Philosophy speaks of three types of men. These three types are physio-psychological in character: the cerebral type, which stresses the activity of the head, belongs to the path of knowledge; the cardiac type, which stresses the heart, belongs to the path of devotion; and the muscular type, which stresses the hand, belongs to the path of action. Dr. Belvalkar very happily has called this triune path by the expression ज्ञानभक्तिकर्मसमुच्चय. We have hitherto seen in works on Indian Philosophy only ज्ञानकर्मसमुच्चय, but we compliment Dr. Belvalkar upon his having introduced that word Bhakti in the scheme, and called it a triune unity of Jñāna, Bhakti and Karma. We are happy to note what he says that 'trichotomy' does not represent the true teaching of the Bhagavadgītā; on the other hand, it is the 'triune unity' of Jñāna, Bhakti and Karma.

Group II : Social Teachings of the Bhagavadgītā

(d) *Dr. K. N. Katju.* When we come to the social implications of the Bhagavadgītā, we may point out what Dr. Katju said in the lecture which he delivered at Nimbal on the 28th December 1954, namely, that all our actions should be intended for the sake of the society and the world. These constitute my God, he said. The three celebrated quotations to which he particularly referred are :—

(1) मन्मना भव मद्भक्तो मद्याजी मां नमस्कुरु ।
मामेवैष्यसि युक्त्वैवमात्मानं मत्परायणः ।। IX.34.

(2) मयि चानन्ययोगेन भक्तिरव्यभिचारिणी ।। XIII.10.

(3) चेतसा सर्वकर्माणि मयि संन्यस्य मत्परः ।
बुद्धियोगमुपाश्रित्य मच्चित्तः सततं भव ।। XVIII.57.

To Dr. Katju, the Ahaṁ which designates God in the above three quotations in expressions such as मन्मनाः, मयि चानन्ययोगेन भक्तिः and मत्परः, points only to the society and the world.

In fact, this is a point which he has stressed throughout his life as well as particularly in his lectures on Karma Yoga in the Bhagavadgītā at Allahabad. The Activism about which he spoke was particularly in relation to the society and the world.

(e) *Shri H. V. Divatia.* Shri. Divatia has written a good book on the Bhagavadgītā in which he stresses the social meaning of self-realisation. Self-realisation, according to him, means the realisation of the self in the wider life of the society. Service of humanity accordingly constitutes the only mode of worship especially for rationalists like himself.

> " Self-realisation means realisation of one's self in the wider life of our fellowmen. The Gītā teaches us that there cannot be self-realisation without the integration of the individual self with the larger social self. (The Art of life in the Bhagavadgītā, p. 173.)..." Service of Humanity is a form of worship of God which can be practised by persons of all religious faiths; and for rationalists such service is the sole religion." Ibid. p. 175.

Group III : Some Brilliant Estimates of the Bhagavadgītā

Let us now go on to consider certain noteworthy observations made recently by different scholars on the teachings of the Bhagavadgītā. We shall begin by calling to mind what Mr. Divatia has said about the unending spiral movement in spiritual life. The spiritual evolution of humanity always goes on upwards, according to him, in a spiral and it is an Avatāra which carries it to its summit.

> " The spiritual evolution of humanity moves in cycles, but this cycle is not a vicious circle; it is the circle of a screw or spiral, which at the end of each circulatory motion, takes us upwards. When evil goes on accumulating, each

cycle is moving to its inevitable end and a new force (Avatāra) arises which destroys the accumulated evil and completes the cycle."

Ibid. p. 135.

(*f*) *Mr. W. D. P. Hill.* Mr. Hill in his Introduction to the Bhagavadgītā makes some very fine remarks. The whole world is regarded as a puppet-show in which the producer, the scenery and the spectator are all Brahman. But let us not be satisfied with this delusion, he says. Let us not regard the performance as absolutely unreal. Let us hope that it constitutes at least a partial reality.

> "The universe is a puppet-show, Brahman is sole producer, Brahman is scenery and players, Brahman is sole spectator. The universe is sportively self-deluded. The means of production is the power of delusion; scenery and puppets are Brahman, self-stamped with 'name and form'. Like every thorough-going monistic system, the system of the Bhagavadgītā robs the universe of meaning. Personality, free-will, good and evil, even Avatāras are incidents in an idle show. The performance is renewed day after day; with each night the curtain falls....But to say that the universe is void of meaning is not to say that the performance is unreal. The Gītā follows rather that doctrine which allows to the universe a temporary reality as such."

The Bhagavadgītā. p. 27.

(*g*) *Shri. C. Rajagopalachari.* Among some of the fine remarks made by Shri. Rajagopalachari in his edition of the Bhagavadgītā, there is one which refers to the verse, बिभर्त्यव्यय ईश्वरः ... In his explanation of the verse, he tells us how we are to regard that there is an identity between God and the Laws of Nature and that the Laws of Nature constitute the Will of God.

> "Notwithstanding the fact that God supports and governs all, बिभर्त्यव्यय ईश्वरः, we are ignorant of it. The Laws of Nature are the Will of God. His Will is manifested in the shape of what we see directly or by investigation but which we choose to call the Laws of Nature. God is the Law and the Law is God. He rules through the Law, and it seems as if the Law rules and not He." The Bhagavadgītā, p. 41.

(h) *Dr. S. Radhakrishnan.* Dr. Radhakrishnan tells us how divine birth occurs in the case of every one of us. Vasudeva and Devakī, the father and the mother of Kṛṣṇa, ought to be allegorically interpreted. Vasudeva means Śuddha Sattva and Devakī means Daivī Prakṛti. Divine birth, therefore, took place not only in the case of Kṛṣṇa, but ought to take place in the case of everyone of us. He says :

> "Kṛṣṇa is said to be born of Vasudeva and Devakī. The Bhāgavata describes Vasudeva as शुद्धसत्त्व. सत्त्वं विशुद्धं वसुदेवसंज्ञितम् and Devakī is Daivī Prakṛti or divine nature. When the divine birth takes place within us, the scales fall from our eyes, the bolts of the prison open. The Lord abides in the heart of every creature and when the veil of that secret sanctuary is withdrawn, we hear the Divine voice, receive the Divine light, act in the Divine power."
>
> The Bhagavadgītā, p. 36.

(i) *Mrs. Annie Besant.* Mrs. Besant in her usual oratorical fashion sums up the teachings of the Bhagavadgītā by telling us that we must bid good-bye for ever to all grief and sorrow, realising the oneness in all things. तत्र को मोहः कः शोक एकत्वमनुपश्यतः । When we have realised the oneness of God, the world and humanity, where will grief remain ? She asks.

> " But one Lord is the object of all devotion, but one Lord is the subject of all wisdom, but one Lord is the source of all activity. One Lord and therefore one humanity ; one Lord and therefore oneness through the entire body of the Lord ; one Lord, one world, one brotherhood, that is the outcome of our study. Thus on from age to age, from universe to universe ; and where, I say again, where is grief, where delusion, when we have thus seen the Oneness ? "
>
> Four Lectures on the Bhagavadgītā. p. 123.

CHAPTER XIII

NUMENISM : OTTO

The Holy as A priori Category

In this and the next chapter we shall deal at some length with the two very significant forms of Gītā interpretation: the one, the Numenism of Otto, and the other, Divinisation of Aurobindo Ghosh. Both these approach the mystical standpoint very closely. Hence we propose to discuss them just prior to our own philosophical exposition of the doctrine of God-realisation in the Bhagavadgītā. Dr. Otto is famous for his doctrine of the Holy. The Holy he regards as a *sui generis* category of value, beyond the categories of the Good, the True and the Beautiful. This is his original contribution to philosophy. His book on the "Idea of the Holy" is very famous. He regards the Holy as an *a priori* category, and speaks of the rational and the irrational as constituting its warp and woof. Somehow he stresses the conception of the irrational, following Bradley, James and Bergson. In fact, it has been a fashion with these philosophers and even an aspiration to bring their philosophy into line with the conception of the irrational. Otto coined the word Numen to signify this category of value which has, according to him, supreme divine power lying inside it. This super-natural divine power is what Otto calls the Extra in explaining the meaning of the Holy, something which cannot be accounted for and which is to be regarded as beyond the scope of reason.

The Numinous as a Complex of the Feelings of Mystery, Wonder, Power, Terror, Reverence and Joy

After having applied this conception of the Holy to philosophy, especially in describing it as a combination of the rational and the irrational, Otto goes on to tell us about the psychological aspect of this 'numinous' category of value. He gives a beautiful analysis of the psychological aspect of the Numinous, and this analysis can be supplemented by our own experience. According to it, the five chief constituents of this conception of the Holy looked at from the point of view of psychology, are the five great spiritual emotions of wonder, power, joy, horror and reverence. These seem to be the ultimate psychological constituents in the conception of the Holy. Otto is also very careful to tell us that the Bhagavadgītā is a sublime illustration particularly of the psychology of horror. Such a psychology of horror has never been written in the West.

Otto on the Original Form of the Bhagavadgītā

Dr. Otto is a great theologian and a very good philosopher and psychologist. His knowledge of Sanskrit also is remarkable, but we do not think that he has succeeded in his eight-tract theory of the Bhagavadgītā. We have already discussed this in our chapter on Interpolationism. According to him, the original form of the Bhagavadgītā consisted of a very short portion which is supplemented both by these tracts and by appendices and marginalia. Even though his theory about the original form of the Bhagavadgītā may not be correct, still his interpretation of the real meaning of the Bhagavadgītā is magnificient. All the more so, because he is a good Christian theologian, has a very wide heart and great sympathy with Indian aspirations, and does not find any ultimate distinction between Indian philosophy and European philosophy. Such people we want today in this world: people who do not stand for Christianity for its own sake, or for Hinduism because it is Hinduism; people who would understand the basis of both Christianity and Hinduism. Otto is one of them. I am glad I met him in the year 1927 at Poona when we exchanged notes on various subjects. The original Bhagavadgītā, according to Dr. Otto, consisted of a few short pithy statements, a few short appealing points, which constituted the entire conversation between Kṛṣṇa and Arjuna and made Arjuna act up to the Will of God. There are only four points, he tells us, as we have seen in a previous chapter, which constitute the original Bhagavadgītā. First, there is the discourse between Kṛṣṇa and Arjuna on the immortality of the soul; second, the vision of the Viśvarūpa of Kṛṣṇa by Arjuna; third, the unfoldment of the doctrine of pre-determination by Kṛṣṇa to Arjuna, showing him a panorama of the future and the way in which God's Will works; and finally, an appeal by Kṛṣṇa to Arjuna to disregard all Dharmas and regard Divine Will alone as his imperative duty:

सर्वधर्मान् परित्यज्य मामेकं शरणं व्रज । XVIII. 66.

The so-called human, social and political duties are no duties at all. The only duty is to reconcile oneself to the Divine Will and Power. This, in short, is the pith of the original Bhagavadgītā, according to Dr. Otto.

The Īśvara of the Bhagavadgītā Wholly Transcendent

Let us now proceed to consider Otto's doctrine of Īśvara as he finds it in the Bhagavadgītā. His doctrine is a wonderful doctrine indeed. It is absolutely un-Christian. He is not unmindful of the claims of the world-whole in the conception of a personal God. It would be interesting to see how Christian theologians would look at such a doctrine from such a great philosopher like Otto. Nevertheless, we welcome it because it is his comprehensive mind which enables him to say so. According to Otto, therefore, the Īśvara of the Bhagavadgītā is a peculiar combination of a personal God and the world-whole. To him personalism and impersonalism do not appear antagonistic. Also, the Īśvara of the Bhagavadgītā is a transcendent God, the wholly other. He is not an ultimate to which other penultimate realities point. We may say that God is super-ultimate. What would Christian theologians say to such a doctrine of a transcendent God from an orthodox Christian theologian? This doctrine Otto finds in the Bhagavadgītā. This doctrine, he tells us, is older than Advaita. Advaita need not feel proud for having discovered this. It was there before the age of the Advaita. We have a very fine parallel in the Book of Job to this doctrine of God in the Bhagavadgītā. The great inscrutability of which that Book speaks is a particular characteristic of the God both of the Bhagavadgītā and of the Book of Job. What else can a man do than be struck dumb before this inscrutable Being? God is super-powerful. We have only to reconcile ourselves to the Will of this Super-powerful. Let us, therefore, as Otto tells us, find peace in the idea that God is so powerful that we have only to surrender ourselves entirely to His Will.

Advaita Bhakti

It is as a consequence of this doctrine of God in the Bhagavadgītā, according to Otto, that he uses the expression, Advaita-Bhakti. He makes here a combination of the two conceptions of Advaita and Bhakti. Of course, that idea is not unfamiliar to us Indians. Jñāneśvara has spoken of Advaita-Bhakti, but for an Austro-German theologian like Dr. Otto, almost to invent this expression Advaita-Bhakti is most remarkable. He tells us that in Bhakti there is room for Advaita of a certain kind.

It is this kind of Advaita-Bhakti, therefore, that we find in the Bhagavadgītā. How does this psychologically arise? Otto tells us that it is from a combination of two feelings, a feeling of dependence on God and a feeling of equality with His greatness. When dependence and equality are combined together, we have the phenomenon of Advaita-Bhakti. After having taught this doctrine of Advaita-Bhakti, it becomes easily possible for Otto to criticise the doctrine of pure Bhakti, as Garbe had stated it, the doctrine of pure, unmixed and unalloyed Bhakti. It is for that reason, says Garbe, that all pantheistic portions of the Bhagavadgītā were later additions and that the theistic portions only were the originals. Otto was a disciple of Garbe and yet he excelled Garbe in his interpretation. In that way Garbe found that the doctrine of Otto superseded his own (शिष्यात् इच्छेत् पराजयम्). One of the fine remarks which Otto makes in this connection is that in the experience of this Advaita-Bhakti, a devotee becomes so merged in God that he becomes one with Him. The devotee, therefore, merges himself in his object of devotion so much so that there comes about an absolute unity between them. Otto tells us :

> " Bhakti means faithful and loving devotion to one's God. It is, as such, a strong emotion which can take the æsthetic form. It is also intelligible that Advaita ideas of a certain kind can find a place in Bhakti, which Garbe has overlooked. Whilst feeling is ecstatically roused, the believer or the lover forgets and feels his unity with Him and therefore extremely high-strung Advaita ideas can precisely give occasion for the expression of his own experience. Pralhāda, the typical representative of the warm personal Bhakti, experiences himself completely as one with, and undistinguished from, Puruṣottama."

Predestination

Dr. Otto tells us that the God of the Bhagavadgītā is the God of Pre-destination. Prior to all human will and work, God has already willed that a certain thing shall happen. This is what might be called the doctrine of pre-destination. Before the fight took place between the Kauravas and the Pāṇḍavas, the fight had already been planned by God. It was the Will and work of God Himself. If, therefore, God creates battles, He has also the power to end them. Dr. Radhakrishnan tells us that God decides the fate of battles. Instead of speaking in the present, we might even speak of the plue-present. Instead of saying that God decides the fate of battles, we might even say that God has already decided them. The future has been already fixed by

God. This is the central point in the doctrine of predestination. Whatever Arjuna may will or may not will, God has already willed that such a thing shall happen, that the Kauravas will be vanquished, and the Pāṇḍavas will win, and that justice and God-devotion will reign supreme in the world. To quote Otto's statements from his Das Bhagavadgītā as translated in English :

> "It is not the work of man, this cruel, horrible fight. The fight is the work and Will of God Himself. This is the meaning of the magnificent theophany and this is the æsthetic purpose of the Gītā in general and of the XI discourse in particular."

> "The God of the Bhagavadgītā is the God of absolute pre-destination, as the verses (XI. 32–33) show Him to be. Here God shows that, independently of and prior to all human will and work, the future has long been fixed unalterably by Him, that all human will, in comparison with Him, is absolutely powerless, and that man is nothing else than a transitory phase of His activity which man's Ahaṁkāra resists."

Man Only an Instrument in the Hands of God

Lastly, we come to what might be called Otto's doctrine of Instrumentalism. Kṛṣṇa tells Arjuna that he is merely an instrument in the hands of God, that he is merely a channel through which His power might flow. As a consequence it behoves Arjuna to reconcile his conception of duty with the Divine Will. This is exactly what is meant by making oneself an instrument in the hands of God. The reconciliation of one's will with the Divine Will involves a moral problem, namely, the problem of Divine Will as being the only Categorical Imperative. Kant and other philosophers might speak of the Categorical Imperative in abstract terms. Here we have got a concrete expression of the Categorical Imperative in terms of the Divine Will. The Divine Will has to dictate and man has to obey. It is in this way, Otto tells us, that Arjuna must regard the fight as a Divine Work. Otto bestows high praise on the author of the Bhagavadgītā for having written one of the most beautiful of the verses in the whole of the spiritual literature. Let us see what Otto says:

> "Give up thy sorrow; fight in the knowledge that thou hast not the power to carry out thy human work, but my work, as my instrument. Thou art nothing but an instrument, that is, an instrument for the most frightful and at the same time sublime majesty of God Himself. These words should be called the Carama Śloka, the highest verse of the Gītā."

CHAPTER XIV

DIVINISATION : AUROBINDO

Introduction

Śrī Aurobindo is the last among our modern interpreters of the Bhagavadgītā. Otto and Aurobindo come very close to a mystical interpretation which it will be our endeavour to expound in the next part of our work. Before, however, we assess the contribution which Aurobindo makes to the interpretation of the Bhagavadgītā, we shall have to dive a little into the various expressions of philosophic thought, which form the background of his interpretation of the Bhagavadgītā. We may say that he is the most distinguished modern Indian interpreter who shows that kind of philosophic grasp of problems, which might be expected from a close student of contemporary thought. Of course, he has got many original suggestions to make and he is never afraid of expressing his opinions in his own way. We shall first consider his contribution to philosophic thought under six heads, and then the application of his doctrines to the interpretation of the Bhagavadgītā.

To begin with, we shall consider his developmental array of categories, so far as his metaphysics is concerned. Then in regard to psychology, we shall consider his scheme of the ascending grades of consciousness, very much resembling that of Leibnitz. Then we shall take up the chief plank of Aurobindo's philosophy, namely, his conception of the Gnostic Ideal. After this we shall proceed to two further doctrines in Aurobindo namely, his conception of the Superman and his doctrine of the relation of Immortality to Divinisation. We shall end this survey of Aurobindo's contribution to philosophic thought by giving a short account of his doctrine of the Ascent of matter into Spirit.

After this survey we shall go on to his interpretation of the Bhagavadgītā proper. Under this head we shall first consider what he has to say about the ethics of the Bhagavadgītā, and then about its social and devotional teachings. We shall next proceed to his conception of the Avatāra, bringing it into relation with some important conceptions of incarnation in the history of thought. We shall conclude the chapter by giving an account of what we ourselves understand by the conception of Avatāra.

Contribution to Philosophic Thought

(*a*) *Developmental Array of Categories.* Let us begin by discussing Śrī Aurobindo's contribution to metaphysical thought, especially his scheme of the developmental array of categories which closely resembles that of Hegel. Sat or Existence, he says, is the highest category from which proceeds Cit–Śakti or consciousness–force, as he calls it, from which issues Ānanda or Bliss. This is exactly what is meant by Sat–Cit–Ānanda. Supermind, according to him, is the connecting link between these higher categories and the lower categories, namely, mind, psyche, life and matter in a descending order. Aurobindo interposes two further categories between mind and supermind, namely, intuition and overmind. There would have been no cause for disagreement with this developmental arrangement, provided he had dropped psyche or soul as below mind, and had not interposed intuition and overmind between mind and supermind.

In Aurobindo's own terminology, psyche, overmind and intuition have only an 'otiose' function to perform. They are not relevant to the picture at all. Aurobindo distinguishes between mind and overmind. What to the mind are contraries are to the overmind complimentaries; but this function can very well be accomplished by the supermind itself. Psyche or soul below mind is inconceivable. Intuition, instead of being a category between mind and supermind, is a power by which mind can rise into the supermind. Further, Aurobindo contradicts himself by calling intuition once a connecting link between mind and supermind and at another time by regarding it as incapable of serving as a connecting link. Compare his utterances: (1) "Intuition establishes the connection between the mind and the supermind." (S. K. Maitra: Philosophy of Aurobindo, p. 34). (2) "Intuition is too flashy, too unstable, too much under the masses of mental stuff that penetrate into it, to enable it to really serve as a link between mind and supermind." (Ibid. p. 40).

Credit must, however, be given to Aurobindo for having boldly initiated this developmental array of categories in the manner of Hegel. In fact, he is the only Indian philosopher who has tried to make this developmental scheme. There would have been perfect agreement with him if his categories had stood like existence, consciousness and bliss on the one hand, and mind, life and matter on the other, supermind constituting the connecting link between the two. Contemporary European philosophers have spoken about "matter, life, mind and God" as constituting the real developmental order which is not an unsatisfactory arrangement.

(*b*) *Ascending Grades of Consciousness.* As regards the psychological account of the developmental grades of consciousness, we may say at the beginning that Aurobindo regards the electrons and the atoms of matter as eternal somnambulists. In the plant we find consciousness in a state of dream, always on the point of waking but never fully awake. The plant is vitally responsive to existence, though not mentally aware. The animal possesses mental awareness, while man possesses reflective self-consciousness. So from the mineral to the plant, from the plant to the animal and from the animal to man, we have in Aurobindo an ascending order of consciousness. It is interesting to see how this scheme is similar to that of Leibnitz who in his Monadology speaks of the sleeping monads, dreaming monads and the self-conscious monads. He crowns his scheme with the conception of the *Monas Monadum*, the Monad of monads, which is equivalent to the Indian conception of Īśvara.

(*c*) *The Gnostic Ideal.* One of the most significant points in Śrī Aurobindo's philosophy is his doctrine of the Gnostic Ideal. Here he not merely defends Christian Gnosticism, but also gives a new meaning to it according to the implications of his own philosophy. Christian Gnosticism laid greater stress on knowledge than on faith. According to the old gnostic sect among Christians, the dictum that the Word became flesh is not true; and also that God manifested Himself in the flesh is not true. So the gnostics quarrelled with the initial and central teaching of St. John : " In the beginning was the Word, and the Word was with God, and the Word was God. " According to the gnostics, there is no place for devotion and no softly-murmured prayers. What is wanted is knowledge and speculation. Aurobindo lays his finger on this point in Christian gnosticism and applies it to his own scheme of supermind. According to him, the gnostic works with the supermind. As the gnostic, true to the derivation of the word, lays stress on knowledge, Aurobindo lays stress upon his conception of the supermind. From that point of view, Yogasiddhis do not seem to be impossible to Aurobindo. This is one of the special points in his philosophical teachings. Jñāna he finds absolutely compatible with Yogic achievements. Applying his doctrine to gnosticism, he tells us further that it is not enough that an individual should become a gnostic, a knower in the philosophical and spiritual sense of the word, but we must see that a community of gnostics or perfected individuals is created leading to the emergence of a whole gnostic race. These are the ideals at which Aurobindo aims. The consequence of all this would be the establishment of the Kingdom of God upon earth.

(*d*) *Superman*. Śrī Aurobindo's doctrine of the superman occupies an important place in his philosophy. We are familiar with Nietzsche's doctrine of the superman. Nietzsche had no sympathy with Christianity and was pro–Hellenic. Hence it was that Nietzsche's superman was almost a Titan or an Asura as the sixteenth chapter of the Bhagavadgītā would call it. Aurobindo's superman is a Sura or God. The distinction between Nietzsche and Aurobindo is like the one between the Āsurī–Sampat and the Daivī–Sampat in the sixteenth chapter of the Bhagavadgītā. An ideal superman, according to Aurobindo, is he who combines in himself not merely Divine Power and Divine Love but also Divine Wisdom.

(*e*) *Immortality and Divinisation.* Aurobindo's doctrine of the relation of immortality to divinisation is very important, because it tells us of a new approach from which he looks at the question of immortality. He does not cut himself adrift from ancient Indian tradition but he introduces certain new concepts which, as we shall see a little later, are worthy of our consideration. He begins by pointing out to us "the normal demand for survival" as well as "the age-long effort of man to conquer physically the death of the body." (Life Divine, p. 731). He has sympathy with the ancient conception of Indian thought, namely, that the subtle body (लिङ्गशरीर) may survive, even after the death of the physical body. "Such a survival", Aurobindo tells us, "could persist only in the subtle body. The Being would have to discard its physical form, pass to other worlds and in its return put on a new body." (L. D., pp. 732–33).

We are told in the Bhagavadgītā :—

शरीरं यदवाप्नोति यच्चाप्युत्क्रामतीश्वरः ।
गृहीत्वैतानि संयाति वायुर्गन्धानिवाशयात् ॥ XV. 8.

Aurobindo tells us that (*a*) "The awakened Mental Puruṣa, and (*b*) the awakened Vital Puruṣa preserve the mind sheath and the life sheath of the subtle body ; while (*c*) the physical survival could only be relative, terminable at will, a temporal sign of the Spirit's victory here over matter." (L. D., pp. 732–33.).

Physical Science. The question of the physical survival of the body should be looked at from three points of view, from the points of view of Physical Science, Occult Science and Theological Science. While discussing the first, Aurobindo gives us an insight into some of his new concepts. Normally speaking, he tells us, "the physical body could only endure if by some means its physical causes of decay and disruption could be overcome." (L. D., p. 732). This, of course, would be a difficult task. A perpetual physical survival would remain only as an "Ideal" in the Kantian sense of the term. But Aurobindo makes two further points of practical spiritual significance. In the first place, he tells us that the body must keep pace with the progress of the Inner Person: "The physical body should be made so plastic and progressive in its structure and functioning that it would answer to each change demanded of it by the progress of the Inner Person." (L. D., p. 732) ; and in the second place, if it does not do so, it is likely to be abandoned by the Inner Being. "If the body could not adapt itself", says Aurobindo, "so as to become a fit instrument of expression of the inner growth, the soul would find some way to abandon it." (L. D., p. 732).

Occult Science. From the point of view of occult science, Aurobindo tells us that "a complete change down to the physical was sought for only by a few and then more as a 'Siddhi' than anything else." (Lights on Yoga, p. 3.). From that point of view, it can hardly be said that occult science has been successful in perpetuating the human body. Many of the great Sādhakas might feel in their highest moments of achievement that there could be no death for their body. But this would be hardly capable of accomplishment in the absence of "the manifestation of a new spiritual nature in the earth consciousness." (L.Y., p. 3).

Theological Science. Thirdly, we learn from Aurobindo: "What our normal demand of survival asks for is a similar survival for our mind, our life, even our body; the dogma of Resurrection of the body attests to this last demand." (L. D., p. 731). Resurrection has indeed played an important part in Christian theology. "Rising from the grave, making appearance before devoted disciples, and even non-believing disciples, talking with them and even partaking of bread with them, making appearance even inside a closed apartment and ultimately ascending to heaven—this may constitute Resurrection but not Immortality. Resurrection implies that a man is to rise from the dead; immortality implies that he never dies at all."

Immortality as Divinisation. Finally, we come to Aurobindo's interpretation of real immortality as divinisation, "the creation of a divine life in matter." (L. Y., p. 1). Elsewhere Aurobindo has also spoken about a "Triple Immortality" (L. D., p. 732). Radhakrishnan in like manner has told us that immortality occurs when "Divine power" pervades matter, life and mind. Aurobindo tells us in a similar spirit that "the aspiration for immortality could succeed only if mind, life, or body could put on something of the divinity and immortality of the indwelling spirit." (L. D., p. 731). It is thus that, according to Aurobindo, real immortality and divinisation go together.

(*f*) *The Ascent of Matter into Spirit.* We are told by Aurobindo that there cannot be any ascent unless there is a descent. There is a descent of spirit into matter; that is why matter seeks to evolve into something higher than itself. Everywhere evolution (ascending process) is conditioned by involution (descending process). Creation, according to Aurobindo, is a plunge of the spirit into ignorance. Ignorance is nothing else than the power of the Divine Consciousness to partially withhold itself.

Our ascent, Aurobindo tells us, brings to us an abiding spiritual sense and awareness of the Infinite and the Eternal. The peace and the joy of the Infinite become concrete and constant in the Being. "In all sights and forms one sees the Eternal, the Reality; in all sounds one hears it; in all touches he feels it; there is nothing else but its forms and personalities and manifestations; the joy and adoration of the heart, the embrace of all existence, the unity of spirit, are abiding realities."

Original Points in Gītā Interpretation

Let us now proceed to note original points in Aurobindo's interpretation of the Bhagavadgītā. Here we shall take six points. In the first four, he goes entirely against the general orthodox interpretation of the Bhagavadgītā, so far as ethics and practical life are concerned, and in the last two, he makes points which might be approved even by old orthodox interpreters.

(*a*) *Gītā not a Book on Ethics but Spiritual Life.* Aurobindo begins by saying that the Bhagavadgītā is not a book of ethics at all. It is a book of spiritual life. What would have Lokamanya Tilak said about this statement? It may be true that the Bhagavadgītā is not primarily an ethical book, that its supreme teaching is that of spiritual life, but it would not be possible to negate the importance of the ethical element in the Bhagavadgītā.

(*b*) *No Disinterested Action.* Secondly, Aurobindo tells us that the Bhagavadgītā does not teach disinterested action. Hitherto all orthodox thinkers, and even

Lokamanya Tilak and Mahatma Gandhi, have said that actions, according to the Bhagavadgītā, ought to be performed in a disinterested spirit, Anāsakti according to them (both) being the highest ethical teaching of the Bhagavadgītā. Aurobindo says that our actions should be interested and not disinterested, interested for the sake of the attainment of God. This is not an unjustifiable proposition, because the supreme aim of ethical life is always the attainment of God.

(*c*) *Abandonment of All Duties.* Thirdly, Aurobindo tells us that we must abandon all standards of duty as orthodoxly conceived. सर्वधर्मान्परित्यज्य मामेकं शरणं व्रज। must be literally interpreted. There are no duties for a man who follows God, says Aurobindo. All social duties in Aurobindo's own phrase are, therefore, otiose. A great thinker has also said in the same spirit that God is a very jealous being, who would not allow any actions to be performed except for His own attainment.

(*d*) *No Social Service.* Social service also is impossible. What we want and what we should have, says Aurobindo, is only action of the God-possessed and for the God-possessed. Novalis in like spirit has said about Spinoza that if there was any God-intoxicated man upon earth, it was Spinoza himself.

(*e*) *Self-Sacrifice.* So far then about Aurobindo's disagreement with the orthodox interpreters of the Bhagavadgītā. Coming to the points in which he agrees with them, we might say that those are of self-sacrifice and self-surrender. Here he is at one with the old orthodox theologians, even with devotional theists. All actions, he says, are to be regarded as a sacrifice to Him, Who stands behind man and nature. Jñāneśvara has said in like manner that we should worship God with the blossomed flowers of our actions:

तया सर्वात्मकां ईश्वंरा । स्वकर्मकुसुमांची वीरा ।
पूजा केली होय अपारा । तोषालागीं ॥ Jña. XVIII. 917.

(*f*) *Self-Surrender.* Finally, Aurobindo emphasizes that our highest ideal ought to be to surrender ourselves to the Master of Existence which, according to him, constitutes the great finale of human achievement. We already know the supreme function which the conception of surrender plays in his philosophy.

All these points have been so beautifully explained by Aurobindo in a few sentences that we cannot but quote his actual words :—

" The Gītā is not a book of ethics but of spiritual life. It teaches not human but divine action; not the disinterested performance of duties but the following of the Divine Will; not a performance of social duties but the abandonment of all standards of duty (Sarva-Dharmān) to take refuge in the Supreme alone; not social service but the action of the God-possessed, the Mastermen, and as a sacrifice to Him Who stands behind Man and Nature (Essays on the Bhagavadgītā, p.43) thus rising to the great finale of supreme self-surrender to the Master of Existence ". (Second Series, Pp. 1-2).

Doctrine of Avatāra

(*a*) *Avatāra not Needed for Preservation of Dharma.* We come finally to Aurobindo's doctrine of incarnation. He makes three points. In the first place, he tells us that according to the Bhagavadgītā an Avatāra is born for the preservation of Right. This, says Aurobindo, is merely an ' otiose ' function. An Avatāra is not needed, he says, for the preservation of Right; that could be accomplished by other people like kings, prophets and sages. The function of an Avatāra is much higher.

(*b*) *Avatāra as both Descent and Ascent.* Secondly, Aurobindo is not content with saying that Avatārahood consists in the descent of spirit into matter, but he also says that we might apply the term to the ascent of matter into spirit. The two might be regarded as different aspects of what might be called Divinisation. Ascent and descent, evolution and involution, he tells us, proceed *pari passu.* It must be remembered, however, that the expression Avatāra connotes descent more than ascent, the prefix 'Ava' meaning 'down'. Avatāra, therefore, literally ought to mean descent of spirit into matter instead of ascent of matter into spirit.

(*c*) *Avatāra as an Effective Channel of God.* Thirdly, Aurobindo is at the height of his interpretation when he defines Avatāra as one who is so possessed by Divine Consciousness that he becomes an effective channel of it. This, it may be easily admitted, is a very important point that an Avatāra is one who realises God within himself and spreads the message of God upon earth.

(*d*) *Other Views.* The suggestion which Aurobindo has made about the Avatāra being the ascent of matter into spirit finds a parallel in some recent writers : (i) Radhakrishnan, for example, tells us that Avatārahood consists in the taking up of our manhood into God. (The Bhagavadgītā, p. 36). This is what he calls the real meaning of resurrection. It is not merely that Christ was resurrected. Every man has the possibility of resurrecting himself, provided he rises from a life of sin to a life of God-devotion and God-realisation. (ii) Miss Underhill talks about the conception of Avatāra in a similar fashion. She likens the development of the rising aspirant to the development of an embryo, which in its upward ascent recapitulates all the stages of racial development. Here the race concerned is the spiritual race. An Avatāra is, therefore, one who exhibits in himself all the stages of the spiritual development of the race. (iii) According to Christianity, as Aurobindo puts it, " On a plane above, which is superconscient to us, the Christians talk of God and man, revealing each one to the other, so that there is co-existence of God and man." Does not the modern Pañca Śīla doctrine talk in like manner and in another connection about the co-existence of nation and nation which is almost on a par with the co-existence of man and God ? According to Aurobindo himself, " the father and son, the devotee and God become one. " "I and my father", says Christ, " are one ". It is in this identification of Self with God, therefore, that, according to Christianity, incarnation consists. (iv) Patmore goes a little further. He tells us that incarnation did not occur only once in history nor did resurrection. They occur in the case of every man who wants to rise to divine consciousness. Incarnation and resurrection, Patmore tells us, are events which occur in the life of everyone who is on the way to the fulfilment of his original destiny.

(*e*) *Our View: Avatāra as Descent of God's Form before a Devotee.* We come, finally, to our own interpretation of Avatāra. We give to the word Ava the meaning which is its due, but at the same time give it a mystical interpretation. Avatāra is the descent of God's form before the spiritual vision of the aspirant. Yāska has said in his definition of the word Ṛṣi in his Nirukta :

तत् ब्रह्म स्वयंभु एतान् ऋषीन् तपस्यमानानभ्यानर्षत् तदृषीणां ऋषित्वम् ।

A Ṛṣi is one who sees the form of God descending before his very eyes.

PART IV

THE CLUE THROUGH THE LABYRINTH

CHAPTER XV

ANTINOMIES OF METAPHYSICS

Antinomy Embedded in the Nature of Thought

We have hitherto considered the labyrinth of modern interpretations of the Bhagavadgītā in full detail. We have passed through various interpretations and have found that one rises almost above the other, and that a definitely mystical interpretation of the Bhagavadgītā in terms of contemporary philosophy has been hitherto lacking. This mystical interpretation is the clue which will enable us to find a way out of the labyrinth. This is like the *cakravyūha* from which Abhimanyu could have got out had he found the proper clue.

In the present part of our work, we shall first show how we may pass through the antinomies that necessarily emerge in the formulation of certain metaphysical concepts. Then we shall proceed to an ethical interpretation of the Bhagavadgītā in terms of the categorical imperative and activism which are the two very important aspects of its ethical teaching. Other ethical theories which the Bhagavadgītā has advanced will occupy our attention next, namely, moralism, supermoralism as well as beatificism. After this we shall consider the nature of God, according to the Bhagavadgītā, as well as the criteria and the search of God. This will be followed by our discussion of the three important methods of meditation advanced by the Bhagavadgītā, namely, the ideological, the moral and the mystical. Finally, we shall end our constructive part by diving into the nature of the sublime vision of God which is the most important teaching of the Bhagavadgītā.

We shall begin our present chapter by considering the antinomies in the Bhagavadgītā. Now 'antinomy' is a very important word in European philosophy, and particularly in the philosophy of Kant. It occupies a very important place in his Critique of Pure Reason. Erdmann has said that Kant's primary desire was to write about the antinomies only, and, in fact, the Paralogisms and the Ideals which he later discussed along with the antinomies were in the first draft included in the antinomies themselves. That is the reason why, along with the discussion of the conception of the world in the Kantian antinomies, there are discussions of the conceptions of the self, freedom and God. We may say that the antinomies in Kant represent one of the foremost watermarks in his Critical Philosophy.

Five Antinomies in the Bhagavadgītā and their Solution

We shall deal here with five antinomies in the Bhagavadgītā : (i) the antinomy of the Personal and the Impersonal ; (ii) the antinomy of the Actor and the Spectator ; (iii) the antinomy of the Transcendent and the Immanent so far as the nature of God is concerned ; (iv) the fourth antinomy refers to the Reality and the Unreality of the World ; and (v) finally, in the fifth antinomy we shall be concerned with the destiny of the Soul. What kind of liberation have we to predicate? Whether it is Krama-mukti, Ante-mukti or Jīvan-mukti? Along with the antinomies we shall discuss also the solutions which the Bhagavadgītā itself offers. We shall cite from the Bhagavadgītā passages, one of which supports one system, another supports another, while a third reconciles them both. Nothing else beyond the Bhagavadgītā itself is needed to reconcile the contradictions which it puts forth as pertaining to opposite systems of thought. We shall divest our mind of the interpretations or the criticisms that have been made on these by the great Vedāntic or modern interpreters. We shall go straight to the originals themselves, and see what evidence there is first for saying that there is any antinomy at all, that is, one law pitted against another, and then find a solution thereof in the Bhagavadgītā itself.

(*a*) *God, Personal or Impersonal? Reconciled in Super-Personalism.* Let us then proceed to the first antinomy, namely, the antinomy of the Impersonal and the Personal, the Nirguṇa and the Saguṇa, with which we are all very familiar and which has divided, for example, interpreters like Śaṁkara, Rāmānuja, Madhva, Vallabha, Nimbārka and others into different schools. In regard to this antinomy, only the most relevant and important passages will be quoted. In regard to the Impersonal characterisation of Reality, no better passage could be found in the Bhagavadgītā than

ज्ञेयं यत्तत्प्रवक्ष्यामि यज्ज्ञात्वाऽमृतमश्नुते ।
अनादिमत्परं ब्रह्म न सत्तन्नासदुच्यते ॥
सर्वतः पाणिपादं तत् सर्वतोऽक्षिशिरोमुखम् ।
सर्वतः श्रुतिमल्लोके सर्वमावृत्य तिष्ठति ॥ XIII. 12-13.

This is an absolutely Impersonal characterisation of the Absolute. That is one part of the antinomy. The second part is, of course, as you know :

उत्तमः पुरुषस्त्वन्यः परमात्मेत्युदाहृतः ।
यो लोकत्रयमाविश्य बिभर्त्यव्यय ईश्वरः ॥
यस्मात् क्षरमतीतोऽहमक्षरादपि चोत्तमः ।
अतोऽस्मि लोके वेदे च प्रथितः पुरुषोत्तमः ॥ XV. 17-18.

Puruṣa is the Personalistic conception of God, which is pitted against the former part of the antinomy, namely, the Impersonalistic conception. We are familiar with solutions of the antinomies in Kant where he gives us probable reconciliations; but here in the case of the Bhagavadgītā, the solutions are found in the words of the text itself. In regard to these solutions we shall take a third passage which puts forth the Personal and the Impersonal characterisations together.

> पिताऽहमस्य जगतो माता धाता पितामहः ।
> वेद्यं पवित्रमोंकार ऋक्साम यजुरेव च ॥
>
> गतिर्भर्ता प्रभुः साक्षी निवासः शरणं सुहृत् ।
> प्रभवः प्रलयः स्थानं निधानं बीजमव्ययम् ॥ IX. 17–18.

Here God is called not only पिता and माता but also प्रभवः, प्रलयः and स्थानम्. In that way there is a reconciliation between those opposite schools of thought which stress the Personal and the Impersonal characteristics of Reality. So then we see in the first antinomy how from one point of view the Impersonalistic conception is stressed, from the other the Personalistic conception and from a third both these views are reconciled together. I do not want to go into the details as every one of you knows the meaning of these passages.

(*b*) *Activity or Passivity? Reconciled in Emanationism.* Let us now take the second antinomy. It is the antinomy of the Actor and the Spectator, which has reigned supreme in the systems of Sāṁkhya and Yoga. Is Reality to be regarded as passive or active? Is God to be regarded as Actor or Spectator? We find in the Bhagavadgītā alternative descriptions on both sides and also their reconciliation as before. (1) (a) In the first place, there is a famous passage—

अधिष्ठानं तथा कर्ता करणं च पृथग्विधम्।
विविधाश्च पृथक्चेष्टा दैवं चैवात्र पञ्चमम्॥ XVIII. 14.

तत्रैवं सति कर्तारमात्मानं केवलं तु यः।
पश्यत्यकृतबुद्धित्वान्न स पश्यति दुर्मतिः॥ XVIII. 16.

All these five causes which constitute Prakṛti may be regarded as fashioning the destiny of the universe. Why should we, asks the Bhagavadgītā, thrust the responsibility upon God for this action and regard Him as Actor ? (b) In another passage all responsibility for action is likewise attributed to Svabhāva :

न कर्तृत्वं न कर्माणि लोकस्य सृजति प्रभुः।
न कर्मफलसंयोगं स्वभावस्तु प्रवर्तते॥ V. 14.

So from this point of view also God must be regarded merely as a Spectator and not as an Actor at all. (2) On the other hand, we have another famous passage in the Bhagavadgītā :

ईश्वरः सर्वभूतानां हृद्देशेऽर्जुन तिष्ठति।
भ्रामयन्सर्वभूतानि यंत्रारूढानि मायया॥ XVIII. 61.

This is exactly in the manner of Goethe who describes God as whirling the world round about His finger in a circle :

" Was war ein Gott, der nur von aussen stiesse
Im Kreis das All am Finger laufen liesse ! "

Action is here attributed to God. So the question arises, shall we regard God as an Actor or as a Spectator? (3) Now in the Bhagavadgītā, we have a reconciliation of these two doctrines of Actor and Spectator in the doctrine of Emanationism ;

मयाऽध्यक्षेण प्रकृतिः सूयते सचराचरम्।
हेतुनाऽनेन कौन्तेय जगद्विपरिवर्तते॥ IX. 10.

The Prakṛti gives birth, no doubt, to all animate and inanimate existences, but it does so on account of the fact that God is its supervisor or Adhyakṣa and is responsible for its स्फुरण. It is on account of the force of the magnet that motion is imparted to the iron filings. It is in this way that Prakṛti is disturbed from its original equilibrium or passivity. It is on account of the combination of this passivity of the Prakṛti and the activity of God that we can speak of Emanationism as a reconciliation of the two conflicting ideas of activity and passivity.

(c) *Immanence or Transcendence? Reconciled in All-Pervasiveness.* We shall now proceed to the third antinomy, namely, the antinomy of the Transcendent and the Immanent. The God of the Bhagavadgītā is like Plato's Sun in the World of Ideas. Just as the sun and the sky remain uncontaminated, similarly God remains uncontaminated.

यथा प्रकाशयत्येकः कृत्स्नं लोकमिमं रविः ।
क्षेत्रं क्षेत्री तथा कृत्स्नं प्रकाशयति भारत ॥ XIII. 33.

यथा सर्वगतं सौक्ष्म्यादाकाशं नोपलिप्यते ।
सर्वत्रावस्थितो देहे तथात्मा नोपलिप्यते ॥ XIII. 32.

So we have this doctrine of Transcendence of God. On the other hand, there are many passages to illustrate the Immanence of God. In the first place, in a well known passage we are told:

मत्तः परतरं नान्यत्किंचिदस्ति धनंजय ।
मयि सर्वमिदं प्रोतं सूत्रे मणिगणा इव ॥ VII. 7.

All the existences in this world are like pearls or jewels woven on me who is their Thread. There are many similar passages where God is regarded as Immanent in the different objects of the world:

रसोऽहमप्सु कौन्तेय प्रभाऽस्मि शशिसूर्ययोः ।
प्रणवः सर्ववेदेषु शब्दः खे पौरुषं नृषु ॥ VII 8.

गामाविश्य च भूतानि धारयाम्यहमोजसा ।
पुष्णामि चौषधीः सर्वाः सोमो भूत्वा रसात्मकः ॥ XV. 13.

And particularly God is immanent not merely in things of nature but also in moral qualities as well as in things, good and bad :

कीर्तिः श्रीर्वाक्च नारीणां स्मृतिर्मेधा धृतिः क्षमा । X. 34.
अमृतं चैव मृत्युश्च सदसच्चाहमर्जुन । IX. 19.

God remains in good as well as in bad things. So God's immanence is to be found not merely in objects of nature but also in objects of morality both good and bad. Now having seen the doctrine of Transcendence on the one hand and Immanence on the other, is there not a way for reconciliation of the two ? There certainly is in the Bhagavadgītā. In the first place, there is a famous utterance in the Tenth chapter :

विष्टभ्याहमिदं कृत्स्नमेकांशेन स्थितो जगत् । X. 42.

By one part of Me, by only an iota of Me, I have filled the whole universe and stand infinitely outside. This means a reconciliation of transcendence and immanence in what we might call the doctrine of Transcendo-Immanence. Secondly, in the tricky expression —

मत्स्थानि सर्वभूतानि न चाहं तेष्ववस्थितः । IX. 4.
न च मत्स्थानि भूतानि पश्य मे योगमैश्वरम् । IX. 5.

That is how neither mere transcendence nor mere immanence is valid. Things are and are not. That seems also to be the reconciliation which the Gītā offers for the difference between transcendence and immanence. And finally, one very important point, namely, the doctrine of Incarnation, is just the reconciling factor between the transcendence and the immanence of God. God stands outside the world but descends inside as an Avatāra. From a transcendent being, He becomes immanent in the world. This is the doctrine of Transcendo-Immanence.

(*d*) *The World, Real or Unreal? Reconciled in Ephemeralism.* We shall now go to the fourth antinomy, namely, the antinomy of the Reality and the Unreality of the world. Kant has also discussed in his latest draft four kinds of antinomies regarding the world, the self, freedom and God. But his antinomial discussion is concerned only with the bounded and the boundless and the simple and the composite, while in our fourth antinomy the discussion is regarding the Reality or the Unreality of the world. It is just these passages which have divided thinkers like Madhva and Śaṁkara, Madhva representing the reality of the world on the one hand and Śaṁkara its unreality on the other. The only reconciling thread through these conflicting views of Madhva and Śaṁkara—pardon me for making that bold statement—is the thread of God-realisation. It is only the mystical view of Reality that will come as a reconciling factor between these different attitudes and different doctrines about God, the world and the self. We have in the Seventh chapter of the Bhagavadgītā a very famous passage about the reality of the world. What better description of the reality of the world can we have than the celebrated passage :

भूमिरापोऽनलो वायुः खं मनो बुद्धिरेव च।
अहंकार इतीयं मे भिन्ना प्रकृतिरष्टधा ॥

अपरेयमितस्त्वन्यां प्रकृतिं विद्धि मे पराम् ।
जीवभूतां महाबाहो ययेदं धार्यते जगत् ॥ VII. 4–5.

Both the conceptions of Parā and Aparā Prakṛti are realistic. The passage speaks of their reality unmistakably. Then as an antidote to this realistic doctrine we have other unrealistic doctrines expressed in terms of either अज्ञान or माया or in the conception of अश्वत्थ. In my book on the Upaniṣads, I have stressed the various conceptions of Māyā to be found in the Upaniṣads. In the Bhagavadgītā, we do not find as many and yet we find a few. I shall lay stress only on three aspects of the nature of unreality in the Bhagavadgītā. Māyā is destroyed by God. Māyā is not a separate entity, but it is only a tool in the hands of God :

> दैवी ह्येषा गुणमयी मम माया दुरत्यया ।
> मामेव ये प्रपद्यन्ते मायामेतां तरन्ति ते ॥ VII. 14.

Secondly, we must not entirely divest the Bhagavadgītā of some kind of consideration about अज्ञान. That is, of course, not the Śaṁkarite अज्ञान, nor the अज्ञान involved in the many post-Śaṁkarite theories. It is more simple. The Bhagavadgītā talks of a certain veil of ignorance that surrounds the world and we must penetrate through it :

> अज्ञानेनावृतं ज्ञानं तेन मुह्यन्ति जन्तवः । V. 15.
> ज्ञानेन तु तदज्ञानं येषां नाशितमात्मनः । V. 16.

This is all that it says. It does not advocate theories of ignorance as in later Vedānta. Thirdly, there is another most important passage in the Fifteenth chapter of the Bhagavadgītā concerning the Aśvattha, where the Gītā is reacting against or even criticising an Upaniṣad. We shall not be very often noticing such a phenomenon. In the very same words in which the Kaṭhopaniṣad speaks of the reality of the world, the Bhagavadgītā tells us about its unreality. According to the Bhagavadgītā, the ultimate type of unreality is what is involved in the conception of the Aśvattha. The etymological meaning of Aśvattha is न श्वोऽपि तिष्ठतीत्यश्वत्थः, that which will not last even till tomorrow. How then are the two conceptions to be reconciled, namely, the conception of the unreality of the world as in माया, अज्ञान and अश्वत्थ and the reality of it as in भूमिरापोऽनलो वायुः ? The reconciliation of the reality and the unreality of the world is achieved, says the Bhagavadgītā, through the doctrine of ephemeralism or evanescence or the doctrine of व्यक्तमध्य.

> अव्यक्तादीनि भूतानि व्यक्तमध्यानि भारत ।
> अव्यक्तनिधनान्येव तत्र का परिदेवना ॥ II. 28.

Things come into existence and depart in a short while. We cannot say they do not exist. They exist but only for a short span of time. They are only व्यक्तमध्य. Behind them there is an infinity, before them there is also an infinity. Only a small speck of our existence is what we might call व्यक्तमध्य. Students of Carlyle know very well his doctrine of ephemeralism. "A little while ago and you were not; a little while after and you are not." You are concerned only with the spacious present, the here and the now, the passing moment which may be regarded either as real or unreal. In this doctrine of ephemeralism then we have a reconciliation of the two opposite doctrines of the Reality and the Unreality of the world.

(*e*) *Videha-mukti or Krama-mukti? Reconciled in Jīvan-mukti*. Now let us pass on to the final antinomy, namely, that of Krama-mukti and Ante-mukti and their reconciliation in Jīvan-mukti. The Bhagavadgītā speaks of both the alternatives and the possibility of Jīvan-mukti. It does not use the word Jīvan-mukti, but the doctrine is there. Krama-mukti in the sense of a passage from one world to another, say from the Moon to Mars, from Mars to Jupiter and so on, is only a doctrine of postponed and procrastinated liberation. We are concerned here only with a successive series of lives. अनेकजन्मसंसिद्धस्ततो याति परां गतिम् । (VI. 45). In that way the doctrine tells us definitely about the post existence of man. It also speaks of the worlds to be obtained by merit:

प्राप्य पुण्यकृतां लोकानुषित्वा शाश्वतीः समाः ।
शुचीनां श्रीमतां गेहे योगभ्रष्टोऽभिजायते ॥ VI. 41.

This is the Krama-mukti of the Bhagavadgītā. Then there is the Ante-mukti or what is also called Sadyo-mukti. We do not, however, prefer this latter expression as it is likely to be confounded with Jīvan-mukti. But if it is only Ante-mukti and nothing more, then it would be quite a welcome expression. In two or three very important passages the Bhagavadgītā speaks about the man who meditates upon God at the time of his death, with his mind full of devotion and concentrated upon God. To remember God at that time will enable him to pass into God at once:

अन्तकाले च मामेव स्मरन् मुक्त्वा कलेवरम् ॥ ... VIII. 5.
......यः प्रयाति त्यजन्देहं स याति परमां गतिम् ॥ VIII. 13.

We are not so much concerned here with what the later Vedānta calls Videha-mukti. It was not given only to Vidyāraṇya or other followers of Śaṁkarācārya to speak of Jīvan-mukti. In the Bhagavadgītā there are definite indications of this doctrine of Jīvan-mukti, even though the expression is not to be found there. Such a man enjoys the peace and tranquillity and joy of God while he is living, and though living. That is the cause of the greatest satisfaction to him. That is what the Bhagavadgītā calls ब्राह्मी स्थितिः, life in God or Brahman:

एषा ब्राह्मी स्थितिः पार्थ नैनां प्राप्य विमुह्यति ।
स्थित्वाऽस्यामन्तकालेऽपि ब्रह्मनिर्वाणमृच्छति ॥ II. 72.

The Gītā tells us also in another way that such a man is surrounded on all sides by Reality or Brahman:

अभितो ब्रह्मनिर्वाणं वर्तते विदितात्मनाम् ॥ V. 26.

So then the doctrines of Krama-mukti and Ante-mukti are reconciled by the Bhagavadgītā in the doctrine of Jīvan-mukti, liberation during life through God-vision. We have not to leave the world. We are full of joy when we are in the contemplation and realisation of God. That state of beatification is itself our liberation. Liberation is not to be found after death. But to know God, to do His work, to enjoy His presence and to devote oneself to His service are exactly what a Jīvan-mukta ought to do and that is the teaching of the Bhagavadgītā.

To sum up: The antinomy of the Personal and the Impersonal is reconciled by the doctrine of Trans-Personalism; the antinomy of the Actor and the Spectator is reconciled by the doctrine of Emanationism and the antinomy of the Transcendent and the Immanent is reconciled by what we may call, for want of a more suitable word, Transcendo-Immanence. The doctrines of the Reality and the Unreality of the world are reconciled in Carlylean manner by Ephemeralism, and finally the antinomy of Liberation through a series of births and liberation at death is reconciled by the doctrine of Liberation Here and Now.

Conclusion

(*a*) *The Mystical Nature of Reality.* We have said at the beginning of the chapter that this reconciliation could be based only on a view of Reality which regards the realisation of God as the be-all and the end-all of all existence. This mystical view of Reality alone will enable us to reconcile all the intellectual dogmas that have infested the philosophies of the world. What we experience, what we feel and what we realise should alone constitute our philosophy. From that point of view, I shall place before you a few utterances from the Bhagavadgītā regarding the nature of mystical Reality. These relate respectively to (1) God as the greatest miracle, (2) the absolute limitations of human knowledge in respect of the knowledge of God and (3) the possibility of the knowledge of God by Himself alone.

(1) A passage in the Bhagavadgītā tells us: "We look upon God as a great miracle; we talk of Him as a miracle; we hear Him as a miracle; and having seen Him, talked about Him and heard Him, nobody has been able to know His ultimate nature."

आश्चर्यवत्पश्यति कश्चिदेनमाश्चर्यवद्वदति तथैव चान्यः।
आश्चर्यवच्चैनमन्यः शृणोति श्रुत्वाऽप्येनं वेद न चैव कश्चित् ॥ II. 29.

(2) According to another passage, "God alone has known all beings in the past, knows them in the present and will know them in the future and that no being whatsoever has ever been able to know Him."

वेदाहं समतीतानि वर्तमानानि चार्जुन।
भविष्याणि च भूतानि मां तु वेद न कश्चन ॥ VII. 26.

(3) Finally, we are told that it is "God alone Who is able to know His ultimate nature."

स्वयमेवात्मनात्मानं वेत्थ त्वं पुरुषोत्तम।
भूतभावन भूतेश देवदेव जगत्पते ॥ X. 15.

From these utterances we shall see that everything about God is miraculous, that nobody has ever been able to know Him and that He alone probably is able to know Himself. Divine Self-Consciousness alone thus constitutes the ultimate Reality.

(*b*) *Self-Consciousness : Human and Divine.* Philosophers have talked of human self-consciousness as the be-all and the end-all of all Reality. The whole range of idealists from Berkeley downwards have made self-consciousness the pivot of all existence. The Gītā dispenses with this human self-consciousness and substitutes instead Divine Self-Consciousness. One of the greatest philosophers of antiquity, Aristotle, was thus able to describe the nature of God as Thought of Thought and to characterise that state as Theoria. Divine Self-Consciousness alone would thus constitute the foundation and the peak of all Thought and Existence.

CHAPTER XVI

THE CATEGORICAL IMPERATIVE, ACTIVISM AND ITS LIMITATIONS

Introduction

After having discussed the question of the Antinomies of the Bhagavadgītā and their reconciliation, we turn our attention to the question of the Theories of the Ethical Ideal in the Bhagavadgītā. The most prominent of these theories is, of course, Activism. It is only with this topic that the present chapter will be concerned; while the next chapter will be devoted to the discussion of the three other theories, namely, Moralism, Super-Moralism and Beatificism. These three together constitute another set of ideas and therefore they require to be treated in a separate chapter.

As regards Activism itself, we might discuss it under the following heads: In the first place, before we go to the study of Activism proper, we must remember that there is a great controversy about the relationship between action and renunciation, or action and knowledge. This controversy has taken various forms. Sometimes it appears as a controversy between Karma and Saṁnyāsa; sometimes it appears as between Sakāma and Niṣkāma Karma and so on. Many times the following words have been used in very different senses in the Bhagavadgītā—Karma, Jñāna, Saṁnyāsa, Sāṁkhya and Yoga. Karma might be used either in the sense of selfless action or of action with a selfish aim. The greatest difficulty lies about the meaning of Jñāna. Jñāna might be taken to mean either knowledge on the one hand or illumination on the other ; and very often illumination is a better word than knowledge. Saṁnyāsa might be understood to mean either the leaving aside of all actions or the renunciatory stage of man's life upon earth. Yoga itself has been used in many senses. It is used as Karma-Yoga. It is evidently used to designate the Pātañjala Yoga. Bhakti is not included in the above list, because it is separate and there is no conflict of views about it. Bhakti is one and unique and all people are agreed as to what the nature of Bhakti is. That Bhakti is possible about a Personal God is evident ; but whether it is possible about an Impersonal Deity is a difficult topic with which we may not be concerned here. But the meaning of Bhakti is clear — attachment, devotion, one-pointed love towards the object of adoration or worship. That is what Bhakti means. So Bhakti unlike other expressions does not come within the arena of verbal interpretations or disputations. It stands apart. Just because the words above-mentioned have been used in different senses that diverse philosophical theories have come into being.

Antinomy of Action and Renunciation

As in the case of Gītā metaphysics, here also in Gītā ethics we find one fundamental antinomy and its solution. This antinomy is between Karma and Jñāna, which can ultimately be reconciled in the conception of sacrifice. It is neither possible nor desirable to cite here all the different passages in which the above words have been used. We shall point out only a few of them ; and these we shall divide under three heads. The first group where Karma is regarded as definitely superior to Jñāna, the second where Jñāna is regarded as definitely superior to Karma and the third where they are regarded as co-equal. All these are utterances from the Bhagavad-gītā itself. Hence the question arises how to reconcile these so-called contradictions. This, however, we shall consider later on. At present, in regard to the first, we shall cite only one passage:

संन्यासः कर्मयोगश्च निःश्रेयसकरावुभौ ।
तयोस्तु कर्मसंन्यासात् कर्मयोगो विशिष्यते ॥ V. 2.

Here Karma is definitely regarded as superior to Saṁnyāsa. Another utterance of the same kind would be

संन्यासस्तु महाबाहो दुःखमाप्तुमयोगतः । V. 6.

So then these establish the superiority of Karma to Saṁnyāsa. A second group where Jñāna is regarded as superior to Karma consists of utterances like

सर्वं कर्माखिलं पार्थ ज्ञाने परिसमाप्यते । IV. 33.

where all action comes to be resolved in Jñāna. Jñānr again is taken as superior to every Karma :

दूरेण ह्यवरं कर्म बुद्धियोगाद् धनञ्जय । II. 49.

where Karma is regarded as very inferior to Buddhi-Yoga or Jñāna-Yoga. So in these two groups we have the two sides of an antinomy, where on the one hand we have the superiority of Karma to Jñāna and on the other the superiority of Jñāna to Karma. And then the most wonderful part which the Gītā plays is that according to it there is no difference between the two opposing conceptions :

यं संन्यासमिति प्राहुर्योगं तं विद्धि पांडव । VI. 2.
सांख्ययोगौ पृथग्बालाः प्रवदन्ति न पंडिताः । V. 4.
एकं सांख्यं च योगं च यः पश्यति स पश्यति ॥ V. 5.

suggesting that there is no distinction between Sāṁkhya and Yoga. What does the author of the Bhagavadgītā mean by Sāṁkhya and Yoga ? Evidently, it is not the Sāṁkhya of Kapila or the Yoga of Patañjali. What the author here means by Sāṁkhya is Jñāna, and by Yoga, Karma. For example, let us compare the following passage :

लोकेऽस्मिन्द्विविधा निष्ठा पुरा प्रोक्ता मयांऽनघ ।
ज्ञानयोगेन सांख्यानां कर्मयोगेण योगिनाम् ॥ III. 3.

How shall we find the way through the dilemma of these conceptions over again ? All the utterances cited above belong to the Bhagavadgītā. We shall see later on that the clue which enables us to emerge out of this labyrinth is through the conception of Yajña. It is the conception of Yajña or sacrifice, that reconciles this antinomy between Karma and Jñāna.

Supremacy of Action

(*a*) *Three Reasons.* Now it cannot be gainsaid that the upshot of the teaching of the Bhagavadgītā is its advocacy of the life of activism. It insists upon Karma-Yoga which is the chief point of its discussion. Kṛṣṇa wanted to put Arjuna on his mettle and to make him fight the battle and Karma-Yoga was the theory which he advocated. If we put together all the utterances in the Bhagavadgītā in this matter, we may say that there are five or six different reasons which the Gītā assigns for the supremacy of this doctrine of activism. In the first, the Gītā relies upon three kinds of laws-the law of the body, the law of society and the law of the universe. Each of these laws supports the doctrine of activism. शरीरयात्राऽपि च ते न प्रसिद्ध्येदकर्मणः । (III. 8.)

is what the law of the body advocates. लोकसंग्रहमेवापि संपश्यन्कर्तुमर्हसि । (III.20) is the law of society which requires us to be active for its welfare. एवं प्रवर्तितं चक्रं नानुवर्तयतीह यः । (III. 16) is the law of the wheel of the Universe which is perpetually and unceasingly rotating and of which we form a part. If we want to be conscious of it we must become a worthy part of it. So these laws—the law of the body, the law of society and the law of the universe—indicate and even vindicate activism.

(*b*) *Criticism.* We may take here the liberty of pointing out certain fallacies which in its poetic oratory the Gītā makes. In the first place, कर्मणैव हि संसिद्धिमास्थिता जनकादयः । (III. 20) which appeals to the personality of Janaka is an *argumentum ad hominem.* यद्यदाचरति श्रेष्ठस्तत्तदेवेतरो जनः । (III.21) is an *argumentum ad verecundium*, as it appeals only to the practice of respectable persons. The third fallacy is what we may call *argumentum ad theonem.* This is a word which I myself have coined on the analogy of *hominem, populem* and *verecundium.* Here we have an appeal to the power and actions of God Himself, for example:

न मे पार्थास्ति कर्तव्यं त्रिषु लोकेषु किंचन ।
नानवाप्तमवाप्तव्यं वर्त एव च कर्मणि ।। III. 22.
यदि ह्ययं न वर्तेयं जातुकर्मण्यतन्द्रितः ।
मम वर्त्मानुवर्तन्ते मनुष्याः पार्थ सर्वशः ।। III. 23.
उत्सीदेयुरिमे लोका न कुर्यां कर्म चेदहम् ।। III. 24.
चातुर्वर्ण्यं मया सृष्टं गुणकर्मविभागशः । IV. 13.

Here God is put on a par with the human activist, and all creative activity in the universe and society is attributed to Him. This is the first point of our discussion in the present chapter where we are setting forth the different arguments in favour of activism.

There is one point which we must make clear. Those who have read Aristotelian Ethics know the great stress which he lays upon the contemplative life. This contemplative life is not very different from what the Bhagavadgītā calls Jñāna Yoga. So can we not borrow a word from Greek philosophy which can be pitted against this kind of activism? We can. In Greek 'theoria' is a very peculiar word. In the first place, it means vision or perception; secondly, it means intellection or knowledge, and thirdly, it means ecstacy or illumination. Similar are the implications of the Sanskrit word Jñāna. A philosophy of Jñāna might well be called a philosophy of theoretism. So we may well regard the contrast between Karma and Jñāna as a contrast between activism and theoretism. This one word theoretism includes in it all the different aspects of perception, intellection and ecstatic enjoyment.

The Categorical Imperative in Kant and the Bhagavadgītā

(*a*) *Three Specifications according to Kant.* We have already seen how there is a great similarity between the author of the Bhagavadgītā and Kant, in regard to their conception of the antinomies. In this chapter we shall deal with something which is still higher, namely, the conception of the Categorical Imperative both in Kant and the Bhagavadgītā about which there is a wonderful resemblance indeed. Those who have studied the Critique of Practical Reason know that the general statement, which Kant makes in regard to the conception of duty, is " act on that principle which may be regarded as a law universal ". Universality is the general characterisation of this law. This general principle Kant had to modify, modulate or specify in course of time. The first specification of this universal law is – " act on that principle which might be regarded as a law of **nature.** " The second specification is –" act on that principle which gamight be rerded as a law of reason." Finally, mere nature and reason are not sufficient. Man must come in. He must be regarded as an end-in-himself. The Kingdom of Ends must justify our practice of the Categorical Imperative. Hence the third specification would be – " act on that principle which will conform to the concept of the Kingdom of Ends." Thus man as an end-in-himself sums up the total teaching of Kant in regard to the Categorical Imperative.

(*b*) *Three Specifications according to Gītā.* **Exactly** in a similar manner, the Bhagavadgītā gives us a certain general formulation of the Categorical Imperative and then its specifications. The procedural similarity as well as the similarity of content is wonderful. This point has not been hitherto noticed by anybody. In the first place, there are these utterances in the Bhagavadgītā in regard to the general formulation :

कार्यमित्येव यत्कर्म नियतं क्रियतेऽर्जुन । XVIII. 9.
कर्मण्येवाधिकारस्ते मा फलेषु कदाचन । II. 47.

You ought to do a thing because it is your duty to do so. This is the general formulation of the Categorical Imperative in the Bhagavadgītā. Then there are three specifications of it. The first specification is that this duty is to be performed leaving away all attachment and desire for the fruit (सङ्गं त्यक्त्वा फलानि च). This rule is applicable, according to the Bhagavadgītā, not merely to ordinary actions but even to holy actions :

यज्ञो दानं तपश्चैव पावनानि मनीषिणाम् । XVIII. 5.
एतान्यपि तु कर्माणि सङ्गं त्यक्त्वा फलानि च ।
कर्तव्यानीति मे पार्थ निश्चितं मतमुत्तमम् ॥ XVIII. 6.

It tells us that we should leave away all attachment and all desire for fruit not merely in the case of ordinary actions but also in the case of holy actions so that even holy actions come within the purview of the Categorical Imperative.

A second specification of the Categorical Imperative in the Bhagavadgītā is योगः कर्मसु कौशलम्। (II. 50). सिद्ध्यसिद्ध्योः समो भूत्वा समत्वं योग उच्यते। (II.48). We are to do our duty skilfully. That is what Mahatma Gandhi claimed to do. He regarded himself as an artist in Satyāgraha. Also one must preserve one's equanimity (समत्वम्). These are the two specifications of the Categorical Imperative in the Bhagavadgītā, namely, (i) leaving aside all attachment and care for fruit ; and (ii) doing actions skilfully and in a spirit of equanimity.

The third specification is the concept of Yajña which is universal in its nature. This corresponds to the Kingdom of Ends in Kant. The Yajña has got both a social and a spiritual value as the Kingdom of Ends itself has. We may also say incidentally that the concept of Yajña reconciles the antinomy between Jñāna and Karma, as we have suggested at the beginning of this chapter. But it is not the conception of Yajña or sacrifice of ghee, sesamum, rice or sheep, which is the reconciler of the antinomy between Jñāna and Karma. It is the general universal conception of Yajña. There are various kinds of Yajñas, एवं बहुविधा यज्ञा वितता ब्रह्मणो मुखे। (IV. 32). It is probably this thing which gave Acharya Vinoba Bhave the impetus towards his conception of Yajña. द्रव्ययज्ञास्तपोयज्ञा योगयज्ञास्तथाऽपरे । स्वाध्यायज्ञानयज्ञाश्च यतयः संशितव्रताः ॥ (IV. 28). But it may mean the sacrifice of material. The Bhagavadgītā even starts with the Dravya Yajña. So whenever we are doing our actions in a spirit of sacrifice we are freed from their contamination. That is the ultimate principle, which reconciles the antinomy between Jñāna and Karma.

Divine Nature of Sacrifice

(*a*) *In Reference to the Individual.* We are also told by the Bhagavadgītā that it is only when we recognise the Divine nature of sacrifice that we can keep ourselves uncontaminated by actions. This aspect of the Divine nature of sacrifice can be discussed in three different ways. First, in reference to the individual; second, in reference to God; and third, in reference to Brahman or the Absolute Reality. In all these cases this freedom from contamination occurs. In the first place, a man who has done his duty is, in spite of himself, filled with a feeling of joy. Kant does not want us to do our duty with a feeling of joy or pleasure. But the Bhagavadgītā tells us that the performance of one's highest duty is attended with a feeling of joy. This is the first effect. The second is the automatic purification of the mind. Man thinks that his bad actions are washed away simply by the performance of his duty; good actions act like a boomerang in a sense. (IV.23). Any good act that is performed reacts upon itself and all the bad effects of a man's actions or even bad thoughts are washed off and purity is produced. And finally, so far as the individual is concerned, he is able to taste what the Gītā calls spiritual ambrosia. Amṛta is the word which it uses in this connection (यज्ञशिष्टामृत). Now what the Bhagavadgītā tells us in regard to sacrifice is this. You must first hand over to men and to God the profits of your actions and any residue that may be left may be partaken of by you: यज्ञशिष्टामृतभुजो यान्ति ब्रह्मसनातनम्। (IV. 31). That gives you the spiritual nectar. This word Amṛta also involves in it the conception of divine flavour. Purity of mind, Grace from above and the tasting of ambrosia in the process of the performance of one's duties are the effects which the individual feels.

(*b*) *In Reference to God.* Then as regards the propitiation of God: if we regard God as a Personal Being, the Gītā tells us what a great dishonesty would a man commit if he does not return to God at least a part of what God has conferred on him. This is a sort of an income-tax which we have to pay to the Divine Power : तैर्दत्तानप्रदायैभ्यो यो भुङ्क्ते स्तेन एव सः । (III. 12). "He who utilises all the products of his work for himself is a thief." So then, return of the effects of one's actions as recompense to God is the first thing which a man owes to Him. Second, the author of the Bhagavadgītā talks in a simple manner पत्रं पुष्पं फलं तोयं । (IX. 26) or else in a little higher vein,

यत्करोषि यदश्नासि यज्जुहोषि ददासि यत् ।
यत्तपस्यसि कौन्तेय तत्कुरुष्व मदर्पणम् ॥ IX. 27.

exhorting us to dedicate all our actions to God. Our actions, says Jñāneśvara in his comment on the line स्वकर्मणा तमभ्यर्च्य । (XVIII. 46), should be like flowers with which we might worship the Almighty. And finally, the Bhagavadgītā tells us, ये तु सर्वाणि कर्माणि मयि संन्यस्य मत्पराः । (XII. 6), that we should deposit our actions in safe custody with God so that we might be recipients of His Grace. This is the second outcome of our sacrificial action.

(*c*) *In Reference to Brahman.* A third reference is evidently to remaining uncontaminated by depositing our actions in the Absolute Reality : ब्रह्मण्याधाय कर्माणि सङ्गं त्यक्त्वा करोति यः । (V. 10). Supposing there are some who believe in an Impersonal Deity, to them also the Bhagavadgītā gives an assurance and a hope. It tells us not merely to deposit our actions with a Personal Being but also of depositing them with even an Impersonal Deity. This is the most important utterance. The omnipresent deity is present in every sacrificial action of ours. तस्मात् सर्वगतं ब्रह्म नित्यं यज्ञे प्रतिष्ठितम् । (III. 15). Our sacrifice is based upon the foundation of God. So the Bhagavadgītā brings out clearly with reference (1) to the Individual, or (2) to a Personal God, or (3) even to an Impersonal Deity, the divine nature of our sacrificial acts. We shall consider one final point, though it is not possible to discuss it here in full. That point is the limitations of the doctrine of activism. What are these limitations?

Limitations of Activism

We have argued so far in favour of activism. But there are also limitations to it which we must now consider. There are, on the whole, four such limitations. In the first place, no universal rule of activism could be laid down in view of temperamental differences. In the second place, God-illumination and God-enjoyment constitute another limitation of activism. The doctrine of ज्ञानकर्मसमुच्चय, a synthesis of action and knowledge, is a third, as it does not allow free scope for activism, while the much debated question as to whether Karma is possible after Jñāna, the doctrine of ज्ञानोत्तरकर्म, implies the last limitation. Let us now consider these limitations in order.

(*a*) *Temperamental Differences.* In the first place, in various contexts we are told by the Bhagavadgītā that Prakṛti or Nature is a powerful instrument; it will ride over us in spite of our philosophical and other attainments:

मिथ्यैष व्यवसायस्ते प्रकृतिस्त्वां नियोक्ष्यति । XVIII. 59.

सदृशं चेष्टते स्वस्याः प्रकृतेर्ज्ञानवानापि ।
प्रकृतिं यान्ति भूतानि निग्रहः किं करिष्यति ॥ III. 33.

कार्यते ह्यवशः कर्म सर्वः प्रकृतिजैर्गुणैः । III. 5.

It is these differences of nature or temperament which constitute one great limitation to the doctrine of activism. That there are temperamental differences among men goes without question. One may be born a thinker, another a worker, a third an artist and a fourth an emotionalist. These temperamental differences have been very cleverly analysed by Jung in his Psychological Types of Men. The broad categories of the introvert and the extrovert which he makes might each be divided under four different heads by reference to feeling, will, intellect and intuition. There are thus eight types of psychological behaviour according to Jung. This is not the only scheme possible ; other schemes might also be suggested. Let us take, however, only four types for our purpose — the philosopher, the mystic, the scientist and the politician. Kant, the philosopher, may be called an intellectual introvert; Blake, the mystic, may be called an intuitive introvert; Darwin, the scientist, may be called an intellectual extrovert; and Nehru, the politician, may be called an intuitive extrovert. The same rule of conduct cannot be applied to all. Similarly, a person who performs Yoga is an activist. A man who engages himself in devotional music is also an activist. A Jñānī who unceasingly engages himself in philosophic speculation is also an activist (ज्ञानं हि मानसी क्रिया). There are different types of activism and the same rule cannot be applied to all of them. Temperamental differences create a difference in conduct. The same kind of activity cannot be prescribed for all. It cannot be a universal rule of life.

(*b*) *Action in Relation to Illumination and God-Enjoyment.* Second, the Gītā itself shows us the relationship between action on the one hand and illumination and beatification on the other;

यथैधांसि समिद्धोऽग्निर्भस्मसात्कुरुतेऽर्जुन।
ज्ञानाग्निः सर्वकर्माणि भस्मसात्कुरुते तथा॥ IV. 37.

The fire of illumination puts a stop to actions and their effects. Similarly, we are told that actions come to an end for a man who is merged in the beatific enjoyment of God:

यस्त्वात्मरतिरेव स्यात् आत्मतृप्तश्च मानवः।
आत्मन्येव च संतुष्टस्तस्य कार्यं न विद्यते॥ III. 17.

So illumination and beatification act as checks to activism. We thus see how the Bhagavadgītā tells us in a mystical spirit the powerlessness of actions before God-vision and God-enjoyment. A kind of a dilemma, as that between action and beatification, presents itself before every person who has made some progress in spiritual life, in a number of instances, as to whether he should select the alternative of action or that of beatific enjoyment. I shall not give illustrations. There are many, but I am putting before you the dilemma as a whole for your consideration.

Examination of the two Theories of ज्ञानकर्मसमुच्चय and ज्ञानोत्तरकर्म

We cannot close this chapter without referring to two theories of classical Vedāntic scholarship, namely, the theory of ज्ञानकर्मसमुच्चय and the theory of ज्ञानोत्तरकर्म.

The theory of ज्ञानकर्मसमुच्चय occupied great attention at the time of Śaṁkarācārya and the Mīmāṁsakas :

उभाभ्यामेव पक्षाभ्यां यथा खे पक्षिणां गतिः ।
तथैव ज्ञानकर्मभ्यां प्राप्यते ब्रह्म शाश्वतम् ॥

says the sage Hārīta. Just as a bird cannot fly without two wings, so Jñāna and Karma are both necessary for the flight of the individual to the Absolute. In the same way there is a passage in the Īśopaniṣad : विद्यां चाविद्यां च यस्तद्वेदोभयँसह । अविद्यया मृत्युं तीर्त्वा विद्ययाऽमृतमश्नुते । (ii) This has been interpreted on the one hand as involving a reconciliation and a synthesis of Jñāna and Karma. Śaṁkara on the other hand has his own arguments to disprove it. He wants nothing else except Jñāna, pure and simple, and has got nothing to do with the Karmas. There is another important theory which is advanced by a great modern Indian scholar, the late Lokamanya Tilak. It is the theory pointed out in a previous chapter, where he is criticising Śaṁkara. According to Śaṁkara, ज्ञानोत्तरकर्म is impossible. कर्म stops as soon as ज्ञान is reached. On the other hand, Tilak advocates that man has a duty to perform even after the realisation of the highest self. In the first place, it is pointed out that action belongs to the body and so long as the body remains, we cannot extricate ourselves from the influence of actions. Then secondly, selfless action or Niṣkāma Karma would alone enable us to move out of thraldom to actions. Hence a man who performs selfless actions cannot be said to be performing any actions at all :

अनाश्रितः कर्मफलं कार्यं कर्म करोति यः ।
स संन्यासी च योगी च न निरग्निर्न चाक्रियः ॥ VI. 1.

Finally, it is the responsibility of a realised soul to point the way to erring humanity and hence action becomes indispensable even for the realiser: लोकसंग्रहमेवापि संपश्यन्कर्तुमर्हसि । (III. 20). Lokamanya Tilak has advanced these and other arguments for proving the imperativeness of actions even after the attainment of the highest knowledge. The question, however, arises whether there is any 'ought' after God-realisation. We shall not go into the details of the controversy, but shall point out only one principle which will resolve not merely this controversy about ज्ञानोत्तरकर्म but also the earlier controversy about ज्ञानकर्मसमुच्चय, a point which has not been hitherto noticed, namely, that Jñāna is not an event but a process. Jñāna might be regarded to be knowledge, but the illumination is its proper meaning for the word. Illumination never comes finally and fully. We always keep making an asymptotic approach to illumination, but never actually reach it. Jñāneśvara has told us that there is always that difference between the aspirant and God as between the gold of fifteen carats and the gold of sixteen carats, or between the moon on the fourteenth day and the moon on the fifteenth. So Jñāna is a process and not an event. The doctrine of ज्ञानकर्मसमुच्चय debated between the Mīmāṁsakas and Śaṁkara and the doctrine of ज्ञानोत्तरकर्म debated between Śaṁkara and Tilak—both fight shy of this principle of the nature of Jñāna as being a process instead of an event. So when we remember that we always keep making an asymptotic approach to the Absolute, then everything else becomes clear. ज्ञानोत्तरकर्म does not occur, ज्ञानकर्मसमुच्चय does not occur. We are free to do our actions as we like in the process of attainment of the highest illumination. If we are activists by temper, nothing can prevent us from doing actions at any stage of our progress towards the attainment of our ideal. If we are contemplatives, nothing can stir us from a life of God-enjoyment to which we are naturally born, though we may not wholly set aside the principle of action to which we are not born. Finally, if we are philosophers, the issue will be how best to determine the nature of the highest Reality and leave the rest to God. Temperamental differences may be modulated but they cannot be so radically changed as to wear an entirely new aspect altogether.

CHAPTER XVII

MORALISM, SUPER-MORALISM AND BEATIFICISM

In the last chapter we were concerned with one chief phase of moral life as depicted by the Bhagavadgītā; and our discussion centered round activism as one of its most important theories. Sometimes activism is regarded as the only theory in the Bhagavadgītā. This is not so. There are other theories also. Those who have studied the Upaniṣads know how many different theories there are in the Upaniṣads. I am reminded here of one particular theory. Years ago Dr. Bhandarkar asked me what was meant by 'theonomy'. People knew what autonomy was; people knew what heteronomy was; but what theonomy was, was something hard to comprehend. We have already discussed activism. We shall now proceed to three other theories. That will complete the ethical doctrine of the Bhagavadgītā. The first of these is what might be called a general theory of moralism. The second as contrasted with the first is the theory of super-moralism; and the third as a reconciliation of the two is the theory of beatificism. Now beatificism is a word which I coined many years ago and with which my old respected friend and teacher, Professor E. A. Wodehouse, was greatly pleased. This beatific theory is exactly the theory of Ānanda as advocated by the Upaniṣads. There are traces of that theory in the Bhagavadgītā also. We shall conclude this chapter with a discussion of the theory of beatificism as found in the Bhagavadgītā.

Moralism

(*a*) *Virtues and their Classification.* The discussion of moral virtues is spread over various chapters of the Bhagavadgītā. We might particularly mention four: (1) In the twelfth chapter we have a series of verses, beginning with

अद्वेष्टा सर्वभूतानां मैत्रः करुण एव च।
निर्ममो निरहंकारः समदुःखसुखः क्षमी ॥ 13.

in which God-devotion is regarded as the supreme virtue. (2) In the thirteenth chapter we have:

अमानित्वमदम्भित्वमहिंसा क्षान्तिरार्जवम् ।
आचार्योपासनं शौचं स्थैर्यमात्मविनिग्रहः ॥
...... एतज्ज्ञानमिति प्रोक्तम् ......॥ 7–11.

where the virtues are regarded as constituting knowledge. (3) In the sixteenth chapter we have:

अभयं सत्त्वसंशुद्धिर्ज्ञानयोगव्यवस्थितिः ।
दानं दमश्च यज्ञश्च स्वाध्यायस्तप आर्जवम् ॥ 1.

where we have got a full moral account of the divine heritage. And (4) finally, in the eighteenth chapter we have:

शमो दमस्तपः शौचं क्षान्तिरार्जवमेव च ।
ज्ञानं विज्ञानमास्तिक्यं ब्रह्मकर्म स्वभावजम् ॥ 42.

and so on, where we have an array of the most important moral virtues characterising the different social orders. These are the four main places where the Bhagavadgītā makes an analytical study of virtues. Whether these could be subjected to a synthetical rule and be comprised under one single head is a question for moral philosophers. To make simply an inventory of the various moral virtues is not a very great thing, but to show how they are all aspects of one central virtue is very important.

This problem of the centralisation of virtues has been tackled throughout the History of Ethics. In

Pythagoras harmony was the highest moral principle. In Plato wisdom, courage and temperance, all were synthesised in the supreme virtue of justice. In Aristotle Measure or the Mean became the central principle, of which all other virtues became specifications. In St. Paul and Christianity generally, and later in St. Augustine, faith, hope and charity, and of all these charity became the fundamental virtue. Charity means love in Greek. And so love of God and humanity was the principle at which Paul and Augustine aimed. After that when we come to Spinoza we find the Intellectual Love of God as the central virtue. In Bentham we have benevolence; in Sidgwick we have equity; in Mahatma Gandhi we have truth and non-violence. So all these great writers and thinkers make it their business to centralise all virtues in one single principle of their choice.

From the four *loci classici* of the Bhagavadgītā enumerated above, we find that an attempt has been particularly made in the twelfth and thirteenth chapters to centralise these virtues either in Devotion or in Knowledge—Bhakti or Jñāna. If we read verses यो मद्भक्तः स मे प्रियः......(16) भक्तिमान् यः स मे प्रियः......(17) भक्तास्तेऽतीव मे प्रियाः......(20) from the twelfth chapter, we will see that all the moral virtues have been regarded there as exemplifications or specifications or exfoliations of the one central virtue of God-devotion. So Bhakti or God-devotion is the central virtue according to the twelfth chapter of the Bhagavadgītā. In the thirteenth chapter the Bhagavadgītā says almost in the spirit of Socrates that virtue alone constitutes knowledge: एतज्ज्ञानमिति प्रोक्तमज्ञानं यदतोऽन्यथा ॥ (XIII. 11). So this Socratic doctrine of virtue being knowledge and the other doctrine, namely, that all virtues are specifications of devotion, may be regarded as illustrations of the attempt of the Bhagavadgītā to centralise all these virtues in a single principle.

As stated above, the problem of finding a guiding thread through the list of virtues is a very difficult and interesting one. The present writer must acknowledge his sense of inspiration when years ago he found the problem first tackled by St. Augustine, who reduced not merely the great Christian virtues of faith, hope and charity but also the Platonic virtues of justice, wisdom, temperance and courage to the one central principle of faith. The present writer has attempted to find a guiding thread through the list of virtues enumerated by the great Hindi saints in his work, "Pathway to God in Hindi Literature". There he has shown how all these virtues could be reduced to one single principle of God-devotion. He has also mentioned therein that the virtues of the Bhagavadgītā itself could be analogously explained by reference to the same principle of God-devotion.

(*b*) *God-devotion as the Central Thread of Virtues.* In the account of the virtues of the Bhagavadgītā which we have referred to above, we have mentioned four *loci classici* in the XII, XIII, XVI and XVIII chapters of the Bhagavadgītā. The task of showing that God-devotion runs like a thread through all the virtues mentioned therein is a long and arduous one. We have, therefore, selected three virtues each from the four different groups referred to above so as to make out of them a necklace of twelve principal virtues. This list would stand as follows :—

Twelfth Chapter

1. करुणा--Compassion 2. समता--Equanimity
3. शौच--Purity

Thirteenth Chapter

4. अहिंसा--Harmlessness 5. आत्मविनिग्रह--Self Control
6. असक्ति--Non-attachment

Sixteenth Chapter

7. अभय--Fearlessness 8. यज्ञ--Sacrifice
9. शान्ति--Peace

Eighteenth Chapter

10. तेजस्--Valour 11. ईश्वरभाव--Lordliness
12. परिचर्या--Service.

This, we hope, would be a fairly representative list to show the supreme moralistic teaching of the Bhagavadgītā. Let us take the virtues in order and show how they are all expressions of the central principle of God-devotion. (1) करुणा or compassion is evidently an expression of praying for mercy from God. One of the cardinal principles of such praying for mercy from God would be to treat others as our own selves. Hence arises the necessity of showing compassion to all creatures whenever and wherever occasion requires it. (2) The other virtue समता or equanimity is both a condition and a result of God-devotion. Unless we preserve equanimity of mind we cannot reach God; and unless we have realised God, we cannot reach the highest stage of equanimity. (3) शौच. One of the evident effects of such God-devotion would be the absolute purification of our mind. No bad idea dare enter our soul if it is once filled with God. Ours is a jealous God and

He would not allow any pretender to the throne. (4) अहिंसा. The same principle of treating equally all created beings results in the virtue of Ahiṁsā which regards all life as inviolable. Hence arises the virtue of harmlessness or non-violence. (5) आत्मविनिग्रह. We cannot hope to reach God unless we have completely controlled our senses. The senses must not compel us to follow the innumerable objects of desire, if we want to achieve the supreme object of desire, namely, God. प्रेयोऽन्यस्माद्वान्तरतरो यदयमात्मा, says the Bṛhadāraṇyaka Upaniṣad. (6) असक्ति. For that same reason we must follow the principle of non-attachment to all external and internal objects. आसक्ति to God means असक्ति to all other things whatsoever. Otherwise, we would be reduced to the plight of जडभरत in the भागवत. (7) अभय. When we have reached a high stage of God-realisation, fearlessness follows on the heels of our experience; as the Upaniṣads have put it—आनन्दं ब्रह्मणो विद्वान् न बिभेति कदाचन । न बिभेति कुतश्चन ॥ This is the reason why a saint is absolutely fearless. (8) यज्ञ. God-realisation also implies a complete sacrifice of all our possessions for the sake of God. This is really what is meant by Yajña. The sacrifice of all objects to God brings in its train the sacrifice involved in our dispassionately doing good to all fellow-beings. (9) शान्ति. Such a life leads us to that cardinal criterion of God-realisation, namely, Śānti or peace. As we have seen elsewhere, Śānti or peace and the bliss of God are interdependent and the two are perfected together. But the peace which follows upon the enjoyment of divine bliss is higher than the peace which precedes it. (10) तेजस्. A man who has reached God must show courage and valour in thought and action. Hence arises the necessity of the virtue of तेजस् or शौर्य. (11) ईश्वरभाव. This brings in its train a state of absolute lordliness in a God-realiser. He does find himself to be the lord of all he surveys. This is what is meant by ईश्वरभाव, the lordliness of the realised saint. He is like a pinnacle. He stands alone to himself in his solitary greatness and with power to do good whenever and wherever he likes. (12) परिचर्या. And in spite of such lordliness he does not find it difficult to do service to humanity. In fact, service to humanity (परिचर्या), even though it might seem antithetical to lordliness, is the result of it. The supreme value of God-realisation for oneself is to create conditions for the realisation of God in and for others. This, in short, is the consummation of the supreme moralistic teaching of the Bhagavadgītā.

Super-Moralism

(a) Actionlessness (Naiṣkarmya)—Going beyond Karma and Dharma. After this analytic and synthetic view of the moral life according to the Bhagavadgītā, let us pass on to what we might call super-moralism. This is something like Nietzsche's doctrine of the superman. Only it must be looked at from the ethical stand-point and not from the social and political points of view. Now there are two different stand-points from which this doctrine of super-moralism may be considered. One is the point of view of नैष्कर्म्यसिद्धि and the other of निस्त्रैगुण्य. नैष्कर्म्यसिद्धि literally means rising superior to Karmas. But it also means rising superior to Dharmas. It is in this latter sense that Śrī Kṛṣṇa asks us to rise superior to all Dharmas, to all duties and all religions and to meditate on Him. सर्वधर्मान् परित्यज्य मामेकं शरणं व्रज। (XVIII. 66). Also he tells us that we may do any Karmas whatsoever. If we only take resort to God we shall be freed from the effects of our actions:

सर्वकर्माण्यपि सदा कुर्वाणो मद्व्यपाश्रयः ।
मत्प्रसादादवाप्नोति शाश्वतं पदमव्ययम् ॥ XVIII. 56.

Śaṁkarācārya has very cleverly interpreted the expression सर्वकर्माण्यपि as निषिद्धकर्माण्यपि कुर्वाणः. We may not go to that length and yet we can legitimately say that the truest morality would lie in going beyond all Dharmas and Karmas.

There is another way in which this नैष्कर्म्यसिद्धि has been interpreted. Most peculiarly the Bhagavadgītā uses the expression नैष्कर्म्यसिद्धि in the famous verse नैष्कर्म्यसिद्धिं परमां संन्यासेनाधिगच्छति । (XVIII. 49), which later became the foundation of Sureśvara's work on नैष्कर्म्यसिद्धि, the main point of which is to prove the supremacy of Jñāna. Had that been the only aim of Sureśvara, it would have been better for him not to have used the word नैष्कर्म्य, but to have directly stated the supremacy of Jñāna. To bring Jñāna by the back door is what Sureśvara has attempted in his work on नैष्कर्म्यसिद्धि. Sureśvara had too much of Vedāntism in him. But the Bhagavadgītā was free from any such encumbrances. Any man who can carry on his Karmas in a spirit of Anāsakti might be regarded as having reached नैष्कर्म्य. This is the नैष्कर्म्यसिद्धि which the Bhagavadgītā aims at. It means rising superior to the *modus operandi* of Karmas and their effects through the principle of non-attachment.

(*b*) *Transcendence of Guṇas* (*Nistraiguṇya*). What is meant by Nistraiguṇya? Its literal meaning is rising beyond the triplet of Guṇas. The Bhagavadgītā makes the following important statement in this connection :

त्रैगुण्यविषया वेदा निस्त्रैगुण्यो भवार्जुन ।
निर्द्वन्द्वो नित्यसत्त्वस्थो निर्योगक्षेम आत्मवान् ॥
यावानर्थ उदपाने सर्वतः संप्लुतोदके ।
तावान् सर्वेषु वेदेषु ब्राह्मणस्य विजानतः ॥ II. 45–46.

The meaning of this statement, however, has not been accurately comprehended. We shall first see what the great Vedāntic commentators have to say on this point and then refer to the view of the poet-saint of Maharashtra, Jñāneśvara. Finally, we shall briefly explain the view which upholds the supremacy of mystical experience.

Śaṁkara says that the same purpose is served by drinking the water in a circumscribed place (well) that is served by drinking the water from an overflowing lake.

परिच्छिन्नोदके स्नानपानादिरर्थः संप्लुतोदके तावानेव संपद्यते ।

The whole purpose served by the Vedic Karmas is included under Jñāna obtained by the realiser. Śaṁkara calls him a Saṁnyāsī. According to Vallabha, the labour involved in the first process is greater: जलाहरणपात्ररक्षणादि क्लेशोऽधिकः । Madhva explains the word ब्राह्मण thus: ब्रह्म अणतीति ब्राह्मणः । According to Madhva, he is a ब्राह्मण who recites the Vedas and he is called अपरोक्षज्ञानी.

Jñāneśvara says that the Vedas contain utterances of all kinds, Sāttvika, Rājasa and Tāmasa. But he who is a Jñānī selects the Sāttvika utterances embodied in the Upaniṣads in preference to Rājasa and Tāmasa utterances embodied in the Brāhmaṇas.

म्हणोनि उपनिषदादि समस्त । सात्त्विक ते ॥
येर रजतमात्मक । जेथ निरूपिजे कर्मादिक ।...
तूं गुणत्रयातें अव्हेरी । मी माझें हें न करीं ।
एक आत्मसुख अंतरीं । विसंब झणीं ॥
जरी वेदें बहुत बोलिलें । विविध भेद सूचिले ।
तरी आपण हित आपुलें । तेंचि घेपें ॥...
तैसें ज्ञानी जे होती । ते वेदार्थातें विचरिती ।
मग अपेक्षित तें स्वीकारिती । शाश्वत जें ॥ Jñā. II. 256–263.

Almost every one of the commentators might well regard the Vedas as the final authority. But the Bhagavadgītā exalts mystical experience above the knowledge of the Vedas. It tells us that we ought to rate the scriptures only for what they are worth, whether they be Hindu, Mohammedan or Christian scriptures. They are all alike. They are like a small well (उदपान) in the all-enveloping sea of the Ātman.

I came across this word उदपान when I took to the study of Jñāneśvarī in 1912 under the influence of my Spiritual teacher, and could then understand it to mean a well. This meaning was corroborated by Jñāneśvara elsewhere, for example कूपतडागादिक. Later on I found Paṇini also using the word in the same sense. उदकस्य उदः संज्ञायाम् (पाणिनिसूत्र) उदपानम् (संज्ञा) = a well and not the drinking of water (उदकपानम्).

Let us not pride ourselves on supposing that we have known the Vedas. That would not help us. The reason why we should rise above the Vedas to the Ātman is that the Vedas are permeated by the three guṇas. God alone is above the three qualities (त्रिगुणातीत). The Gītā therefore teaches us to rise beyond the triplet of the guṇas, wherever they may be found, the Vedas being only one of the instances subject to the influence of the three guṇas.

There are two ways, according to the Bhagavadgītā, in which one can go beyond the three guṇas, (i) by being नित्यसत्त्वस्थ and (ii) by अव्यभिचारिणी भक्ति. As regards the first, the question arises whether this state is to be reached by positively continuing to stay in the purified Sattva or by transcending all the three qualities. Shri Mukunda Shastri used to quote the verse from the

Bhāgavata : सत्त्वेनान्यतमौ हन्यात् सत्त्वं सत्त्वेन चैव हि ।. The two other guṇas, namely, Rājasa and Tāmasa, are to be destroyed by Sattva, and Sattva is to be destroyed by Sattva itself. The Nitya Sattvahood is reached when the Rājasa and Tāmasa are thus destroyed : निर्द्वन्द्वो नित्यसत्त्वस्थः. This, however, is not the ultimate end. It is a very difficult doctrine almost like the one we meet with in the आनन्दमयाधिकरण. Is God bliss or blissful ? Similarly, the question posed here is : Can our highest ideal be described in terms of नित्यसत्त्व or निस्त्रैगुण्य ? The author of the Bhagavadgītā draws our attention to the superiority of निस्त्रैगुण्य over नित्यसत्त्व.

The Bhagavadgītā points out the second way of reaching निस्त्रैगुण्य. The state of निस्त्रैगुण्य is to be reached not merely by killing the other two guṇas by Sattva and Sattva by itself, but by pursuing the path of अव्यभिचारिणी भक्ति or one-pointed and unswerving devotion to God. It is only अव्यभिचारिणी भक्ति which ultimately takes us beyond the three guṇas.

मां च योऽव्यभिचारेण भक्तियोगेन सेवते ।
स गुणान् समतीत्यैतान् ब्रह्मभूयाय कल्पते ॥ XIV. 26.

It is only Bhakti-yoga which enables us to go beyond the three guṇas and thus to attain the highest ideal.

(*c*) *Characteristics of an Equanimous Man* (*Sthitaprajña*). Now the question before us is : what is the highest moral ideal realisable by man, according to the Bhagavadgītā ? The answer to this question is found in its famous doctrine of स्थितप्रज्ञ. In the history of Greek and Indian philosophy we find that the sage of the Stoics is characterised by *apathia*, the sage of the Epicureans by *ataraxia* and the sage of the Bhagavadgītā by Anāsakti. These are all on the same level. These sages point to an ideal which we have to realise by our own effort and by our fortune if possible. The Bhagavadgītā goes to the length of calling the स्थितप्रज्ञ a कूटस्थ himself. (कूटस्थो विजितेन्द्रियः VI. 8.). Now what is the meaning of the word कूटस्थ ? It is a very peculiar and important word. My own Vedāntic teacher used to explain the word कूटस्थ as meaning unmoving like an iron anvil (कूटवत् तिष्ठतीति). In that sense it occurs in Vedānta Paribhāṣā ; but कूटस्थ also means the soul and very peculiarly also God in the head, as Kabīra has put it :

दसवे द्वारे ताली लागी, अलख पुरुख, जाको ध्यान धरै।

—Paramārtha Sopāna, Part I. 5. 16.

'The top-most part of the brain' is a very famous meaning of the word कूट. It is the summit or the pinnacle. Now when the Bhagavadgītā speaks about this स्थितप्रज्ञ or कूटस्थ, it implies automatically that he is the individual soul, the soul in the head, or the soul above the head, or the soul all-governing. Many people have known from the Bhagavadgītā what are the various characteristics of such a स्थितप्रज्ञ. We shall not cite all the passages from the Bhagavadgītā relating to the characteristics of a स्थितप्रज्ञ, but refer to only a few of them from which we shall gather together the chief characteristics and describe them briefly under four heads : psychological, ethical, social and mystical.

(1) *Psychological.* The psychological characteristic consists in withdrawing the mind from the organs of sense. Let not our mind be subjected to the influence of the sense-organs.

इन्द्रियाणां हि चरतां यन्मनोऽनुविधीयते ।
तदस्य हरति प्रज्ञां वायुर्नावमिवाम्भसि ॥ II. 67.

Man's mind is tossed to and fro on the sea of sensual enjoyment like a boat, helpless and hapless. One who is able to conquer his senses is compared to a कूर्म or a tortoise which can withdraw its organs within itself at will:

> यदा संहरते चायं कूर्मोऽङ्गानीव सर्वशः ।
> इन्द्रियाणीन्द्रियार्थेभ्यस्तस्य प्रज्ञा प्रतिष्ठिता ॥ II. 58.

Such is the psychological characterisation of a स्थितप्रज्ञ.

(2) *Moral.* The second characteristic is the moral. We have a very famous verse in the Bhagavadgītā:

> आपूर्यमाणमचलप्रतिष्ठं समुद्रमापः प्रविशन्ति यद्वत्
> तद्वत् कामा यं प्रविशन्ति सर्वे स शान्तिमाप्नोति न कामकामी ॥ II. 70.

The ocean is full. Hundreds of rivers flow into it, but the ocean is not increased by the inflow of these waters. If it increases, it is due to the influence of the Moon, but not to the inflow of the waters of the rivers. As the inflow of the waters of the rivers has no influence on the sea, similarly the senses have no influence over a poised mind. This is the moral characterisation of a स्थितप्रज्ञ. But there is another aspect of this moral characterisation which we might consider. It is what may be called the moral Jīvan-mukti as distinguished from the metaphysical Jīvan-mukti. He who is able to bear the ferocious onslaught of Kāma and Krodha before he bids good-bye to his body may be called a moral Jīvan-mukta:

> शक्नोतीहैव यः सोढुं प्राक्शरीरविमोक्षणात् ।
> कामक्रोधोद्भवं वेगं स युक्तः स सुखी नरः ॥ V. 23.

(3) *Social.* As regards the social characteristic of the स्थितप्रज्ञ, we may refer to the following famous verse in the Bhagavadgītā:

विद्याविनयसम्पन्ने ब्राह्मणे गवि हस्तिनि ।
शुनि चैव श्वपाके च पण्डिताः समदर्शिनः ॥ V. 18.

For such a man there is equality of vision everywhere. Whether it is a cow or a bullock, a bird or a buffalo, a dog or a dog-eater, a Cāṇḍāla or a Brahmin, there is the same vision for him in all cases. This is what we might call the social characteristic of the स्थितप्रज्ञ.

(4) *Mystical.* Finally, we come to the mystical characterisation. In the first place, it may be noted that such a man is always in an equanimous state of mind :

इहैव तैर्जितः सर्गो येषां साम्ये स्थितं मनः ।
निर्दोषं हि समं ब्रह्म तस्माद्ब्रह्मणि ते स्थिताः ॥ V. 19.

He lives in साम्यावस्था; therefore, he is God. समता is, therefore, the ethico-mystical characteristic of such a स्थितप्रज्ञ. The purely mystical characteristic, however, would be as implied in the line अभितो ब्रह्मनिर्वाणं वर्तते विदितात्मनाम् । (V. 26). Round about him is moving the Brahman ; wherever his eye is cast he sees God. If he looks ahead of himself he sees God ; if he looks behind, he sees God. This is exactly how Jñāneśvara has described the vision of God as experienced by Arjuna. In like manner does Tukārāma speak about his own experience. Inside you can see God ; outside you will be able to see God. You can see God inside, outside, to the left, to the right, above, below and everywhere. हरि हा भोंवे भोंवताला is what Tukārāma says in this connection. When you can see God in such a manner then alone you may be entitled to the name of a स्थितप्रज्ञ. So far then about the mystical characterisation of the स्थितप्रज्ञ.

Beatificism

(*a*) *Beatification, the Crown of Equanimity.* We have discussed above the last element in the conception of the स्थितप्रज्ञ which introduces us to the doctrine of beatificism which, as we saw at the beginning of the chapter, reconciles moralism and super-moralism. In स्थितप्रज्ञ we have a peculiar compound of all the three shades of the ethical theory. But in order to have a correct statement about the स्थितप्रज्ञ, the beatific element must rank the highest. What is the nature of this beatificism? For a full doctrine of beatificism we shall have to go to the Upaniṣads. The doctrine has been fully discussed by the present writer in his "A Constructive Survey of Upaniṣadic Philosophy." As we have said above, the Bhagavadgītā only adumberates the doctrine though for its full statement we must go to the Upaniṣads. Socrates used to say that his happiness was far above the pleasure of the Cyrenaics. Mill has well contrasted the pleasure of a pig and the happiness of Socrates. We may say that to the extent to which the happiness of Socrates rises above the pleasure of a pig, to the same extent does the bliss of a saint rise above the happiness of Socrates. In the Upaniṣads we have a very celebrated beatific doctrine which proceeds by multiplying every smaller unit of happiness a hundred times, this again by another hundred and so on until the bliss of the realised saint has been reached. That is the doctrine of Ānanda in the Upaniṣads. Of course, the Bhagavadgītā does not rise to this high analytic level of the Upaniṣads, but still gives us in its own way a characterisation of Ānanda or Bliss as the chief element in the doctrine of beatificism.

(*b*) *Analusis of Beatification.* There are three points to be noted in this connection. (1) The first is contained in

युञ्जन्नेवं सदाऽऽत्मानं योगी विगतकल्मषः ।
सुखेन ब्रह्मसंस्पर्शमत्यन्तं सुखमश्नुते ॥ VI. 28.

I am indebted to my friend and former colleague and now the Vice-President of the Indian Union, Dr. S.

Radhakrishnan, for having brought to my notice this conception of ब्रह्मसंस्पर्श. I never knew that though I had read the Bhagavadgītā so many times. Touching God, coming into direct *contact* and communion with Him, that is the first element in beatificism. (2) The second point is the *identification* of the Saint and Brahman :

योऽन्तःसुखोऽन्तरारामस्तथाऽन्तर्ज्योतिरेव यः ।
स योगी ब्रह्मनिर्वाणं ब्रह्मभूतोऽधिगच्छति ॥ V. 24.

Having enjoyed the highest bliss inside and having become one with the Brahman, a man reaches the state of Nirvāṇa, the highest bliss. (3) The third point is the identification of the blissful state itself with Brahman : *Bliss is Brahman.*

प्रशान्तमनसं ह्येनं योगिनं सुखमुत्तमम् ।
उपैति शान्तरजसं ब्रह्मभूतमकल्मषम् ॥ VI. 27.

Here I might make a small suggestion. The expression ब्रह्मभूत might go either with the स्थितप्रज्ञ or with the सुख which he enjoys. ब्रह्मभूत is a lamp which gives light both ways by a sort of a देहलीदीपन्याय. That the Saint is full of joy or that he has become one with the Brahman goes without saying. But to say that the bliss which he enjoys is the same thing as Brahman itself involves a certain element of चमत्कृति which will not come in the way of philosophic speculation. The identification of happiness with Reality, the axiological conception of bliss and the metaphysical conception of Brahman are the same. So the enjoyment of ecstatic bliss inside ourselves is the same thing as becoming one with Brahman. Many philosophers have regarded self-consciousness to be the central principle of Reality. If philosophers have prided themselves upon making self-consciousness the pivot upon which all existence turns, why not make beatification itself the pivot and fulcrum of Reality? If we have Idealism in the one case we have Beatificism in the other.

CHAPTER XVIII

THE PROBLEM OF GOD

After considering the antinomies of metaphysics and the ethical problems in the Bhagavadgītā, we shall pass on to the consideration of the general problem of God in the Bhagavadgītā. This problem falls under three major heads, to each of which we shall devote a chapter in the remaining part of our work :–(1) The Nature, the Criteria, the Aspirations and the Search of God; (2) Methods of Meditation for the attainment of God and (3) The Vision of God. The first topic will be discussed under the four following heads:— (i) The Nature of God; (ii) the Criteria of God-realisation; (iii) the Levels of God-aspiration and (iv) the Perils in the Search of God.

The Nature of God

The problem of the nature of God has been tackled times out of number in different countries, in different philosophies and in different languages. Of course, the discussion of this problem in the Bhagavadgītā is a comparatively small one. The only place where it is somewhat philosophically treated is the twelfth chapter of the Bhagavadgītā, where a distinction is drawn between Saguṇa Upāsanā and Avyakta Upāsanā. As we shall see very soon, the chief object of the Bhagavadgītā is a practical one and instead of spending much labour upon a theoretical discussion of the Nature of God, it suggests to us certain methods by means of which God could be practically attained. These methods, as we shall see in the next chapter, are the ideological method, the moral method and the mystical method. After a consideration of these methods, we shall proceed to tackle the problem of the Vision of God in the chapter after the next. Both in respect of the Nature of God and the Vision of God, the Upaniṣads stand as an ideal to which the Bhagavadgītā always points. In fact, we may say that the highest peak ever reached in the whole range of Indian or European thought in regard to the nature and vision of God is to be found in the Upaniṣads themselves. We shall not, however, enter into a detailed discussion of these problems here. We have dealt with them thoroughly in another work " A Constructive Survey of Upaniṣadic philosophy." It is only necessary to point out here that the Bhagavadgītā is regarded and justly regarded as offering a faint replica of the doctrines of the Upaniṣads. We must, however, remember that though the Gītā derived its inspiration from the Upaniṣads, it had to consider the problem in a setting peculiarly its own.

Just before the times of the Bhagavadgītā, Sāṁkhya and Yoga had attained to a certain height of speculation. They were passing through various stages of formulation. No rigorous systems had yet been evolved. The whole philosophical atmosphere was surcharged with Sāṁkhya and Yoga speculations. The Bhagavadgītā was naturally influenced by these speculations of Sāṁkhya and Yoga. Also contemporaneously with this were probably the systems of the Brahmasūtras which were coming into being. It is a question as to what is the exact meaning of the Brahmasūtras referred to by the Bhagavadgītā in the thirteenth chapter. It is not unlikely that they refer to the Bādarāyaṇa Sūtras. Scholars are divided on this point. Nevertheless, the Bādarāyaṇa

Sūtras formulated the different problems of Vedānta Philosophy. The Brahmasūtras of Bādarāyaṇa and the Bhagavadgītā inter-referred to each other, the Gītā referring to the Brahmasūtras by name and Brahmasūtras referring to the Bhagavadgītā by doctrine and making a logical improvement upon it. All this is familiar to students of Indian Philosophy. Though the Buddhist and the Jain systems had not begun their speculative formulations at the time of the Bhagavadgītā, they closely followed it. The Bhagavadgītā does not seem to have been influenced in any way by the speculations of these systems; their denial of God had its nemesis only in the Apotheosis of their Founders. As we have seen elsewhere in this book, there are only a few references to Nirvāṇa in the Bhagavadgītā, for example:—

(1) लभन्ते ब्रह्मनिर्वाणमृषयः क्षीणकल्मषाः । V. 25.

(2) अभितो ब्रह्मनिर्वाणं वर्तते विदितात्मनाम् । V. 26.

where the meaning is bliss rather than annihilation. The source of the reference to Ahiṁsā in the Bhagavadgītā (XVI. 2) is traceable to the Cāndogya Upaniṣad.

अहिंसा सत्यवचनमिति ता अस्य दक्षिणाः । III. 17. 4.

The Buddhistic doctrine of Nirvāṇa and the Jain doctrine of Ahiṁsā came a little later. At the present stage of our discourse, therefore, it will be only necessary to consider the Gītā doctrine of God with reference to the systems of Sāṁkhya and Yoga and the Brahmasūtras of Bādarāyana.

(*a*) *God in Sāṁkhya.* The Sāṁkhya system was a negation of God in favour of what its author chooses to call the Puruṣa. There must be indeed a plurality of Puruṣas according to the author, but there is a sub-conscious reference to a single Puruṣa in the first Kārikā, न प्रकृतिर्नापि विकृतिः पुरुषः । It is a psycho-analytical indication that he believed not in a plurality of Puruṣas but in one single Puruṣa which was the nearest approach to the conception of God. Somehow the Sāṁkhya philosophers seemed to be afraid of God, while the "last of the Romans", Pañcaśikha, felt the necessity of such a one in the Twenty-sixth Principle which he chose to call God. Puruṣa, according to the Sāṁkhya system, was absolutely uncontaminated by actions ; in other words, he is केवल, अकर्ता and द्रष्टा while Prakṛti alone is the कर्त्री. This peculiar doctrine of the activity of Prakṛti and the uncontaminated perceptive isolation of Puruṣa influenced the Bhagavadgītā to a very great extent. In fact, there are many passages in the Bhagavadgītā which have been written under that influence. For example, look at the passage :

> कार्यकारणकर्तृत्वे हेतुः प्रकृतिरुच्यते ।
> पुरुषः सुखदुःखानां भोक्तृत्वे हेतुरुच्यते ॥ XIII. 20.

Stress is laid only on the activity of Prakṛti while the fruit of the action falls to the lot of Puruṣa. In fact, instead of regarding Puruṣa as absolutely uncontaminated, the Sāṁkhya would regard him as suffering vicariously for the actions of Prakṛti. In tune with it we find an utterance in the Sāṁkhya Kārikā, 65, which tells us that Puruṣa cannot be regarded as entirely unconcerned. Also an utterance is to be found in Kārikā 36 :

> एते प्रदीपकल्पाः परस्परविलक्षणा गुणविशेषाः ।
> कृत्स्नं पुरुषस्यार्थं प्रकाश्य बुद्धौ प्रयच्छन्ति ॥

which speaks about पुरुषार्थ or the purpose which Puruṣa has in view. It does away with the isolation or the mere perceptive function of Puruṣa and puts an irremovable break in the activity of Prakṛti with the result that the entire structure of the Sāṁkhya Philosophy falls to the ground.

(*b*) *God in Yoga.* The Yoga system does not fare better. It may be regarded as a half-way house between Sāṁkhya and Vedānta. Yoga allows God but cripples His supreme function. In fact, it seems that people in those days were living in a region of non-contamination, and even the God of Yoga is uncontaminated as Puruṣa of Sāṁkhya is : क्लेशकर्मविपाकाशयैरपरामृष्टः पुरुषविशेष ईश्वरः। Yoga Sūtra (1, 24). Yoga speaks about पुरुषविशेष, while Sāṁkhya speaks only about पुरुष. While Puruṣas in Sāṁkhya are all on a level, the God in Yoga is a पुरुषविशेष, a *primus inter pares.* Again, from a different point of view, Yoga makes some concession to the devotional element by postulating that ईश्वर may 'also' be regarded as a way to realisation. It may be noted that ईश्वर is not regarded here as the only way to realisation but may be permitted to be so regarded. In fact, the God of Yoga is nothing but an epiphenomenon or an appendix to the Sāṁkhya system. Yoga occupies a halting position ; it does not allow the element of activity to its God. We are told, of course, that ईश्वर is to be regarded as the one Reality (एकतत्त्व), as being omniscient (सर्वज्ञ), as being the remover of obstacles or Antarāyas and as being the supreme teacher (Parama Guru) who lives beyond time. There is, however, one very important contribution which the Yoga system makes to the doctrine of realisation, namely, its identification of God with the Ātman. तदा द्रष्टुः स्वरूपेऽवस्थानम् is the ideal teaching of its practical philosophy ; and even though the God of Yoga might be admitted as a mere necessity of thought, the practical and the most important ideal which the Yoga system aims at is the realisation of the Ātman.

(c) *God in the Brahmasūtra.* If we analyse the conception of God in the Brahmasūtras of Bādarāyaṇa, we find that it has two aspects, the personal and the impersonal. We may take the liberty of quoting four epithets for each to designate the highest Reality. In the Brahmasūtras the Impersonal God has been described as अव्यक्त, अदृश्य, अक्षर, अरूप; and the Personal God as अन्तर्यामिन्, शारीर, अनन्त and वैश्वानर. This double formulation of the conception of God in the Brahmasūtras was responsible for the later Advaita and non-Advaita systems. In fact, it is this conception of the personal and the impersonal aspects of God that has reigned supreme in all philosophies. Śaṁkara and Rāmānuja, Kabīra and Tulasīdāsa, Bradley and Ward, Mansūr and Mahomed have all been divided among themselves according to the difference in their attitudes towards the impersonalistic and the personalistic aspects of God.

(d) *God in the Bhagavadgītā.* It is no wonder that the Bhagavadgītā should have also been influenced by this difference between the personal and the impersonal aspects of the God. Though the Bhagavadgītā does not devote much attention to this difference, still in the beginning of the twelfth chapter it makes a distinction between Saguṇa Upāsanā and Avyakta Upāsanā. The stage at which the Bhagavadgītā recommends Avyakta Upāsanā is a very difficult one indeed (क्लेशोऽधिकतरस्तेषामव्यक्तासक्तचेतसाम् । XII.5), because, according to it, it is most difficult to reach the Avyakta ideal so long as one lives in the body. अव्यक्ता हि गतिर्दुःखं देहवद्भिरवाप्यते । The general upshot of the teaching of the Bhagavadgītā in this respect seems to be that the Saguṇa Upāsanā might be regarded as even higher than the Avyakta Upāsanā. ते प्राप्नुवन्ति मामेव सर्वभूतहिते रताः। (XII.4). We cannot, however, afford to enter here into the relative values of the personalistic and the impersonalistic conceptions of God. It forms an independent subject and it must be viewed not merely from the point of view of the Bhagavadgītā, but also from that of the different Vedāntic systems, schools of contemporary philosophy and the religious systems of the world, where great philosophers and sages have tried to determine the nature of their highest God. The most important point, however, which the Bhagavadgītā makes is not the determination of the nature of God, but the way for the practical attainment of Him. In this respect we shall later deal with three different methods enabling us to attain practically to the God-head. In fact, to come to grips with the attainment of God from the practical point of view is a far greater achievement than to determine the nature of God from the philosophical point of view, which would merely plunge us into a bog of intellectual warfare.

The Criteria of God-realisation

We now proceed to a discussion of the criteria of God-realisation. I myself have discussed the question in many places. When I wrote the introductory section to my book, "Pathway to God in Hindi Literature", I summarised and presented in a slightly different form how the problem appeared to me in "Mysticism in Maharashtra." Here I am not going to enter into the details of a full theory of mystical experience. I am concerning myself only with what the Bhagavadgītā itself tells us about the criteria of mystical experience. In one famous line of the ninth chapter, the Bhagavadgītā speaks of the mystical experience as प्रत्यक्षावगमं धर्म्यं सुसुखं कर्तुमव्ययम्। (IX. 2). These are very pregnant words, प्रत्यक्षावगमं, सुसुखं and अव्ययम्. They contain in themselves all the criteria of mystical experience that could be imagined.

(*a*) *Super-sensuousness, Intuition and Central Initiation*. Let us see what these terms mean. The first is प्रत्यक्षावगमम्. The Bhagavadgītā tells us that our experience would be real only if it becomes an object of प्रत्यक्ष. Now what is this प्रत्यक्ष ? Is it an actual demonstration ? Is it what the physical eye sees or is it what the inner eye might be expected to see ? The Bhagavadgītā uses the word प्रत्यक्ष not in the physical or physiological sense, but in the super-sensuous and mystical sense. In these three words, प्रत्यक्षावगम, सुसुख and अव्यय, all the main criteria of mystical experience have been well expressed. प्रत्यक्ष is super-sensuousness; सुसुख, सुतरां सुख is beatification or bliss and अव्यय is permanence or continuity. Suppose I get an experience to-day and I fail to get it or lose it tomorrow, that is no real experience at all. The mystical experience must pervade our states of consciousness, for example, जाग्रत्, स्वप्न and तुर्य. The experience which Akrūra got as described in the Bhāgavata (X. 39.39-45) of the form of Kṛṣṇa while he had dipped in the Yamunā, and again while he was looking at Kṛṣṇa's form in the chariot outside is a compound of the mystical and the visual, each being a corroboration of the other. We may note that super-sensuousness, intuition and central initiation are merely different ways of speaking about the same matter. Super-sensuousness is what corresponds to transcendence of senses. Intuition refers to the faculty by which we get that spiritual experience. 'Central initiation' is a peculiar expression. In the physiological sphere it is opposed to what we may call peripheral initiation. It is not anything impinging upon our senses from the outside that constitutes beatific experience; it is something which comes from inside. As psychologists of mystical experience are aware, the different forms which the mystic sees, the sounds that he hears, the smells that he enjoys and so on, are not drawn from the outside world. They come from within. They are centrally initiated. Hence प्रत्यक्ष—super-sensuousness, intuition and central initiation as opposed to peripheral initiation—is what constitutes the first criterion.

(*b*) *Beatification.* The second is सुसुख, beatification or bliss. As we have pointed out elsewhere, this bliss is as much above what we call happiness as happiness is above pleasure. The bliss of a saint is as much above the happiness of Socrates as the happiness of Socrates is above the pleasure of a pig.

(*c*) *Permanence or Continuity.* अव्यय, continuity or permanence, subsumes under it universality, both metaphysical and logical, which philosophers like Kant have carefully considered. Incidentally, we may say that this continuity subsumes under it what saints like Mirābāī have spoken about the growth of spiritual experience. Daily growth in spiritual experience is also a vital factor in its continuity or permanence. दिन दिन बढत सवायो. The Bhagavadgītā thus speaks about the different criteria of mystical experience. Our mystical experience must not only be super-sensuous and blissful, but it must also be continuous and permanent. It must not desert us; we may desert it, because at the time of death we are nowhere but that experience remains. That Anāhata Śabda which we hear remains, that mystical form which we see remains, while our body falls off, as a great saint used to say. They are continuous and permanent. There are other criteria of mystical experience but we are not concerned with them in this chapter.

Levels of God-aspiration

(*a*) *Six Categories of God–seekers.* The next point which we shall consider in this chapter is the levels of God-aspiration in the Bhagavadgītā. The Bhagavadgītā writes its new divine comedy. In his Divine Comedy Dante has described the *Inferno*, the *Purgatorio* and the *Paradiso.* The Bhagavadgītā speaks about six different categories so far as aspirations towards God are concerned. There is this one great similarity between the Bhagavadgītā and Dante that they both relegate the unrepentent sinners for ever to the *Inferno*, who are thus condemned for ever.

तानहं द्विषतः क्रूरान् संसारेषु नराधमान् ।
क्षिपाम्यजस्रमशुभानासुरीष्वेव योनिषु ॥
आसुरीं योनिमापन्ना मूढा जन्मनि जन्मनि ।
मामप्राप्यैव कौन्तेय ततो यान्त्यधमां गतिम् ॥ XVI. 19–20.

They are not allowed to rise. (1) The unrepentent sinners, therefore, constitute the first category. They cannot hope to do anything to better their lives. Both the Bhagavadgītā and Dante deny the possibility of any reformation in their character. I think we should be a little generous. Even they should be allowed to come up somewhat nearer to the life of spirit, as the Bhagavadgītā later on itself admits. (2) (a) The second category consists of those who are merged in the miseries of existence. People suffer from various kinds of miseries in this life. Some people fall dangerously ill, some meet with dangerous accidents, some are subject to dangerous epidemics, some are subject to bomb-falls, thunderbolts, earthquakes and so on; everywhere there is a miserable state of existence.

> बाप दुःखाचें केणें सुटलें । जेथ मरणाचें भरे लोटले ।
> तेथ मृत्युलोकींचें शेवटिलें । हाटवेळे येणें जाहलें ॥ Jñā. IX. 496.

says Jñāneśvara. That is what prompted Buddha to go out of the miseries of life to a superior state. So those who are plunged in misery draw therefrom an incentive towards spiritual life. (b) Then there are those who are afraid of Jarā and Maraṇa, old age and death, as is so often emphasised by the Hindi saints.

> घर बनाया, तैयार यह जब घर हुवा ।
> मौतका डंका बजा, बेहद दिलमें डर हुआ ।

In that way an unprecedented terror takes hold of the heart of a man when he reaches the age of seventy, not to speak of the age of eighty. So Jarā and Maraṇa constitute, like miseries of life, powerful incentives for turning a man's attention towards God. This is the second category of those people who go in search of God. (3) The third is the category of the end-seekers, those who have got a particular desire to be fulfilled. A man might wish to go into the I.A.S., a man might aspire to become the President of the Union, he might aim at winning victory in war, or he might desire to be a Hitler or a Roosevelt and so on. All these are end-seekers. The category of end-seekers may also include those who propitiate God for the fulfilment of a particular end. Even the great Shivaji was prompted to follow the path of spirit in accordance with the instructions of Rāmadāsa, with a national and political end in view, because he thought that the life of spirit alone would come to his help. We have considered three categories so far, namely, the unrepentent sinners, the miserable and the end-seekers. (4) The fourth is the category of repentent sinners. The Bhagavadgītā has got a very open heart and is very charitable towards these people. It seems that the Bhagavadgītā has also 'repented' for the repentent sinners. Show me a man, says a passage from a sacred book, who has never looked at another man's woman with an eye of lust. It does not matter if you sin, but repent you must.

अपि चेत्सुदुराचारो भजते मामनन्यभाक् ।
साधुरेव स मन्तव्यः सम्यग् व्यवासितो हि सः ॥ IX. 30.

I think no better lines could have been written about the future of a repentent sinner. It is not impossible for him to hand himself over to God. St. Augustine's mother wept before St. Ambrose and St. Ambrose promised that the child of those tears would never perish, and so St. Augustine became the second founder of Christianity. Similarly the Bhagavadgītā holds out a hope for the repentent sinners. (5) and (6) Then there are two more categories to be discussed: those who are intellectual seekers of God, and those who have reached their spiritual end—the जिज्ञासु and the ज्ञानी. These have been also otherwise described by the Bhagavadgītā as the आरुरुक्षु and the आरूढ, those who want to ascend and those who have ascended. The question arises whether anybody in this world has hitherto climbed absolutely to the top of existence (कीर्तिः पृष्ठं गिरेरिव.). That was what a great Upaniṣadic sage said after having reached, according to his lights, the top-most part of existence. The only criterion for the reality of a man's experience is himself and God and nobody else. There is no intellectual argument, no logical proof which can either support or refute or deny what he might say. The reality of his experience and the heights which he has reached are known only to himself and to his Maker. Those who have reached the end might thus constitute the top-most part of the *paradiso* in Dante. These on the whole, then, by an analysis of the teachings of the Bhagavadgītā, might be regarded as constituting the six different categories of God-seekers.

(*b*) *The Perils in the Search of God.* Now we come to the last problem, the perils in the search of God. The path of the seekers of God is beset with immense difficulties. क्षुरस्य धारा निशिता दुरत्यया, says the Upaniṣad. They have to walk on the edge of a razor. (1) God is a great artificer, he is a juggler, he hides his art and the powers of his art. It is for that reason, says the Bhagavadgītā, that the spiritual life goes underground from time to time. स कालेनेह महता योगो नष्टः परंतप । (IV. 2). The river of spiritual experience hides itself like the Phalgu. By the evidence of Kṛṣṇa himself, we understand that the river of spiritual experience had gone underground with the passage of time and it was for God-men like him to remove the sands and to bring it to light. The great artificer God thus finds it necessary—for what purpose we do not know— to hide the river of spiritual experience for the time being. (2) Secondly, it is extremely difficult to meet a man who has reached the highest spiritual end. The Kaṭhopaniṣad has pointed out the difficulty of meeting such a man. अणीयान्ह्यतर्क्यमणुप्रमाणात् । (I. 2. 8.) If you are fortunate enough to meet an आत्मज्ञ, then that would be another matter. It is only he who has realised his identity with God, who is capable of imparting the secret of spiritual life. अनन्यप्रोक्ते गतिरत्र नास्ति । (I. 2. 8.) Such persons are rare. It is the rarity of such persons which constitutes another obstacle for those who want either to enter the spiritual path or to rise to the full stature of mystical experience. Now the question is how to approach such a teacher. The Bhagavadgītā answers it in the following words: तद्विद्धि प्रणिपातेन परिप्रश्नेन सेवया। (IV. 34). You have to bow before him, you have to serve him. Your salutations and your services are not enough. Ask him all sorts of circumlocutory questions if you have got the power and if he has the time and the inclination to answer. In that way you might be able to get an iota or a fraction of insight into the spiritual life if he condescends to reply to your परिप्रश्नs. (3) We now go to the third peril. Even supposing that a man is fortunate to commence his journey on the spiritual path, a vast amount of time is necessary to enable him to go ahead, not to speak of reaching the end. तत्स्वयं योगसंसिद्धः कालेनात्मनि विन्दति। (IV. 38.) It is not a two years', three years' or a five years' plan that would be enough to enable him to reach the God-hood. In fact, time has got nothing to do with it. What is wanted is the inner quality of the heart which may enable him to conquer time. In order, however, that that quality might be attained, अभ्यास may be necessary but it is not all. If you have reached a particular stage of भाव, then neither much time nor much practice would be needed. Normally, however, people are not endowed with that kind of भाव. Therefore, they have to depend both upon practice and time (अभ्यास and काल). Suppose a man has spent about fifty years of his life in the spiritual pursuit; of course, it may be granted that he may be on a comparatively higher level than what he occupied a few years ago; but he can never be said, only on that account, to have reached the Absolute End. (4) It is just here that we meet with the fourth difficulty in the way of our spiritual life, namely, destiny or what the Greeks would call *moria*. Crores of people might try to heighten their spiritual life, but there is an element of chance, what in philosophical terminology may be called indeterminism or in theological terms the Will of God. It is only by the Will of God that one among millions of people is able to attain to the highest end. These then are the perils which stand in the way of our consummation of the spiritual life.

CHAPTER XIX

METHODS OF MEDITATION

The Ideological Method

Meditation on Ten Conceptions. We shall now proceed to the three chief methods of meditation. The first is the ideological method. We shall stress ten different points in this ideological meditation. We are to meditate on the idea of God. Absolutistic philosophers, those who are intellectually inclined, those who want to reach their highest end by philosophical pursuits, would find this a very helpful device. Let us concentrate on these ten different conceptions of meditation :

(*i*) *Puruṣottama.* The first is the conception of पुरुषोत्तम. Now this उत्तम पुरुष is here contrasted with the क्षर पुरुष and the अक्षर पुरुष. The Bhagavadgītā has here used the word पुरुष in a very loose sense. All existences in the universe are called क्षर पुरुष. The Self that is immanent in them is called अक्षर पुरुष, while the परमात्मन् who rules over all is called उत्तम पुरुष. It is a very peculiar doctrine to call all existences in the universe by the name of पुरुष, unless one takes a fully pantheistic view without making a distinction between the material and the spiritual existences. It may not be wrong to call the Self that resides in these as well as the Self that rules all material and spiritual existences by the name of पुरुष. But to call all elemental and animate existences by the name of पुरुष is a travesty of words. We are, however, here concerned with meditation on the उत्तम पुरुष, the all-pervading परमात्मन् who rules over all material and spiritual existences alike. It is a very good conception indeed.

(*ii*) *Sūtra.* The second is the ideological meditation on the Sūtra. This word is familiar to students of Upaniṣadic philosophy. Sūtra is a thread that passes through the pearls of a necklace. God is such a Sūtra, as He calls Himself, which passes through all objects, mental as well as physical : मयि सर्वमिदं प्रोतं सूत्रे मणिगणा इव । (VII. 7). The author of the Bhagavadgītā, does not use the word अन्तर्यामिन्. He uses the word Sūtra only, and the Upaniṣads and the Vedānta systems use both सूत्र and अन्तर्यामिन्. But we might take the word Sūtra as coming up to the level of the अन्तर्यामिन्, that is immanent in all the existences of the world.

(*iii*) *Vaiśvānara.* The third is a very important conception, namely, that of वैश्वानर. It is not merely the gastric fire that is spoken of in अहं वैश्वानरो भूत्वा प्राणिनां देहमाश्रितः । (XV. 14), not the terrestrial fire, nor the fire on the hearth, but the celestial fire as in Herakleitos and Zoroaster. It implies that spiritual entity which lives in all human beings as well as in all material objects of existence. By a sort of अजहल्लक्षणा, the word नर not merely implies all human beings, but includes also all other beings as well as material objects. So contemplate on God, if you like, by regarding Him as वैश्वानर, the individual and supreme spirit, which inhabits and enlivens all animate and inanimate existences.

(*iv*) *Ravi.* You might, if you like, contemplate on God as Ravi, the Sun of the World of Ideas as in Plato. Plato tells us that the Sun is responsible for generation and growth of things in the world. Similarly is the Ātman responsible for generation and growth of all objects in the world: यथा प्रकाशयत्येकः कृत्स्नं लोकमिमं रविः। (XIII. 33). The word Ravi also connotes the quality of transcendence. Just as the Sun and the Sky are uncontaminated by any existences whatsoever, similarly is the Ātman uncontaminated by any existences, being transcendent to all of them. So we can even meditate on God as a great transcendent Being.

(v) *Māyī.* Again, you can contemplate on God by regarding Him as Māyī as the Upaniṣads put it. The word Māyā occurs in the Upaniṣads in many senses as we have shown in "A Constructive Survey of Upaniṣadic Philosophy." But the Bhagavadgītā uses it principally in the sense of power, though it does not deny to it a touch of illusion in another connection. भ्रामयन्सर्वभूतानि यन्त्रारूढानि मायया। (XVIII. 61), मम माया दुरत्यया। (VII. 14). We do not propose to enter into the question as to whether Māyā may be regarded as realistic or unrealistic. Still it is undoubted that God possesses this Māyā. He may be described as मायावी, मायी, मायावान् or मायापरिवृत. But He certainly lives in a camouflage and does not allow Himself to be seen. Let us try to penetrate the camouflage. In that way we may be able to reach at least the outskirts of some concrete reality. That is another way of the ideological meditation.

(vi) *Rasa.* Another way of meditation is to regard God as Rasa. The word Rasa has been used in three different senses, as taste, essence and bliss. When the Bhagavadgītā says रसवर्जं रसोऽप्यस्य परं दृष्ट्वा निवर्तते। (II. 59), it refers to taste. Rasa may also be regarded as essence. And finally, it may also mean as in the Upaniṣadic expression, रसो वै सः। रसं ह्येवायं लब्ध्वाऽऽनन्दीभवति।, mellifluous juice or bliss. Rasa is that Amṛta by tasting which one reaches supreme beatification. So let us meditate on God as Rasa, the mellifluous supreme spiritual nectar.

(*vii*) *Tajjalān.* You may also contemplate on God as तज्जलान्, to use a very famous Upaniṣadic expression, that from which all things proceed, that in which all things are ultimately resolved and that in which they live and move and have their being. Aristotle has defined the word Substance exactly in the same manner, that from which all things spring, that in which all things live and that to which they ultimately repair. The Bhagavadgītā likewise has told us that we should contemplate on God as the source of all things, the annihilation of all things and the life of all things. These conceptions exactly correspond to what the Upaniṣads suggest in that cryptic expression तज्जलान् (छां. III. 14). We might incidentally mention that the same function which may be served by meditation on the cryptic formula तज्जलान् would be accomplished still more elaborately by meditation on the comprehensive twelve-pointed verse from the Bhagavadgītā :

> गतिर्भर्ता प्रभुः साक्षी निवासः शरणं सुहृत् ।
> प्रभवः प्रलयः स्थानं निधानं बीजमव्ययम् ॥ IX. 18.

which is one of the finest verses in spiritual literature. This verse brings together the personalistic and impersonalistic conceptions of God. Think of God in any way you like; but if you meditate upon this one single verse, it will bring you nearer to the knowledge of God.

(*viii*) *Atiṣṭhāna.* There is a further way of meditation on God by regarding Him as अतिष्ठान. Of course, everybody knows that God is the अधिष्ठान, the substratum of all existence. But what is meant by this अतिष्ठान ! The

Bhagavadgītā tells us विष्टभ्याहमिदं कृत्स्नमेकांशेन स्थितो जगत्। (X. 42). I have pervaded the whole universe, says the Lord, by a part of me and have remained infinitely outside. In this way not merely all objects of excellence, call them विभूतिमत्, श्रीमत् or ऊर्जित, have sprung from a portion of God; but God has remained infinitely outside, an absolutely transcendent Being.

(*ix*) *Jñeya*. The next category of ideological meditation would be to meditate on God as the supreme ज्ञेय, either in the philosophical or the mystical sense. Philosophically, we might contemplate on God as transcending all dualities, as being beyond both existence and non-existence, beyond good and bad, as being beyond the qualities and the qualityless, as being untouched and yet the support of all and as being too subtle to be comprehended.

ज्ञेयं यत्तत्प्रवक्ष्यामि यज्ज्ञात्वाऽमृतमश्नुते ।
अनादिमत्परं ब्रह्म न सत् तन्नासदुच्यते ॥ XIII. 12.

This, of course, is a very difficult way of meditation. Mystically, we might 'think' about it as having its hands and feet everywhere, its eyes, ears and faces in all directions, as being within and without all existing objects and as being both far and near (XIII 13). This, however, is only mystical thought and not yet mystical experience.

(*x*) *Āścarya*. Finally, you might contemplate on God as the supreme object of wonder, almost tantamount to the Unknowable of Spencer or the x^n of Huxley. The Bhagavadgītā tells us :

आश्चर्यवत् पश्यति कश्चिदेन-
माश्चर्यवद्वदति तथैव चान्यः ।
आश्चर्यवच्चैनमन्यः शृणोति
श्रुत्वाऽप्येनं वेद न चैव कश्चित् ॥ II. 29.

Śaṁkarācārya explains श्रुत्वा as including, by a sort of an अजहल्लक्षणा, both दृष्ट्वा and उक्त्वा. Nobody has yet ever been born upon this earth who has known this God. God cannot be seen, God cannot be expressed by word of mouth and God cannot be heard. God is the greatest wonder of all existence.

If you gather together all these different conceptions, you can meditate on God ideologically in any one of these ten different ways as (1) the highest person, (2) the immanent thread of all existence, (3) the highest individual and supreme spirit, (4) the Sun of the World of Ideas, (5) the great artificer, (6) the mellifluous essence of all existence, (7) the supreme source of all generation, growth and decay, (8) the absolutely transcendent Being, (9) the highest object of knowledge or (10) the greatest wonder of all wonders. What a great panorama of supreme objects of meditation would there be now for you! You may not be sure that such an ideological meditation would put you in possession of God. But at least it will take you a few steps ahead in your spiritual pursuit. This is a point which has not been so elaborately discussed anywhere else.

Moral Method

(*a*) *Meditation on Virtues, Individual and Social.* The conception of ideological meditation sprang in my own mind, but the idea of moral meditation came to me from other sources. Now what is moral meditation? There are many persons in this world who do not regard God as a Personal Being, who do not believe in God at all, but who believe in ethical values. Let them contemplate on God as an ethical value. In the year 1908 when I had been to Shanti Kunj in Banaras along with prof. E. A. Wodehouse, I met there two persons of the Theosophical Society, Mr. Samant and Mr. D. K. Telang. Mr. Samant was a very fine man and we had a heart-to-heart talk. I already had some spiritual experiences at that time, and, therefore, whatever he said was to me of great value. He said, " The practice in Esoteric Section of our Theosophical Society is to contemplate on virtues." " Upon what virtues do you contemplate ? ", I asked. He quoted the first two verses of the sixteenth chapter of the Bhagavadgītā :

अभयं सत्त्वसंशुद्धिर्ज्ञानयोगव्यवस्थितिः ।
दानं दमश्च यज्ञश्च स्वाध्यायस्तप आर्जवम् ॥
अहिंसा सत्यमक्रोधस्त्यागः शान्तिरपैशुनम् ।
दया भूतेष्वलोलुप्त्वं मार्दवं ह्रीरचापलम् ॥ XVI. 1–2.

We have already seen how from four different chapters the Gītā has gathered together different series of virtues. Most probably as I had already got some spiritual experience, even though I was not a theosophist, Mrs. Besant admitted me to the Esoteric Hall. Contemplation on these virtues is what is inculcated in this Esoteric Section of the Theosophical Society. This is a very healthy principle. For the sake of such meditation we might select a few of these moral virtues and try to inculcate them firmly in our mind.

1. Fearlessness......... अभयम्
2. Purity .... शौचम्
3. Self-Control........ आत्मविनिग्रहः
4. Equanimity......... समत्वम्
5. Equality of life..... अहिंसा
6. Bravery .... शौर्यम्

7. Compassion......... दया
8. Humility........... अमानित्वम्
9. Forbearance......... क्षमा

For example, if you want to develop the virtue of fearlessness, you should try to do one fearless action every day. After a number of days you will find that that virtue is gathering force in you. There is also another method for the stabilising of a particular virtue in our mind. I had recently a conversation with another old member of Esoteric School of the Theosophical Society, Mr. Dastoor at Nasik, who told me that if we wanted to develop a particular virtue we should harbour it in our mind for three months. What did Buddha contemplate on except these social and ethical virtues? He could not contemplate upon a non-entity. What did Patañjali suggest in regard to the contemplation on such moral virtues as मैत्री, करुणा, मुदिता and उपेक्षा? Our mind becomes pure, he tells us, our mind gathers a force and a power, when we concentrate upon such ethical conceptions as sympathy, compassion, contentment and detachment. In a celebrated Sūtra, Patañjali has also advised us to contemplate on Ananta, the thousand hooded serpent-God who holds the worlds securely on his crest, if we want to develop the virtue of स्थैर्य or stability.

(*b*) ἔθος (*Custom*) and ἦθος (*Character*). Even Aristotle, the great author of Nicomachean Ethics, tells us 'ἔθος is ἦθος.' No virtue could be contemplated on unless we have practised that particular virtue day after day in our life. In that way habit becomes character, as Aristotle tells us. This is exactly what the Theosophists did. A great modern psychologist, William James, has told us that even though we may not believe that God and freedom and immortality are real, let us act from day to day as if they are real, and one day, they will become real for us. The practice of ethical virtues is higher than these metaphysical ideas. Tulasīdāsa uses the expressions निरंतर and बहुकरमा as helps to our stabilising these virtues in us. So great is the value of contemplation on moral virtues which we have noticed. They may not take you to God. They will give you the gunpowder; only a spark might be required and then there might be a spiritual explosion. Thus this moral meditation also is of great value.

Mystical Method

Let us now pass on to the third method of God-realisation. We have hitherto spoken about the ideological method and the moral method, which are suitable more or less for philosophers and moralists; but the mystical method I am going to expound is suitable for any human being according to the level of his qualifications and ideals. This is a very practical method and has been practised by all great aspirants. What we have to do here, however, is to distinguish the relevant from the irrelevant. I myself had known about this method in my boyhood when I used to recite the Bhagavadgītā and began to practise it at the age of eighteen. I shall stress here some points which might be useful for beginners, seekers as well as those who have made some advance in their spiritual realisation. Under the mystical method, we shall deal with four points. There is a physiological element in this mystical method, then there is what we might call a psycho-ethical element, thirdly, there is the devotional element, and finally, the element of Grace. When all these are fully present, we might say that the mystical method has achieved its purpose.

(*a*) *Physiological Element.* What is meant by the physiological element in the mystical method of realisation? It has been customary among people to suppose that it is the posture or Āsana which has got everything to do in the matter of meditation; it is not so at all. Many people have spent their time and labour for many years in the performance of Āsanas in the hope that they might be able to achieve their end. This method of postures cannot take us far in achieving our spiritual end. But it has its own use of which we must take advantage. We hear of our Prime Minister Shri Nehru performing शीर्षासन and thereby filling his own body and mind with energy which is really wonderful. I have also seen other Āsanas being performed and great energy of body and mind being achieved. But the energy of body and mind does not mean either moral energy or spiritual energy, so that the method of postures fails in the achievement of our spiritual ideal. The moral energy might be dependent to a certain extent upon mental energy, and people might become more or less moral, but the spiritual experience is *sui generis* and cannot be given by the method of Āsanas alone. Patañjali in his *Yogasūtra* has told us that the only Āsana that a Sādhaka should perform is one in which he can sit or lie down for a long time and at the same time fill himself with joy in such a way that he may not be required to move from his seat: स्थिरसुखमासनम् (II.46). Any Āsana, therefore, in which we can continue our God-meditation for a long time and in a happy mood is the Āsana that is useful for us. I have myself used four or five different Āsanas in my early spiritual career, but that Āsana alone has value which enables us to sit for a long time in our contemplative mood.

The second point in the physiological element is breath-control. A good number of things barring probably the highest have been achieved by breath-control. We have heard various recipes for breath-control. A good number of Kumbhakas have been regarded as having some function to perform in the matter of God-realisation. They might, like the Āsanas, put the mind in a certain equable mood, no doubt, but in themselves they cannot lead to spiritual realisation. In the Upaniṣads we are told about ऊर्ध्वं प्राणमुन्नयत्यपानं प्रत्यगस्यति । मध्ये वामनमासीनं विश्वे देवा उपासते ॥ (Ka. Up. V. 3). Between the up-going breath and the down-coming breath there is a beautiful or dwarfish God, Vāmana, whom all the gods adore. We have heard of a method suggested by Ignatius Loyola that each of the words in the Lord's prayer beginning with "Our Father which art in heaven, hallowed be Thy Name" should be interspersed with an incoming breath and an out-going breath. So also there is a method suggested by the Bhagavadgītā in that cryptic utterance, प्राणापानौ समौ कृत्वा नासाभ्यन्तरचारिणौ । (V. 37). It was in the year 1905 when Lok. Tilak was speaking and Dr. Garde of Poona was presiding at a summer lecture in Poona that Dr. Garde who, as you might be knowing, had dedicated his life to spiritual realisation in his own way, invited the audience to find out the meaning of the expression, प्राणापानौ समौ कृत्वा, which was highly thought-provoking. The Prāṇa and Apāna must be equalised. Anyone who has tried this experiment will see that they are generally never equal, that one is always longer than the other; and it is only when Prāṇa and Apāna become equal that a mental equilibrium is created. Sometimes it also happens that both Prāṇa and Apāna might stop altogether, a Kevala Kumbhaka might be produced and the man might live without breathing. This state would certainly be useful for spiritual contemplation. Śaṁkarācārya has said that there might be a thousand kinds of Kumbhakas but the best of them all is the Kevala Kumbhaka : सहस्रशः सन्तु हठेषु कुम्भाः सम्भाव्यते केवलकुम्भ एव । (Śaṁkara : Yogatārāvali, 10.)

Then the third point in the physiological element is that of sight. We are told by the Bhagavadgītā that we should look at the tip of the nose (नासिकाग्र). What is meant by नासिकाग्र ? Evidently there are two meanings; it might mean either the tip of the nose or the top of the nose. They are both useful only so far as they would draw the sight of the man from the external objects to something internal which he wants to see. But दृष्टि or sight by itself and in itself is not of much consequence. Our sight must be directed to the spiritual object of perception, but not to the physiological tip of the nose, either up or down. That is intended only to fasten the mind and to make it a little composed, and to draw it away from the objects of sense-perception. No further value can be attached to this process of looking at the tip of the nose or the root of the nose. So far then about the physiological element in the mystical method.

(*b*) *Psycho-ethical Element.* Let me now proceed to the psycho-ethical element in the mystical method. This is rather important, because without it no spiritual realisation is ever possible. (1) The Bhagavadgītā in a very famous passage tells us that the objects of our senses must be sacrificed in the senses, that senses must be sacrificed in breath, breath in mind and mind in Ātman :

श्रोत्रादीनीन्द्रियाण्यन्ये संयमाग्निषु जुह्वति ।
शब्दादीन्विषयानन्य इन्द्रियाग्निषु जुह्वति ॥
सर्वाणीन्द्रियकर्माणि प्राणकर्माणि चापरे ।
आत्मसंयमयोगाग्नौ जुह्वति ज्ञानदीपिते ॥ IV. 26-27.

It is only when this kind of 'sacrificial process' is carried on from point to point and Ātman reigns supreme that we may be said to have reached a very powerful stage in the mystical life. (2) Speaking from the ethical point of view, Kāma may be regarded as the chiefest enemy of man. To conquer Kāma is a most difficult job and he who has been able to conquer it will make easy progress on his spiritual path. We are also told that this Kāma or lust takes its seat in the senses, mind and reason or intellect : इन्द्रियाणि मनो बुद्धिरस्याधिष्ठानमुच्यते । (III. 40). The Bhagavadgītā also tells us about the sorites of passions—lust, rage, infatuation and ruin.

ध्यायतो विषयान्पुंसः सङ्गस्तेषूपजायते ।
सङ्गात्संजायते कामः कामात्क्रोधोऽभिजायते ॥
क्रोधाद्भवति संमोहः संमोहात्स्मृतिविभ्रमः ।
स्मृतिभ्रंशाद् बुद्धिनाशो बुद्धिनाशात्प्रणश्यति ॥ II. 62-63.

So Kāma is the chiefest enemy which must be first conquered. What in modern psycho-analysis is regarded as a powerful element in human nature must be conquered, if moral and spiritual progress is to be made. Even to talk about lust, as the psycho-analysts do freely, would itself be an act of lust. The Bhagavadgītā has no difficulty in saying that as a mirror may be covered by dust, as fire may be covered by smoke or as a fœtus might be covered by amniotic membrane, even so our spiritual life may be covered by lust (III.38-39). We have to drive it away; then alone would the Ātman be born. (3) Further, the Bhagavadgītā speaks of the great value of concentration for the process of meditation. It is a very important element which almost everybody, who practises meditation, tries to achieve :

यतो यतो निश्चरति मनश्चञ्चलमास्थिरम् ।
ततस्ततो नियम्यैतदात्मन्येव वशं नयेत् ॥ VI. 26.

Any man who by looking within finds that his mind is wandering all round must turn it away from all objects and ideas and concentrate it on the one object, namely, God :

प्रशान्तात्मा विगतभीर्ब्रह्मचारिव्रते स्थितः ।
मनः संयम्य मच्चित्तो युक्त आसीत मत्परः । VI. 14.

Just look at these conditions. Let our mind be composed; let fear be away from our mind; let there be no regnant emotion in our system. Then alone would we be able to concentrate on God. All these, however, are negative elements. About the positive elements we shall speak presently. But even these three, drawing the mind away from the objects of sense, would constitute some equipment for spiritual achievement. (4) Finally, the Bhagavadgitā tells us that even though we may seem to have conquered our senses and mind, the flavour for sensual and sexual enjoyment remains, and like the cat in Aesop's Fables would throw away the guise of a woman and pounce upon the mouse. The inner flavour, therefore, must be destroyed and this cannot be done without a previous vision of God : रसवर्जं रसोऽप्यस्य परं दृष्ट्वा निवर्तते । (II.59). The word Para has two meanings; either it might mean that God is above Rasa, or it might mean that God is the enemy of Rasa. In either case, we have to note that in order to reach the pinnacle of spiritual life, the sub-conscious flavour or Rasa which lies latent in our mind must first be destroyed, and this cannot be done without a previous vision of God.

(c) *Devotional Element.* We shall now pass on to the devotional element in the method of mystical meditation. This is very important. What is the use of merely looking at the tip of the nose or even controlling breath or trying to purge the mind of all sensual and sexual ideas? Unless we feel an earnest devotion to God, i.e. Bhāva or Bhakti, nothing would be of any avail whatsoever. In one famous passage the Bhagavadgītā sums up all the elements that are necessary for the success of devotional meditation. Let us recall to our mind the lines:

अनन्यचेताः सततं यो मां स्मरति नित्यशः ।
तस्याहं सुलभः पार्थ नित्ययुक्तस्य योगिनः ॥ VIII. 14.

We are told in this verse, in the first place, that we should be inspired with one-pointed devotion towards God. We should have no other object of attachment –अनन्यचेतस्त्वम्. Then secondly, we are told that we must practise meditation without sacrificing a single moment –नित्यशः and finally we are told that this must be continued from day to day, month to month and year to year to the very end of our life—नित्ययुक्तत्वम्. These are exactly the three requisites which Patañjali has spoken of in his most famous Sūtra:

स तु दीर्घकालनैरन्तर्यसत्कारासेवितो दृढभूमिः । I. 14.

When all these things have been accomplished, then alone does the success in spiritual life become assured. We must not, however, fail to note that Bhāva or Bhakti, an unexplained and inexplicable love of God, is a fundamental requirement; meditation from hour to hour and day to day and even concentration on the name of God are of secondary importance. The Bhagavadgītā further tells us that unless there is the element of शरणगमन or surrender in our devotion and unless we resign ourselves completely to the Power and Will of God, no great achievement in spiritual life is possible तमेव शरणं गच्छ सर्वभावेन भारत। (XVIII.62). Finally, the Bhagavadgītā tells us that it is only through one-pointed devotion to God that one may be able to know Him, see Him and enter into Him :

भक्त्या त्वनन्यया शक्य अहमेवंविधोऽर्जुन।
ज्ञातुं द्रष्टुं च तत्त्वेन प्रवेष्टुं च परंतप॥ XI. 54.

This constitutes the devotional element.

(*d*) *Element of Grace*. The last element necessary for the success of our spiritual meditation is the Grace of God. It is not simply by performing our devotional acts that we may be able to achieve our highest goal. God must be moved and it is only when He is moved that He will move the world by His Grace. There are three points in this element of Grace as we may be able to see from the Bhagavadgītā. Let us quote three important utterances in this connection:

(1) ददामि बुद्धियोगं तं... X. 10.

(2) तेषामेवानुकम्पार्थं... X. 11.

(3) तत्प्रसादात्परां शान्तिं... XVIII. 62.

So the Grace of God descends upon the aspirant who is nearing his perfection in three stages. In the first place, God gives a particular bent to his intellect and volition, a stimulus and a direction in which he might work. That is बुद्धियोग. Secondly, after he has worked unceasingly in this direction for a long time, he becomes the recipient of God's अनुकम्पा or compassion. And finally, God crowns his efforts with the gift of His blessing.

तत्प्रसादात् परां शान्तिं स्थानं प्राप्स्यसि शाश्वतम्। (XVIII. 62). God actually delivers His goods. It is only when the aspirant has passed through all these three stages, namely, बुद्धियोग, अनुकम्पा and प्रसाद, that we might say that the Grace of God has fully descended on him.

CHAPTER XX

A SUBLIME VISION OF GOD

Root Source of the Experience of Ātman

The utterances of the Bhagavadgītā in regard to the ecstatic vision of God are neither many nor explicit. In one cryptic passage the Bhagavadgītā tells us :

यत्रोपरमते चित्तं निरुद्धं योगसेवया ।
यत्र चैवात्मनात्मानं पश्यन्नात्मनि तुष्यति ॥ VI. 20.

This is the place where the Bhagavadgītā specially refers to the vision of the Ātman by the Ātman. Elsewhere it does speak briefly of the cosmic vision of God as we shall see towards the end of this chapter. It does speak explicitly of the personal relationship of Kṛṣṇa to Arjuna; but rarely, as in this peculiar passage, it describes the ecstatic vision of the Self by the Self. One does not know whether there is any value in being so chary of describing mystical experience; and yet this is what the Bhagavadgītā does. In fact, it is just here that the Bhagavadgītā speaks of the vision of Ātman, following what the Yoga Sūtras of Patañjali have set as an ideal for our realisation, तदा द्रष्टुः स्वरूपेऽवस्थानम् । (I. 3). In that state the seer lives in his own form. Patañjali also does not exfoliate the full meaning of this utterance. In the Bādarāyaṇa Sūtra particularly there is a famous passage, संपद्याविर्भावः स्वेन शब्दात् । (IV. 4. 1.), which gives the quintessence of the vision of the Self by the spiritual aspirant. The words there might be noted : संपद्य, आविर्भावः and स्वेन. All these words refer to a famous passage in the Maitrī Upaniṣad, as we shall see very soon, where the author describes the way in which God appears to the mystic's vision in a flood of illumination. It is unfortunate that this peculiar Sūtra of Bādarāyaṇa has not been properly interpreted by any great Vedāntic writer except Śaṁkarācārya. It is only he who understood the full meaning of the Sūtra, and there he quotes the Maitrī Upaniṣad (...अस्माच्छरीरात्समुत्थाय परं ज्योतिरुपसंपद्य स्वेन रूपेणाभिनिष्पद्यत इत्येष आत्मा । II. 2.) to which the Sūtra may be said to refer. In fact, this might be regarded as the great achievement of Śaṁkarācārya, so far as the interpretation of that Sūtra is concerned. Other Vedāntic commentators have failed here for the simple reason that they did not understand the inner meaning of this mystic vision. So far about the analogues (in old Sanskrit works) of the experience of Ātman as adumbrated in the Bhagavadgītā.

The greatest commentator on the Bhagavadgītā that ever lived, namely, Jñāneśvara, has elucidated the above verse from the Bhagavadgītā in his own exquisitely poetic and allegorical way. We can do nothing better than quote the passage from his Jñāneśvarī in order to bring out the full meaning of the utterance of the Gītā itself. So far as the present writer is aware, there has been no other writer except Jñāneśvara who draws out the secret meaning of this verse of the Gītā in such an excellent manner. Jñāneśvara tells us what happens when this vision of the Ātman is attained :

> " When the tree of unreality has been cut down by the sword of Self-knowledge, then ...one is able to see one's own form, one's own Self. This is, however, not to be compared to the vision of the reflection in a mirror ; for, the reflection in a mirror is simply an ' other ' of

the seeing man. The vision of the individual Self is as a Spring which may exist in its own fullness even when it does not come up into a well. When water dries up, the image goes back to its proto-type; when the pitcher is broken, space mixes with space; when fuel is burnt, fire returns unto itself; in a similar way is the vision of the Self by the Self.....One must see without seeing. One must know without knowing. That is the primary Being from which everything comes.....It is for seeing this original Being that seekers have gone by the path of Yoga, after having become disgusted with life, and with the firm determination that they would not return again.....They have given over their egoism, and have reached their Original Home. That is this Existence, which exists in itself and for itself.....after reaching which, there is no return."

Jñā. XV. 266...283.

Upaniṣads on the Experience of Ātman

We have seen hitherto how the fundamental idea in the Bhagavadgītā about the vision of God is paralleled by similar conceptions in Patañjali, Bādarāyaṇa and Jñāneśvara. But we shall now go to the fundamental source (the Upaniṣads) of the experience of Ātman which has been the eternal spring of such an experience in India and has been paralleled by similar experiences almost everywhere in the world. We cannot think of better passages than the following ten which we have selected in order to point out the real nature of the experience of Ātman as given by the seers of the Upaniṣads. As is well known, the doctrines of the Bhagavadgītā are merely a microcosmic representation of the teachings of the Upaniṣads and in the case of God-vision particularly we might even say that they are even ultra-microcosmic. Let us, however, give to the passage from the Bhagavadgītā quoted at the beginning of this chapter the benefit of a full exposition in terms of what the Upaniṣads have taught us, so far as the experience of Ātman is concerned. This will stand as an eternal pattern not merely for students of Indian mystic thought but for parallel considerations to students of any mystic thought whatsoever. We shall divide the ten utterances of the Upaniṣads into five groups of two each. In the first group, we are told how the vision of Ātman takes place inside us. In the next two, we are shown how the vision of God is to be had in the external world. Then thirdly, we are told about the activity or no-activity of the Ātman, his motion and no-motion, his joy and no-joy. In the fourth group, we have two utterances which bring the mystic into moral and axiological relationship with the Ātman. And finally, we have two utterances in which the post-ecstatic monologues of two Upaniṣadic seers have been preserved for us as a perpetual treasure.

(*a*) *Vision of God in Internal Consciousness.* Coming to the first group we are told :

अथ य एष सम्प्रसादोऽस्माच्छरीरात् समुत्थाय परं ज्योतिरुपसंपद्य स्वेन रूपेणाभिनिष्पद्यत इत्येष आत्मेति होवाच । एतदमृतमभयमेतद् ब्रह्मेति । Mai.Up.II.2.

That luminous reality which comes out of us in the ecstatic state of consciousness and appears to our vision in our own form, is what we might call the Ātman, says the Upaniṣad. This passage is from the Maitrī Upaniṣad. In the same manner the Katha Upaniṣad also tells us that the aspiring mystic must extract very courageously the form of the Ātman out of his own body, as a blade of grass might be extracted from its sheath. तं स्वाच्छरीरात्प्रवृहेन्मुञ्जादिवेषीकां धैर्येण। The Saint of Nimbargi has told us in the same strain the significance of the extraction of the Self from the human body : हींगे ई जन्म इरुवदरोळगे आत्मनन्नु कडेगे तेगेदुकोंडु नोडिद्रे आ मनुष्यनु मराळि जन्मके बरुवदिल्लु। So these passages speak of the presentation, to the vision of an aspiring mystic, of the Form of God standing alone by itself without reference to the body.

(b) *Vision of God in the External World.* While the first group of extracts refers to our vision of God in ecstacy, in the second there is a reference to our vision of God in the external world.

> य एषोऽन्तरादित्ये हिरण्मयः पुरुषो दृश्यते हिरण्यश्मश्रुर्हिरण्यकेश आ प्रणखात् सर्व एव सुवर्णः। Chān. Up. I. 6. 6.

The mystic is able to see on the Sun, for example, the full Form of God, clothed in golden radiance, with golden mustaches, with golden hair and up to the tip of his nails full of golden appearance. This passage is from the Chāndogya Upaniṣad, which is supported by another passage in the Īśa Upaniṣad, which tells us that this golden person, whom one is able to see on the Sun, is the same being as our own self. (योऽसावसौ पुरुषः सोऽहमस्मि) Īśa. Up. 16). Here the mystic feels the identity of the person within himself with the person outside, whom he is able to see projected, for example, on the Sun.

(c) *Reconciliation of Contradictions in God-experience.* In the next group, we are told of the motion or no-motion of God :

तदेजति तन्नैजति तद्दूरे तद्वन्तिके
तदन्तरस्य सर्वस्य तदु सर्वस्यास्य बाह्यतः । Īśa. Up. 5.

God moves and does not move ; He lives inside and outside ; He is both far and near. Such contradictions exist in God. Similarly, in another famous passage the Kaṭha Upaniṣad tells us :

आसीनो दूरं व्रजति शयानो याति सर्वतः ।
कस्तं मदामदं देवं मदन्यो ज्ञातुमर्हति । I. 2. 21.

Sitting, the Ātman is able to move far off, and lying, he is able to travel the whole universe. Who save myself is there in this world, asks the poet, who has been able to know this God, who is intoxicated and not intoxicated or who is intoxicated with his own rejoicings ? This passage has had analogues in the teachings of almost every mystical literature. Tukārāma has told us :

निजल्यानें गातां उभा नारायण । बैसल्या कीर्तन करितां डोले ॥
उभा राहोनियां मुखीं नाम वदे । नाचे हा गोविंद नाना छंदे ॥

We have utterances of the same kind in two great Kannada Saints, Purandaradāsa and Jagannāthadāsa :

मलगि पाडिदरे कुळितु केळुव । कुळितु पाडिदरे निंतु केळुव ।
निंतरे नलिव, नलिदरे ओलिव निमगेंव ।

So these visions of God, which have been experienced in all ages and lands by the Upaniṣadic seers, Tukārāma, Purandaradāsa, Jagannāthadāsa and others, cannot be lightly set aside by saying that they are only imaginative conjurations. There is in fact a certain universality in their statements, which confers an objective validity upon them. So far about the seeming contradictions of experience in God.

(*d*) *Moral and Axiological Relationship with God.* Now let us see in another group the way in which the mystic comes to be morally and axiologically linked up with the Ātman whom he has realised :

आत्मानं चेद् विजानीयादयमस्मीति पूरुषः ।
किमिच्छन् कस्य कामाय शरीरमनुसंज्वरेत् ॥ (Bṛ. Up. IV. 4.12.)

Why should such a man enter upon any feverish bodily or mental activity when once he has realised that the Ātman whom he has seen is really himself? The vision of the Self would put an end altogether to any such feverish activity. If such a mystic finds himself in extraordinarily difficult circumstances from which there is no escape except by praying to God, then the Chāndogya Upaniṣad tells us that he should approach God in an unperturbed state of mind remembering the end he has in view. Immediately will the end be fulfilled for him if it has not been already fulfilled.

आत्मानमन्तत उपसृत्य स्तुवीत कामं ध्यायन्नप्रमत्तोऽभ्याशो ह यदस्मै स कामः समृध्येत यत्कामः स्तुवीतेति । (Chān. Up. I. 3. 12)

In this way, we know from the Upaniṣads how God may come to the rescue of the aspiring devotee and quickly fulfill his aims.

(*e*) *Post-ecstatic Ejaculations.* Finally, let us make a mention of the monologues of the two realised Upaniṣadic saints :

अहं वृक्षस्य रेरिवा । कीर्तिः पृष्ठं गिरेरिव ।
ऊर्ध्वपवित्रो वाजिनीव स्वमृतमस्मि ॥ (Tai. Up. I. 10).

"I am the mover of the tree, namely, the tree of the body or the tree of the world. My fame is like the top of a mountain, lofty and super-eminent. My source lies in the holy original Being. I live immortally like the luminous Being in the Sun." This is one post-ecstatic monologue. There is another still more famous :

एतत्साम गायन्नास्ते । हा३वु हा३वु हा३वु ।
अहमस्मि प्रथमजा ऋता३स्य । पूर्वं देवेभ्योऽमृतस्य ना३भायि ।
यो मा ददाति स इदेव मा३वाः । अहमन्नमन्नमदन्तमा३द्मि ।
अहं विश्वं भुवनमभ्यभवा३म् । सुवर्न ज्योतीः ॥

(Tai. Up. III. 10. 5-6)

in which we are told that such a mystic sits in ecstatic contemplation singing the song of universal unity. "How wonderful! How wonderful! How wonderful! I am the first born of the Law. I have lived before the Gods. I am the source of immortality. He who gives me keeps me. I devour as food the devourer of all food, which is as much as to say that both the objective and the subjective worlds are resolved in me." Finally, the same mystic tells us "I fill the whole universe with splendour as of the Sun."

In the above ten utterances, we have the quintessence of the mystical experiences of God-realisation in all ages and climes, and particularly as given in the Upaniṣads. It is only an infinitesimal spark of this experience which the Bhagavadgītā has portrayed for us in that one cryptic utterance, यत्र चैवात्मनात्मानं पश्यन्नात्मनि तुष्यति । (VI. 20). Probably there was no occasion for the writer of the Bhagavadgītā to expand or expatiate on this theme. The present writer has done the work of that expatiation on behalf of the Bhagavadgītā.

Gītā on the Effects of God Vision

We have seen what the meaning of Self-vision or God-vision is according to the Bhagavadgītā, Patañjali, Bādarāyaṇa and the Upaniṣads. Though the problem of God-vision is tackled summarily in the Bhagavadgītā, the account it gives of the effects of God-vision is exceedingly good. This description is scattered throughout the work. But if we gather together the utterances of the Bhagavadgītā in regard to Self-vision, we shall get an extremely good description of the results of the vision of God.

(*a*) *Joy and Peace.* In the first place, we are told in the Bhagavadgītā that God-vision is accompanied with two seemingly incompatible emotions, namely, joy and peace. The question is whether they are really incompatible in the last resort. The present writer thought for a long while that joy was elative and peace was equanimous and therefore there could not be any compatibility between the two. Joy lifts us upwards and peace keeps us on a level. The one is anatropic and the other is metatropic. He has, however, now come to the conclusion that ultimate peace would be even a higher category but that peace could not be attained except through joy. The Bhagavadgītā tells us that no grief would be able to stir a man who is enjoying this great bliss from his position.

यं लब्ध्वा चापरं लाभं मन्यते नाधिकं ततः ।
यस्मिन् स्थितो न दुःखेन गुरुणाऽपि विचाल्यते ॥ VI. 22.

Of course, a man attains to this exceeding peace only after the attainment of God-realisation. Peace does not lead to joy but joy leads to peace, and hence it is that peace might be regarded as the apex of joy, even though its nature seems to be incompatible with the beatific experience.

(*b*) *Disgust for Worldly Things.* In the second place, we are told in the Bhagavadgītā that when a man reaches God, he has a feeling of disgust for all worldly things. He takes no interest in things to be heard and seen.

तदा गन्तासि निर्वेदं श्रोतव्यस्य श्रुतस्य च । (II. 52.)

The only object of hearing and seeing for such a person is God. If, therefore, anything comes to disturb him from that position, it is natural that he should not merely feel apathy for it, but even disgust. This kind of Nirveda of which the Bhagavadgītā speaks has been often referred to by writers on religion and rhetoric. The Upaniṣad speaks of निर्वेदमायान्नास्त्यकृतः कृतेन । (Muṇ. Up. 1. 2. 12). Unless this attitude of disgust is produced, man's mind cannot be turned towards God. The Bhagavadgītā has also said elsewhere :

स निश्चयेन योक्तव्यो योगो निर्विण्णचेतसा । (VI. 23.)

The highest kind of Yoga cannot be practised unless man feels disgust for all things worldly. If we however read an अवग्रह between योगः and निर्विण्णचेतसा, the meaning would be that a man must practise Yoga with a heart fully devoted to it. In fact, Yoga must be practised with an attitude of highest joy. Rhetoricians speak of निर्वेद as a स्थायीभाव of शान्तरस. In any case this attitude of apathy, indifference and disgust for all things which do not belong to God is a sure requisite of man's search after God.

(*c*) *Sinlessness.* The third effect of God-vision is sinlessness. A man is freed from his sins as soon as God reveals Himself to his vision. As a lit-up fire reduces the entire firewood to ashes, similarly, all sins of man are burnt away by the fire of God. Here a question arises whether sinlessness is a pre-condition of God-vision or whether it is only when you attain to God-vision that you become sinless. In other words, is sinlessness a cause or an effect of God-vision? This is a case of reciprocal causation. Unless all our sins are burned away, the path of God will not open out to us, and unless we are successful in reaching the God-head, we shall not become sinless.

(*d*) *Origin of True Bhakti.* In a similar manner, we are told in the Bhagavadgītā that it is only after God-vision that true Bhakti is generated in man. Very often a novice thinks that he has no element of devotion in him and that, therefore, any progress in the spiritual line is impossible for him. This is not so. A great Bhakta like Tukārāma has told us that true Bhakti is attained only after the vision of God. होईल सद्भक्ति येणें पंथें। सद्भक्ति झालिया सहज साक्षात्कार। The Bhagavadgītā has said :

> यो मामेवमसंमूढो जानाति पुरुषोत्तमम् ।
> स सर्वविद् भजति मां सर्वभावेन भारत ॥ XV. 19.

It is only when a man has attained to the full knowledge of God that he is able to meditate on Him with full devotion. In fact, as in the previous case, highest devotion and highest realisation seem to be in reciprocal causation. Unless a man comes to possess the highest devotion, he will not have a vision of God, and unless he has the vision of God, true Bhakti will not spring in him.

(*e*) *Warding off of all Perils.* The fifth effect of God-realisation is the warding off of all perils by the power and the Grace of God :

> मच्चित्तः सर्वदुर्गाणि मत्प्रसादात्तरिष्यसि ।
> अथ चेत्त्वमहंकारान्न श्रोष्यसि विनङ्क्ष्यसि ॥ XVIII. 58.

Unless you set your heart fully upon Me, you will not cross this ocean of perils, says Lord Kṛṣṇa ; but if you turn a deaf ear to my advice through egoism, then ruin will be your only lot. May I confess to a friend's personal obligations which saved me in 1909 at the Deccan College and at my home at Poona, when I was hovering between life and death? At that time I fastened my mind upon this verse in the course of the full recitation of the Bhagavadgītā, which by the Grace of God led me successfully through a sea of perils.

(*f*) *Solution of World-Riddle*. Sixthly the Bhagavadgītā says that it is only as a result of God-vision that one is able to solve the world-riddle :

यदा भूतपृथग्भावमेकस्थमनुपश्याति ।
तत एव च विस्तारं ब्रह्म सम्पद्यते तदा ॥ XIII. 30.

We may be said to have attained to the God-head, when we see all things concentred in God and see all things issuing from Him and being resolved in Him. This is almost in the spirit of the Upaniṣadic expression 'TAJJALĀN' which, as we have seen, makes God responsible for the generation, governance and annihilation of all things whatsoever. So when we have known God as the centre of the universe, we may certainly be said to have solved the world-riddle. Bādarāyaṇa has told us that a saint who has realised God gets all the powers of God, except the power of creation. But unless at least an iota of that power has descended upon the God-realiser, he may hardly be said to have realised God at all.

(*g*) *Vision of Equality*. Seventhly, we are told in the Bhagavadgītā that a mystic attains to a vision of absolute equality ; समं पश्यन्हि सर्वत्र समवास्थितमीश्वरम् । (XIII. 28.) Now this expression is capable of various important interpretations. In the first place, a mystic sees God in all beings and on all beings. May not the feeling of social equality of all beings be an outcome of this mystic vision? Secondly, he sees God in a symmetrical and harmonious fashion. The same meaning is conveyed by the expression of Tukārāma, समचरण दृष्टि विटेवरि साजिरी । or the expression in the Sanskrit verse from Śaṁkarācārya, समचरणसरोजं सान्द्रनीलाम्बुदाभम् । ... which tells us that proportion, symmetry and harmony are the essential features of the form and experience of God. Finally, the mystic must see the form of God continuously or लगातार as the Hindi saints would put it. So this kind of harmonious, symmetrical and continuous vision of God, immanently in the universe and transcendentally above it, constitutes the quality of समत्व in the experience of God.

(*h*) *Community of Saints.* Finally, a saint who has realised God in that manner cannot remain to himself like the rhinoceros of Khagga Visāṇa, of which Buddha speaks. He must come into contact with souls similar to himself. Communion of the saints, therefore, becomes not merely an ideal but the practice of such a saint. मच्चित्ता मद्गतप्राणा बोधयन्तः परस्परम् । (X. 9). says the Bhagavadgītā. Even contemporary philosophers have stressed the value of such a society of saints. Communion has been and is an essential feature of the Christian religion also. There is an inexpressible joy in the partaking of bliss not merely for oneself but in the company of those who have been recipients of a similar bliss. It is in this manner that the saints become responsible for the spreading of God's Gospel. Jñāneśvara, the greatest expounder of the doctrines of the Bhagavadgītā, has brought out this point so beautifully that we cannot do better than quote his passage, which tells us exactly how like two adjacent lakes, sending out their waves into each other, one saint sends out the waves of joy into the other and receives back from him similar waves of joy, when the wind of God's Grace blows over both of them :

> " In their hearts, they have become one with Me and I have become their very life. By the power of their realisation, they have forgotten life and death. By the power of that great illumination, they dance in the bliss of communion. They now give to each other illumination of Self, and nothing else. As two lakes, which are in close proximity to each other, send their waves into one another, and as the mingling waves form as it were a crest-house for them, similarly, the waves of the joy of the two lovers of God mix with each other, and become ornaments of illumination for both. As the Sun may waive lights before the Sun... or as in full equality one stream may mix with another, similarly, the equal love of these Saints makes a happy confluence, on the top of which rise the crest of the Sāttvika emotions... Then by the power of that great beatification they move out of themselves, and being filled with Me, they begin to proclaim Me to the world. The word, which had passed between the pupil and the teacher in their privacy, these Saints now proclaim to the whole world like a rumbling cloud. As when the unblown lotus flower begins to open, it cannot contain within itself its own perfume, but must necessarily distribute it to king and pauper alike, similarly, these realisers of God proclaim Me to the whole

world, and in the joy of the proclamation they forget the process of proclamation itself."

Jñā. X. 119–128.

Cosmic Vision of God

In the great theophany in the eleventh chapter of the Bhagavadgītā, we are lifted from the earthly region to the celestial, and there brought face to face with the manifestation of God, as He pervades the whole universe. Under this head we shall discuss six points. First, we shall speak about the wondrous manifestation of God, secondly, about His dazzling splendour and thirdly, about His terror-striking form. We shall next deal with the competition of the feeling of fear and joy as they arise in the mind of the aspirant (in the present case, Arjuna) during such a state of God-experience, and then with the vision of the future which was shown to Arjuna by Kṛṣṇa. Finally, we shall speak about the divine determinism, (as in the Tenth Book of Plato's Republic), according to which the universe is ruled by one principle only, namely, the Will of God.

(*a*) *A Wondrous Manifestation of God.* In regard to the first point, the wondrous manifestation of God, we are told in the Bhagavadgītā how when Kṛṣṇa showed his cosmic form to Arjuna, Arjuna saw that there was neither any beginning, nor any middle nor any end to the vision which he had seen. नान्तं न मध्यं न पुनस्तवादिम् । (XI. 16.). The entire space between earth and heaven seemed to have been occupied by God. द्यावापृथिव्योरिदमन्तरं हि व्याप्तं त्वयैकेन दिशश्च सर्वाः । (XI. 20). The form of God reached almost the top of the sky, being illumined with beautiful colours and lights. नभःस्पृशं दीप्तमनेकवर्णम् । (XI. 24). Inside this space-filling appearance, Arjuna saw various forms of God with an infinite number of colours and celestial shapes. पश्य मे पार्थ रूपाणि...नानावर्णाकृतीनि च। (XI. 5). Beyond these morphic and colour experiences Arjuna saw that God showed Himself to him an infinite number of faces and eyes and hands and feet. So the entire space of the universe seemed to be filled with God. As to how far this space-filling form of God, as itself filled with an infinite number of divine faces, eyes, hands and feet, could be regarded as a mystical fact or a poetical description, we leave it to the judgment of those who have spent their lives in a spiritual endeavour for God-realisation and who can see behind both poetry and mysticism.

(*b*) *The Dazzling Splendour of God.* The Bhagavadgītā offers the following description of the dazzling splendour of God. The Sun and the Moon serve as his eyes. God is regarded as शशिसूर्यनेत्र. His mouth is described as emitting a blazing fire, दीप्तहुताशवक्त्रम्। and the dazzling splendour of His form is regarded as equalling the splendour of a thousand Suns, simultaneously illuminating the sky. दिवि सूर्यसहस्रस्य भवेद्युगपदुत्थिता। (XI. 12.). Beyond the morphic and colour experiences of God, as described above, we have here a description of photic experience which has many parallels in the mystical literatures of India and elsewhere.

(*c*) *The Terror-striking Form of God.* We now proceed to what, according to the Bhagavadgītā, may be called the terror-striking form of God. In that terrible theophany God shows Himself with a number of mouths having terrible fangs; दंष्ट्राकरालानि च ते मुखानि। (XI. 25). All the beings that exist in the world are there shown to be crushed to death with their heads pounded between the teeth: केचिद्विलग्ना दशनान्तरेषु संदृश्यन्ते चूर्णितैरुत्तमाङ्गैः। (XI. 27).

This is as much as to say that God here takes on the form of the Terrific Death. कालोऽस्मि लोकक्षयकृत्प्रवृद्धः। (XI.32). He is also described as not being satisfied with the crushing of all beings in the world. The form of God is also described as devouring the worlds themselves with flaming mouths and licking His tongues for want of satiety. लेलिह्यसे ग्रसमानः समंताल्लोकान्समग्रान् वदनैर्ज्वलद्भिः। (XI. 30).

(*d*) *Competition of the Feelings of Fear and Joy*. It is no wonder that such a terrible form should fill Arjuna with fear. We find here a striking description of the competition of the feelings of fear and joy, of pain and bliss. Arjuna confesses that he was greatly satisfied with having seen the form which he had not seen before; but at the same time he confesses that the form he had seen was so terrible that it inspired him only with mortal fear. अदृष्टपूर्वं हृषितोऽस्मि दृष्ट्वा। भयेन च प्रव्यथितं मनो मे। (XI. 45). Fear entered the very marrow of his system and there was a sort of tremor that he experienced; horripilation was also there. He also saw all the three worlds quaking with fear on account of the terrific form of God. लोकत्रयं प्रव्यथितं महात्मन्। (XI. 20) and consequently, he said, he had lost all sense of direction and neither could he gather courage nor find peace, and the flow of his vital forces seemed to have been absolutely checked. दिशो न जाने न लभे च शर्म। (XI. 25) and धृतिं न विन्दामि शमं च विष्णो। (XI. 24). Here we can only cite a parallel from the experience of a modern mystic who described himself as absolutely powerless even to lift his hand from his heart in mortal fear and exclaimed that it would have been much better if he had not been privileged to have that experience. There was terrific fear inside, no doubt, but there was also at the same time abounding joy. He wanted to have a re-vision of that experience over again, but re-visions are not in man's hands, and one has to leave them to the sweet Will of God.

(e) *Vision of the Future.* In the situation in which Arjuna was placed, Kṛṣṇa showed him the vision of the future in order that he might be encouraged to fight to the end the battle in which he was engaged. Kṛṣṇa showed him a panorama where Bhīṣma and Droṇa and Karṇa along with the foremost warriors even on the side of the Pāṇḍavas were rushing headlong with great speed into the opened mouths of Kṛṣṇa like moths in flaming fires :

...भीष्मो द्रोणः सूतपुत्रस्तथाऽसौ
सहास्मदीयैरपि योधमुख्यैः ॥ XI. 26.
वक्त्राणि ते त्वरमाणा विशन्ति .... XI. 27.
यथा प्रदीप्तं ज्वलनं पतंगा विशन्ति नाशाय समृद्धवेगाः ॥...XI. 29.

The vision which Kṛṣṇa showed to Arjuna was the vision not merely of speed but of acceleration (समृद्धवेगाः) with which the contending armies were rushing into the mouths of Kṛṣṇa. To God there is neither friend nor foe. He treats all things alike. Earthquakes, pestilences and bombs do not make any distinction between one man and another, between prince and pauper, between friend and foe. Kṛṣṇa showed His cosmic form to Arjuna in order to give him a glimpse of the vision of the future.

(f) *Divine Determinism.* It was for that reason that Kṛṣṇa told Arjuna that there was Divine Determinism shaping the destinies of the world. "All those heroes who were standing in the opposite ranks had already been killed by me." मयैवैते निहताः पूर्वमेव (XI. 33). "Leave away, therefore, all sense of egoism and conquer your enemies." ऋतेऽपि त्वां न भविष्यन्ति सर्वे । (XI. 32). They will be killed in spite of you. Be, therefore, a willing instrument in the hands of God and take the credit of killing your enemies. निमित्तमात्रं भव सव्यसाचिन् । (XI. 33). These were the prophetic words which Kṛṣṇa uttered to Arjuna. At the end Kṛṣṇa assured him that if he did so, he was sure to obtain victory in the contest. Fight and thou shalt win. युध्यस्व जेतासि रणे सपत्नान् । (XI. 34). This was the message which Kṛṣṇa delivered to Arjuna. It was, therefore, the duty and the privilege of Arjuna to fight as the result had been already vouchsafed to him by Kṛṣṇa.

(*g*) *A Picture on the Divine Canvas.* We thus see from the Bhagavadgītā how a combination of the vision of the future and Divine Determinism paved the way for the victory of the friends of God in the great Mahābhārata war. Can we cite any modern example in which this combination has worked similarly ? The greatest war that was fought on earth after the Mahābhārata war was the last world war between the Germans and Italians on the one side and the English and the Americans on the other. The course of the war falls into two stages, one from 1939-1942 and the other from 1942-1945. There is a clear indication that Hitler and Mussolini always won in the first stage, and that Montgomerry and Eisenhower won continuously in the second. How are the two different strata to be seen in the divine picture ? If there was Lord Kṛṣṇa to show Arjuna a vision in which he could see the form of God devouring and annihilating the enemies with his flaming mouths, we wonder how a similar picture could have been imagined in the last World War, where there was an almost antithetical representation of the two stages on the heavenly canvas. Artists and poets may try to depict it in their own way. Would not the necessities of mystic experience, however, require a pictorial representation of the changing fortunes on the heavenly canvas, in which God with an uplifted flaming thunderbolt might strike mercilessly at one side of the battle during the first period and at the other side in the reverse direction with the same uplifted thunderbolt in the second? A Divine Thunderbolt is probably the best weapon to annihilate the contending armies. It would have been extremely fortunate if one had been privileged to see the changing fortunes of the war on the heavenly canvas, and to interpret the Will of God accordingly.

PART V

CONCLUSION

CHAPTER XXI

CONCLUSION

*The Sublime and the Divine : A Study in Comparative Thought

Introduction

I am very thankful to you, Revered President, for the signal honour you have done me in asking me to speak here this time on the subject which I propose to designate "The Sublime and the Divine: A Study in Comparative Thought". This could also be otherwise called a "Critique of Spiritual Experience, Intuition or Self-Realisation". The word Critique is used here in the sense in which Kant has used it. It does not mean criticism, it does not mean a denial, but it means a very careful study and a critical investigation of any philosophical problem. Kant was probably one of the greatest of European philosophers that have ever lived and his three works are most remarkable, namely, the Critique of Pure Reason, the Critique of Practical Reason and the Critique of Judgment, one rising on the top of the other. When I was young, I looked upon them like works of philosophy, but now they appear to me like works of poetry. When a thinker like Kant has given us his most abstruse ideas upon every single topic of thought and experience in these three Critiques, it would be a very hard task for any layman or even a philosopher to propose any new problems which might go beyond these three Critiques.

---

* A lecture delivered at the Rashtrapati Bhawan, New Delhi, in April 1954.

And yet those who have studied contemporary philosophy and those who have studied Indian and Western thought from the spiritual point of view, will see that Kant is lacking in one element, namely, the element of intuition. The translators of his works in English have used the word 'intuition' no doubt but in a different sense. They have used the word 'intuition' (Anschauung) in the sense of perception. Now the sense in which I am going to use it and in which it is used in contemporary thought is that super-sensuous faculty which goes beyond reason and which puts us in possession of things unknown to reason. The faculty by means of which we can enter into the spiritual life is intuition. It might correspond to what Śaṁkarācārya calls Anubhūti. So I felt the necessity of supplementing the three great Critiques of Kant—those of Pure Reason, Practical Reason and Judgment—by a new Critique, namely, the Critique of Intuition or Spiritual Experience as we may call it. Now this idea arose in my mind from the study of the Bhagavadgītā. For a long time since 1928, when I delivered my lectures on the Bhagavadgītā at the Nagpur University, I have been pondering over that subject ; but many pre-occupations have prevented me from publishing the lectures till now. The three important topics which I discussed at that time were : (i) the Antinomies in the Bhagavadgītā, (ii) the Categorical Imperative and the Bhagavadgītā, (iii) the nature of the Sublime in the Bhagavadgītā with reference to the philosophy of the Bhagavadgītā. Very peculiarly these are also the three most important topics in Kantian philosophy and these have been dealt with respectively in the three great Critiques, Critique of Pure Reason, Critique of Practical Reason and

Critique of Judgment. Anyone who will read the present work even cursorily will see that these are the most important problems which have been dealt with therein.

The Sublime in Western Thought

In the last part of our work we discussed in detail the nature of the Antinomies in the Bhagavadgītā, its doctrine of the Categorical Imperative, and other theories of the ethical ideal. The problem of the Sublime was just touched upon while dealing with the Vision of God in the last chapter, but its full philosophical implications were not brought out. If there is any great philosophical work which has fully brought out the relation of the Sublime to the Divine, it is the Bhagavadgītā.

(*a*) *The Concept of the Sublime in Kant.* Kant had seen the relation of the Sublime to the Divine only as through a glass darkly, and hence he was not able to portray the conception of the sublime in its full lineaments. For example, Kant was not right in putting the category of the sublime in between the categories of the beautiful and the teleological in his Critique of Judgment. Kant included sublimity along with taste in the æsthetic judgment and left teleology for a later part, namely, the teleological judgment. I think that instead of putting sublimity in between taste and teleology, Kant should have put the teleological in between the beautiful and the sublime. The sublime might well be taken to be a synthesis of the beautifu and the teleological. Incidentally, we might also mention that this would have helped Kant in his usual scheme of tripartite development as between taste, teleology and sublimity. In spite, however, of Kant's interposition of the sublime between taste and teleology, his description of sublimity remains wonderful. What tempted me to take this subject was this kind of sublimity which occurs in poetry, in art, in human life and in spiritual experience. The Taj might be a beautiful building, but the laying out of the three-mile long avenue to the President's Chamber studded on both sides by Governmental buildings and the Houses of Parliament, is sublime. The distinction between beauty and sublimity, according to Kant, is that while in beauty, which aims at order, symmetry and harmony, man's mind becomes assimilated and attuned to the objects perceived, in sublimity, it is conquered by them. What happens when earthquakes take place? In hurricanes, in great fires, in wars, during pestilences and high floods? Man's mind is conquered by nature and hence sublimity comes in. And yet, says Kant, man's mind is so great that he must not allow these to overpower it. It may be that these forces might make a man succumb for a while; but he knows that man's inner self is ultimately higher than any of the forces of nature, and that the inner conquest is on a higher level than the conquest of nature.

(*b*) *The Idea of the Holy in Otto.* Kant's idea of the sublime resembles that which has been explained so well in recent times by a writer of great note, Dr. Rudolph Otto, in his remarkable book, the Idea of the Holy. I was fortunate to meet Dr. Otto in Poona in 1927. I had read his book and he also had read mine on the Upaniṣads, and he sent a note to me saying that he would come to see me. I replied, "Sir, you are very old. You need not come to me, but I will myself go to see you." And so I went to him along with Dr. Macnicol and

Dr. Belvalkar and had good discussion with him. He spoke English so well. And when I parted company with him, I said, "Sir, you are a real professor." I have not seen another Christian who was so open-minded and who read and prized the religious books dealing with religions other than his own as Otto. Otto has translated the Eleventh chapter of the Bhagavadgītā in verse and added it as an appendix to the Idea of the Holy. The Idea of the Holy is a wonderful book even from the point of view of literature, not to speak of philosophy. In this book Dr. Otto has advanced a new conception like our own conception of intuition. Our intuition rises on the top of pure Reason, Practical Reason and Judgment. So also, he says, his Idea of the Holy rises above the conceptions of the True, the Good and the Beautiful. It is a category *sui generis*. It cannot be reduced to any other. The Holy is the category of God. It is what Otto calls '*Mysterium Tremendum*'. It is full of mystery and full of the highest terror which God inspires. Such a terror was inspired in the mind of Arjuna by the विश्वरूप of Kṛṣṇa. We may see from the above how Kant's idea of the Sublime, Otto's idea of the Holy and our own idea of Intuition stand on the same level.

The Sublime in Indian Spiritual Literature

We have already described in the last chapter the nature of the Cosmic Vision of God which Arjuna had through the Grace of Kṛṣṇa. The eleventh Chapter of the Bhagavadgītā is a classical illustration in Sanskrit literature of such Cosmic Vision or विश्वरूपदर्शन. The various provincial literatures of India also are not wanting in a portrayal of this kind of experience. Let us illustrate the idea of the sublime from three Provincial literatures of India—Hindi, Kannada and Marathi. Of course, these are only specimens and the same idea of the sublime may be illustrated from other provincial literatures also. We shall take three illustrations from Hindi spiritual literature, from Kabīra, Gulāla and Tulasīdāsa ; one from Kannada literature, from Bhavatāraka ; and finally, one from Marathi literature from Jñāneśvara. These will support, from the point of view of mystical experience, the discussion of the sublime which we have already given from the Bhagavadgītā. These five specimens would be enough to let us know the real nature of the sublime in mystical experience, the characteristics of the Holy and the intuitional method by which they have to be apprehended.

(*a*) *Kabīra.* Let us begin by taking three great poems from Hindi spiritual literature. In the poem चुवत अमी रस भरत ताल जहँ, Kabīra tells us that the river became so powerful that it devoured the ocean. The individual self devoured the existence of God. (सरिता उमाहि सिन्धु को सोखै). This is sublime, human existence devouring God. Kabīra also tells us, दस अवतार एक रत राजैं अस्तुति सहज से आनी हो.... " I see the entire panorama of the ten Avatāras passing before me in a single night, and at the same time my mind is filled with soft and delicate sounds of रामरामध्वनि. Will it not fill me with great wonder and astonishment ? Words of praise fall automatically from my lips ", says Kabīra. This is sublime.

(*b*) *Gulāla.* We have another sublime experience in Gulāla. He tells us that the human children, little selves as we are, are in a small cradle which has been provided for us by our mother. This cradle in which God has put man, has neither poles to support it nor ropes to bind it: बिन ड़ोरी बिन खंभे पौद़ल. The bells of the cradle are making an unceasing musical sound for all twenty-four hours: आठ पहर झनकार. Let us sing this song in the Hindol Rāga: गावहु सखि हिंडोलवा हो. He further tells us that when the spiritual teacher gave a push to the cradle, the cradle lost all moorings, lost all connection of poles and ropes which did not exist and evaporated in the air, and that the 'spiritual article' that was inside it mixed with the whole universe (as Wordsworth has also put it): छुटल जगत कर झुलना हो। प्रेम पदारथ भइल निनार ॥ So, such a kind of sublime experience a mystic can get provided he regards himself as a child of God.

(*c*) *Tulasīdāsa* We now pass on to some fine verses from Tulasīdāsa in which we are given the instance of a Cātaka. It was pelted by Nature with pebbles of ice with the consequence that its feathers were reduced to pieces. In addition, a huntsman came and discharged a mortal arrow at the bird. Then what did it do? It fell into the Gaṅgā, no doubt, but it did not turn its beak downwards. It refused to partake of the holy waters of the Gaṅgā. It lifted its beak upwards towards the cloud in order that it might gather some drops of rain from it. This is an illustration to show how a man must be a one-pointed Bhakta if he wants to receive drops of mercy from God. The goal of the attention of the Cātaka was the drops of water from the cloud. The goal of the attention of a Bhakta should be drops of mercy from God. This is an illustration of the sublime. Of course, I leave it to those who are students of Alaṁkāra Śāstra and to those who are students of poetry—Indian and European—to consider this question of the sublime in its spiritual aspect.

(*d*) *Bhavatāraka.* Let us now proceed to a famous poem in Kannada literature, namely that from Bhavatāraka दृष्टियोळगे दृष्टि निंतिरु । When the Eye has stood before the eye, says the poet, a great phenomenon occurs; the world disappears दृश्यवेल्ल नष्टवाइतु, the vision of the Eye before the eye implies an absolute destruction of the vision of the world. Bhavatāraka further tells us that when he, as an individual spirit, made his appearance in the world, he descended into the complex of the twenty-five elements, reminding us of similar utterances from other great writers. Aristotle talks of a god-like activity from without to inhabit this complex of different elements. The Bible tells us that God breathed into the nostrils of man the breath of life and vivified a tenement of clay. And in the Vedas we have a famous utterance अस्थन्वन्तं यदनस्था बिभर्ति । (R. V. I. 164.). The boneless entity made a bony tenement for itself. This is the literal meaning of the word अवतार. Finally, in a couple of famous lines Bhavatāraka tells us that after spiritual realisation, he saw a new glory in the world. It seemed as if there was a regeneration or a re-creation of the entire world. The whole world from the earth to the top of the mountain seemed filled with immaculate spirit: पर्वताग्र भूमियिन्नु निर्विकार तोरितल्ल. These are excellent illustrations of the sublime.

(*e*) *Jñāneśvara.* As an illustration of the sublime we shall take only one passage from Marathi literature. The passage given below is taken from Jñāneśvarī. It shows how its author, the great poet-saint of Maharashtra, develops the idea of the sublime :

> " Arjuna saw himself along with God in God and God saw Himself along with Arjuna, and Sañjaya saw both of them together...When

one mirror is placed in front of another, which shall we say reflects which ? The difference between the original and the image vanishes and each will give an infinite number of reflections of the other. Supposing another Sun arose before the Sun, who is the illuminator and who is the illumined ?... So Kṛṣṇa and Arjuna reached a state of unison. I myself, said Sañjaya, found my at-one-ment with them."

XVIII. 1592-1607.

The Sublime in the World of Nature

After these illustrations of the sublime in the mystical experience drawn from the various provincial literatures of India, we shall proceed to discuss the question of the sublime in its other aspects. We have hitherto taken into account only the world of spirit; but the world of nature also is no inconsiderable field for the operation of the sublime. It has been well said that any spiritual experience whatsoever hides in it an element of sublimity. It may be said similarly that every department of Nature is filled with the operation of the sublime. We shall here consider only three branches of science, namely, geology, meteorology and astronomy to understand the nature of the operation of the sublime. The earth, the sky and the heavens might well be taken to be the three fields where the principle of the sublime operates.

(*a*) *Geology.* So far as geology is concerned, (i) we have merely to look at the phenomenon of the earthquakes to see how and to what heights the sublime might rise. The present writer had an experience of an earthquake at Allahabad in 1934 when a palatial building opposite his own house swung to and fro on account of the internal vibrations of the earth, calling forth from a devout Mullah in the vicinity an expression of prayer 'Alla Ho Akbar'. It was feared that the earth was almost breaking in twain. (ii) The same thing happens when volcanic eruptions take place. The whole history of volcanic eruptions upon the earth and the succeeding geological formations show what great power there is in these eruptions to produce a feeling of the sublime. The celebrated Mānasa Sarovara on the top of the Himālayas in Tibet, encircled by the two mountains, Kailāsa and Māndhātā, is a typical example of how at the beginning of the formation of the earth, volcanic eruptions came from craters like the one in Mānasa Sarovara and produced mountains of lava on both sides of the crater, which stand even today as monuments of the power of the internal forces of the earth. We have merely to carry our imagination back to the beginning of the earth when such a tremendous natural phenomenon was occurring. (iii) Then again, anyone who has seen the entire region of the delta between the Gaṅgā and the Yamunā, with its tip at their confluence at Allahabad upwards to a distance of about two to three hundred miles, will know that the whole region is covered merely by sand, and not a single piece of stone is to be found there. When the present writer, after going to Allahabad in 1928, wanted to fix a nail in a wall, he could not find a single stone even after an amount of search. He greatly wondered at this phenomenon and inquired why it was that he could not find a stone? The reply came that in order to find a stone

one had to go up a hundred miles to the Himālayas in the North or to go down almost as many miles to the Vindhya in the South. The whole region is covered by sand. What a great phenomenon must have occurred when this sandy plain was brought into being by the withdrawal of the waters from the Arabian sea and the Indian ocean, reminding us perpetually that every particle of sand in the delta is a memento of eternal history, crying out "शतं भीष्म शतं भीष्म."

(*b*) *Meteorology.* Another illustration of the sublime might be drawn from the science of meteorology when we consider such phenomena as the Aurora Borealis in the Arctic regions and the Aurora Australis in the Antarctic. The Latin word **Aurora** and the Greek word **Eos** are connected with the Sanskrit word उष् to illumine, from which the name of the deity उषस् is derived. It is one thing to read of the phenomenon of various colours in the Aurora and another altogether to be a witness to the manifestation of this phenomenon before one's eyes. A friend of mine, who was able to see it at Oslo about a quarter of a century ago, described to me what a great panorama of colours is exhibited in the Aurora Borealis. Various colours such as orange, blue, red, yellow and green are exhibited, the green being the most predominant of them all. The colour phenomenon is due to the electric disturbances in the Arctic and Antarctic regions when disturbances occur at the Magnetic Poles. The description of the Aurora is indeed a vivid illustration of the sublime.

There is also a description of the उषस् so far back as the times of the Ṛgveda which might well have prompted Tilak to point out that this description could be experienced only by one who has lived near about the Arctic region.

चक्रमिव नव्यसि आववृत्स्व । R.V. (III.61.3) is a celebrated prayer which is offered to the Goddess Dawn by her Vedic devotees. She moves round about the horizon like a wheel, separating day and night approximately by a period of two months, the day consisting continuously of about four months, the night again continuously of about four months. These are joined together by the dawn and the twilight of two months duration each, when either before sunrise or sunset we find these variegated multi-coloured phenomena on the canvas of the horizon. Uṣas is described as coming in a golden chariot with her horses bedecked in prismatic colours:

आ त्वा वहन्तु सुयमासो अश्वाः ।
हिरण्यवर्णां पृथुपाजसो ये । (RV. III. 61.2)

Though old, she is ever young. ... She is regarded as a banner of immortality: अमृतस्य केतुः । She follows the eternal law and is an ideal of vision and aspiration for all humanity: अनुव्रतं चरसि विश्ववारे । It is this sublime experience of the dawn which has made the prayers to Uṣas in Ṛgveda the most classical illustrations of poetic imagination and devotional fervour.

(c) *Astronomy*. Not less important nor less significant are the astronomical phenomena which from the points of view of intensity and operation in imagination might be supposed to excel any other description of the manifestations of the sublime in the world of nature. What a great description we find in the Bhāgavata of the so-called Śiṁśumāra Cakra or the Divine Alligator, as it is called, with its tail originating at the North Pole and its mouth at the Canopas, its spherical body moving in the heavens situated up and down the milky ways, with the great bear and the small bear constituting its waist, with stars, planets and constellations constituting the other parts of the body; the stars constituting the numberless hairs of the alligator, the planets constituting the internal organs such as thorax, throat, navel, heart and the rest, and the constellations constituting its external limbs such as ears, eyes, legs, ribs and so on. The heavenly motions are due entirely to this whirling round of the alligator from end to end in the heavenly regions. No better example of the sublime from astronomy clothed in poetic imagination and with an element of devotion added to it could be thought of. In fact, this form of the alligator is supposed to have been revealed to Vāsudeva, as the Bhāgavata tells us, during his state of meditation. In addition, any one who contemplates on this form of the alligator, the Bhāgavata tells us, will thereby be freed from all his sins.

We have hitherto taken specimens of the sublime from the world of spirit and the world of nature. It now behoves us to make a short philosophical investigation of the nature of the sublime. This will be done from the points of view of (1) metaphysics, (2) psychology of religion and (3) morality.

The Sublime in Metaphysics: (Conquest of mind by Nature. Infinitude. The Divine)

As regards metaphysical analysis of the conception of the sublime, we have to point out at the outset what Kant has so much insisted on in his Critique of Judgment, namely, that the distinction between the beautiful and the sublime is the distinction between assimilation and conquest. While in the experience of the beautiful the mind of man becomes assimilated to the object perceived, in the case of the sublime it is conquered by outside experience. A second point in the metaphysical analysis would be the distinction between magnitude and force, what Kant calls the mathematical and the dynamical aspects of the sublime. We might, for our purpose, call these respectively extensity and intensity of sublime experience. The third, and this is the most important point, is the nature of the Infinitude that is portrayed in the manifestations of the sublime. The experience of the sublime seems to be almost transcendent and baffling even for the imagination to reach. Anaximander was not wrong when he regarded the Apeiron as his most fundamental category. The Peras is a small conception, but the Apeiron brings us quite near to Divinity. In other works of mine I have already stressed this aspect of the element of Divinity in all cases of Infinitude as, for example, in the बेहद of Kabīra and निर्बैलु of Kannada saints. I was very glad to find that when Professor Burch of America came to Nimbal, he stressed exactly in the same manner the divine aspect of Anaximander's Infinitude in one of his recent contributions to the American Review of Metaphysics.

The Sublime in Psychology of Religion

As regards the analysis of the sublime from the point of view of the psychology of religion, we must make it clear that here, so far as the relation between the internal and the external experiences is concerned, the tables are turned. In the metaphysical aspect of the sublime, nature dominates the mind of man, but in the psychological aspect it plays a subservient role. Inner consciousness rises superior to nature in the case of psychological experience, while in the case of metaphysics it is subordinated to nature. Then again, the total compound state of emotions, which a man is enjoying while he is experiencing the sublime, is what as we might call, according to the diary of a modern mystic, a "compound of reverence, fear, joy, wonder and love." Fear and joy, of course, are predominant as we have already seen in the case of Arjuna, but the other experiences of reverence, wonder and love also are not less important. These along with fear and joy make up the total compound of emotions which a mystic enjoys during his experiences of the sublime. Finally, we pass through the three-fold process of purification, clarification and sanctification from the moral, intellectual and spiritual points of view respectively. In the first place, our mind must become pure before we could have any experience of the sublime. Secondly, this purity must lead to the clarification of intellect, and finally this clarification must culminate in a state of sanctification. It is not without reason that people, who have come out of spiritual meditation, have described how a new world has been created for them. Bhavatāraka had such an experience as we have seen elsewhere, and even Ruskin has referred to it in his Modern Painters. This is the highest state to which a man can rise, so far as the psychology of religious experience is concerned.

The Sublime in Morality: Kant's New Copernican Revolution in his Opus Postumum: Three Stages

As regards the analysis of the sublime from the moral point of view, no better proposition can be put forth than the one suggested by Kant that the moral may be regarded as the most sublime conception of experience. No man has spent greater labour upon the justification of the moral life than Kant; no better book has been written on ethics than his Critique of Practical Reason; and no more important statement has been made by anybody than by Kant that the proof of God was to be found through an analysis of the conception of the Summum Bonum from the point of view of the adjustment of merit and reward. This is a very classical statement of moral philosophy. It is really a great wonder that after he had written his Critique of Pratical Reason, Kant continued to ponder on its tenets till the time of his death. Certain manuscripts in his handwriting were discovered with him at the time of his death, which were published posthumously by Erich Adickes in 1920 and in which we find Kant entirely revolutionising his old conceptions of the Summum Bonum and the Categorical Imperative.

Kant's statements which Erich Adickes has published under the title 'Opus Postumum' are most wonderful, showing to us how a deep thinker like Kant, not being satisfied with some propositions which he had enunciated early in his career and upon which he constantly meditated till the time of his death, should have come to certain new conclusions which change entirely the aspect of his moral philosophy. These statements put together might, in our opinion, be taken to indicate the three stages, the negative, the positive and the constructive, if we follow the usual Kantian synthetic method.

(*a*) *Negative.* Negatively, we might say that Kant now entirely denies to the conception of the Summum Bonum the power to prove the existence of God. Students of Kant are aware how the upshot of his Critique of Pure Reason was to show the invalidity of the intellectual proofs of God, the ontological, the cosmological and the physico-theological, while the only proof of God upon which he could rely in the Critique of Practical Reason was the moral proof based upon an analysis of the conception of the Summum Bonum, involving adjustment of works to recompense. In the Opus Postumum of Kant above referred to, even this moral proof of God is regarded by him as entirely "untenable and illegitimately theoretical." The powerlessness of the Summum Bonum to prove the existence of God and the illegitimateness and the untenability of the moral argument for the proof of God would have been sufficient to give the old purist interpreters of Kant a nervous shock from which it would have been hard for them to recover.

(*b*) *Positive.* Positively, we may say that (1) Kant now credits the Categorical Imperative itself with the power of leading us directly to God. Kant thus tells us that the Categorical Imperative might be regarded as the "Command of the Inner Being," the voice of the "Imperantis who holds universal sway." From this point of view, all duties become the Commands of God Himself. We have pointed out in a former chapter that the one main distinction between Kant and the Bhagavadgītā, so far as the Categorical Imperative is concerned, is that while in Kant the old Categorical Imperative is self-justified, in the Bhagavadgītā it is justified by reference to God. The Bhagavadgītā has insisted upon the divine nature of all dutiful actions as we have already seen. The position at which Kant has now arrived is exactly the position of the Bhagavadgītā. (2) Kant goes on to say now he "stands under the awful but at the same time salutary guidance and surety of God; and it is He," he tells us further, "who either justifies or condemns my actions." (3) Kant is not satisfied with the mere statement that the Categorical Imperative issues from God; he makes further statements in which we find the moral purist arriving at the position of a theist. Kant says in a theistic manner that it is "God Himself and not merely the Idea of God who is immanent in the human spirit." (4) It is this God, he further tells us, "this Being (Wesen) in him who stands in causal relationship with him, and what is strangest of all is that this causality is a determination to freedom." (5) Kant even speaks about the personality of God. "Personality could be ascribed to God," he tells us, "as a result of the singleness of its object." (6) Further, almost in a theological fashion he speaks about God as "the Ideal of Power and Wisdom in one." (7) Finally, in almost a mystical manner, Kant tells us that it "is God who is not merely in him but about him and over him." What an extraordinary change we find here from the mere Idea of God with which Kant began his philosophic career to this conception of an all-pervasive Spirit with which he ends it!

(*c*) *Constructive*. Beyond these negative and positive aspects of the new Kantian ethics is his constructive statement, a very extraordinary statement, indeed, in which he asserts his identity with this Supreme Being. One stands gaping to see how he should have arrived at the conclusion: "I, AS MAN, AM MYSELF THIS BEING." What better enunciation can we have than this of an intrepid Identitate philosophy? On the whole, we thus see Kant rising, through his Critiques and Opus Postumum, from a mere agnosticism to moral purism, from moral purism to theism, from theism to theologism and from theologism to a mystical Identitate philosophy. What difference would there be now between Kant's perfected philosophy and the philosophy of the Bhagavadgītā which synthesises the moral, the sublime and the divine in a crowning Philosophy of Spirit. One need now no longer ask, "what is the relation between the moral and the sublime? Is the moral more divine than the sublime or the sublime more divine than the moral?" It is enough for us to know that the Moral, the Sublime and the Divine all merge in one consummate Philosophy of Spirit like that of the Bhagavadgītā.

INDEX

[Numbers refer to pages. BG stands for Bhagavadgītā]

INDEX
